Midsummer

MEDIEVAL TEXTS AND CULTURES OF NORTHERN EUROPE

3

Midsummer

A Cultural Sub-Text
from Chrétien de Troyes to Jean Michel

by

Sandra Billington

BREPOLS

British Library Cataloguing in Publication Data

Billington, Sandra
    Midsummer : a cultural sub-text from Chretien de Troyes
    to Jean Michel. – (Medieval texts and cultures of Northern Europe ; 3)
    1.French literature – To 1500 – History and criticism
    I.Title
    840.9'001

    ISBN 2-503-51084-1

ᐸ

© 2000 Brepols Publishers n.v., Turnhout, Belgium

D/2000/0095/97
ISBN 2-503-51084-1

Printed in the EU on acid-free paper.

Dedicated to
Fortune, with her right arm in a sling
—
and in memory of
David Robert Billington

Contents

List of Illustrations

Acknowledgements

Embarking on this kind of project has something in common with a pilgrimage and although travelling in hope is meant to matter more than arriving, yet one does become immensely thankful, finally, to come to a point which can be called 'completion'. Many colleagues have been involved. The research could not have continued without the patient support for funding from Herman Braet and Hilda Ellis Davidson, who did not blench at this being needed twice yearly for a number of years, and who also suggested some key exempla. So, too, did Derek Brewer and my gratitude to him includes his continuing help towards a successful outcome for the work.

Others who kept the momentum going, and to whom I am also very grateful, are Alison Adams, Madame Danièle Alexandre-Bidon, Jean-Claude Aubailly, Marie and Richard Axton, Natalie Zemon Davis, Marjoke de Roos, Wim Hüsken, Alexandra Johnston, Angus Kennedy, Meg Mumford, D. D. R. Owen, Stephen Rawles, John S. Richardson, Claude Schumacher, Malcolm Underwood, Kenneth Varty, Bart Westerweel, and Nicholas Wyatt. My thanks, too, go to James R. Simpson for his help with tricky translations and to Isabelle Lazier, of the Musée Dauphinois for helping me track down material. Librarians in Glasgow, Edinburgh, and Cambridge University Libraries, often working in difficult circumstances, have always been extremely helpful; so too librarians and archivists in The British Library and The Warburg Institute; also in French public libraries and regional archives in Angers, Brussels, Laon, Louvain, Luxembourg, Lyon, Metz, Nancy, Toul, Troyes, and Verdun. I would particularly like to thank Mr Jean Lefèbvre, Conservateur, Bibliothèque Municipale, Laon, Mr Louis Torchet, and Madame Deschères of the Bibliothèque Municipale, Angers, and Mr Guy Parguez, Conservateur adjoint, Bibliothèque Municipale, Lyon.

It gives me pleasure, too, to thank Wendy Scase for her guidance and the readers for their criticism and essential advice in the last stages of preparation. I am especially grateful to Alan Hindley, not only for reading the text and picking up linguistic slips, but also for his thoughtful and perceptive interventions. Any remaining slips, however, are entirely the author's responsibility. My thanks also go to Dr Simon Forde of Brepols for his planning, and to Elizabeth Wall for patient and thorough work in editing the text.

Finally, I am much indebted to The British Academy, The Carnegie Trust for the Universities of Scotland, and to Glasgow University for funding my research visits, also to The Carnegie Trust for meeting the cost of reproduction 'permissions', and to the Department of Theatre, Film, and Television Studies, Glasgow University for negotiating time when it was needed.

The material on Arnoul Gréban's *Mystère de la Passion* in Chapter 9 first appeared in 'King and Queen Play in English Mystery and French Passion Plays', *Custom, Culture and Community*, ed. by T. Pettitt and L. Søndergaard (Odense: Odense University Press, 1994), pp. 85–104. The study of Jean Michel's *Passion JesusCrist* first appeared in 'Social Disorder, Festive Celebration, and Jean Michel's *Le Mistere de la Passion JesusCrist*', *Comparative Drama*, 28 (1995), 216–47, while some of the material in Appendix C first appeared in 'The Cheval Fol of Lyon and Other Asses', *Fools and Folly*, ed. by Clifford Davidson (Kalamazoo: Western Michigan University, Medieval Institute Publications, 1996), pp. 9–33. I would like to thank the editors, the University of Southern Denmark, and the Board of the Medieval Institute, Western Michigan University for permission to reproduce this material.

Sandra Billington
July 2000

Abbreviations

Bibl. Mun.	Bibliothèque Municipale
BL	British Library
BnF	Bibliothèque nationale de France
CFMA	Classiques Français du Moyen Age
CNF	*Chroniques Nationales Françaises*
EETS	Early English Text Society
LGF	Librairie Générale Française
LCL	Loeb Classical Library
Migne	*Patrologiae Cursus Completus*, Series Latina (Paris: Migne 1844-)
SATF	Société d'Anciens Textes Français
SEDES	Société d'Édition et d'Enseignement Supérieur

Moveable Feast Days in Summer—deduced from C. R. Cheney, *Handbook of Dates*, Royal Historical Society Guides and Handbooks no. 4 (London: Royal Historical Society, 1945):

Ascension: 30 April to 3 June
Pentecost: 10 May to 13 June
Corpus Christi Day (after 1317): 21 May to 24 June

All ellipses within quotations indicate my truncations, not gaps in the manuscript or printed text.

Introduction

Any study of seasonal celebration in medieval and Renaissance Europe leads to the conclusion that the most sophisticated popular culture developed at feast days between December and February, since the details which survive give a clear understanding of the Christmas festive ethos. As is well known, the custom at the winter solstice was to present a mock mirror image of the world, copying and inverting normal behaviour and social order. Winter festive days were often organized as inverted kingdoms governed by Lords of Misrule, *reges stultorum,* Abbots of Unreason, Boy Bishops, Epiphany Kings, or *princes des sots,* and traditions under their rule can be studied in relation to 'normal' society: for their association with pre-Christian culture, their association with the theatre, and also for their volatility.

Summer festivities did not have such a high profile and so far, today, no coherence has been found for the May to August period, beyond the observation that all feast days were Bacchic and folly was made official.[1] The election of May kings and queens involved the disorders of romance, events on Ascension day and Pentecost were usually under the control of the Church while, at the midsummer festival of St John the Baptist, celebrations usually returned to secular control and appear to have centred on fires and semi-magical rites. Historians have noted riots which occurred in summer months yet, in the study of social disorder, winter has again been found the more prolific time and the best known festive rebellion is the one at Shrovetide, explored in Emmanuel Le Roy Ladurie's *Carnival in Romans.*[2]

---

[1]   Yves-Marie Bercé, *Fête et révolte* (Paris: Hachette, 1976), p. 24.

[2]   E. Le Roy Ladurie, *Le Carnaval de Romans* (Paris: Gallimard, 1979), trans. by M.

Further, Shrovetide customs, perceived as carnival, have provided a theoretical dimension for social and literary studies. In Mikhail Bakhtin's words: 'carnival laughter...is universal in scope; it is directed at all and everyone, including the carnival's participants', resulting in a 'second world...outside officialdom.'[3] This method of applying carnival as a *speculum* of the dominant hegemony illuminates some historical events. For example, Yves-Marie Bercé finds the carnival season, chosen for the revolt in Romans, itself symbolic of the people's struggle against the puritanical Huguenots, with the usually festive battle between Carnival and Lent played out in the streets of the city for real.[4] On the other hand, Natalie Zemon Davis's article, 'Scandale à l'Hôtel-Dieu de Lyon (1537–1543)', reveals an inverted world in one apparently normal—even sanctified—social structure in Lyons, and the clues are in the festive sobriquets given to those involved.[5]

The use of carnival in literary studies was also introduced by Bakhtin whose concept of 'carnivalization' has provided a way to understand any work containing a separate world-view, consciously mirroring and parodying reality.[6] This form of analysis has been applied to the multi-faceted nature of much English Renaissance drama, as explored by Neil Rhodes, Michael Bristol, and others[7] although C. L. Barber retained the more general, 'festive' for his inquiry into Shakespeare's comic charac-terisation. In festive comedy, he wrote, '"events" put its persons in the position of festive celebrants: if they do not seek holiday it happens to them'.[8] Yet carnival remains the dominant term and, as Stallybrass and White have observed, there is now 'a large and increasing body of writing

---

Feeney (Harmondsworth: Penguin, 1981).

[3] Mikhail Bakhtin, *Rabelais and his World*, trans. by H. Iswolsky (Chicago: MIT, 1968), pp. 8–11.

[4] Bercé, p. 78.

[5] N. Z. Davis, 'Scandale à l'Hôtel-Dieu de Lyon (1537–1543)', in *La France de l'Ancien régime: études réunies en l'honneur de Pierre Goubert*, ed. by Société de démographie historique (Toulouse: Privat, 1984), pp. 175–87 (p. 181).

[6] M. Bakhtin, *Problems of Dostoevsky's Poetics*, trans. by R. W. Rotsel (Ann Arbor: Ardis, 1973), pp. 129–31.

[7] N. Rhodes, *Elizabethan Grotesque* (London: Routledge and Keegan Paul, 1980), and M. Bristol, *Carnival and Theater* (London: Methuen, 1985).

[8] C. L. Barber, *Shakespeare's Festive Comedy* (Princeton: Princeton University Press, 1959), p. 6. Bakhtin had originally written, 'Carnival is not a spectacle to be seen by the people; they live in it.' *Rabelais and his World*, p. 7.

which sees carnival not simply as a ritual feature of European culture but as a *mode of understanding*, a positivity, a cultural analytic.'[9] Carnival was more than unregulated time; it was one whose disorder could be theoretically justified. The complexities of the concept, along with twentieth-century interest in ambivalence, have created a carnivalesque mode of interpretation.

By contrast, midsummer has almost gone unnoticed. One might say it has been eclipsed: a fate which is highly appropriate but, nevertheless, one which I shall try to change.

For none of the carnival studies would have been possible without the extant records of customs from Christmas day to Shrovetide. The ecclesiastic feast of fools at New Year—the first to attract scholars' attention—was not welcome to the authorities but, since it was a fundamental part of the life of the lower clergy, the Church was compelled to respond with written comments and attempted prohibitions: similarly from civic authorities at Shrovetide, when whole towns united in a last subversive challenge to the stringent order to be imposed from Ash Wednesday.[10] Obviously, celebrations controlled or sanctioned by authority have an advantage for the twentieth-century historian and, since many winter activities needed indoor accommodation, another source of record becomes available. At Christmas, all social classes were united in honour of Christ's birth; a celebration which contains a Christianized concept of festive inversion in the form of a weak child who was born to overcome kings. This principle helped unite high and low and gave licence to other, more pagan, traditions of reversals, some of which were also Christianized as, for example, Boy Bishops. The other crucial factor which helped mid-winter customs to thrive was the weather: neither fighting nor farming made much progress; therefore serious business was forced to come to a halt for all but the bourgeoisie, and whole courts and communities turned to play.

The feast of the Nativity of St John the Baptist was held in quite opposite circumstances. Since the weather was warm, indoor shelter was not needed; games could take place in various locations without any

---

[9]   Peter Stallybrass and Allon White, *The Politics and Poetics of Transgression* (London: Methuen, 1986), p. 6.

[10]   These authorities were frequently cajoled into taking part. See Marjoke de Roos, 'Carnival Traditions in the Low Countries', in *Custom, Culture and Community in the later Middle Ages,* ed. by T. Pettitt and L. Søndergaard (Odense: Odense University Press, 1994), pp. 17–36 (p. 28).

4

official eye taking note. At this season, society was divided by the separate interests of different classes. From chronicles it would appear that much of the nobility spent the summer disputing territory; the bourgeoisie had commercial concerns, and the artisans, on their own, had little means of leaving a record. Yet, sometimes, the lack of comment is itself eloquent, as in the account of the Angevin lawyer, Jacques Bruneau, writing in 1626. In his section on 'the revels, pleasures and delights of the country of Anjou' there is a notable contrast between the detail on customs up until May and an attempt to skate over those held later. Bruneau mentions two winter kings and gives details on Carême Prenant, Easter (Shrovetide), and Pentecost (Whitsuntide). But, as he approaches midsummer, vagueness enters in. 'All summer each man goes to indulge his pleasure outside the town [some working] others diverting themselves with various amusements, which they enjoy and wish for, in the fields.'[11] Bruneau clearly knew what went on and his silence suggests self-imposed censorship over a subject which was not socially acceptable. The title of his book includes the phrase, 'some of what can be reported about the town of Angers'.[12] Fortunately, Claude de Rubys, a local historian from Lyon, wrote a 'real history of Lyon' in 1604 and he gave details which could explain Bruneau's reticence. The possibility is that, not only were midsummer amusements more dispersed and harder to document or define, some were harder to accommodate within an ethical code. In a list of activities on and around St John the Baptist's day, which include jousting and *charivari*, de Rubys comments: 'if *charivari* are banned, the people return to the taverns where after much drinking they stamp their feet under the table...they pull to pieces the king, princes, governor, the State and the legal system. They write scandalous and defamatory leaflets which they pin up at crossroads or pass around in the streets'. Such diversions are allowed 'following the advice of that great politician, Theodore Amatus, king of the Ostrogoths...who said that it was expedient

---

[11] 'Tout l'été, un chascun va prendre son plaisir hors de la ville [some working] les aultres se recréent aux divers contentemens qui se peuvent désirer et souhaitter aux champs' from 'Des esbatz, plaisirs & delices du paie d'Anjou', Angers Bibliothèque Municipal MS 994 [870], pp. 345–46. See S. Billington, 'Social Disorder, Festive Celebration, and Jean Michel's *Le Mistere de la Passion JesusCrist'*, *Comparative Drama*, 95 (1995), 216–47 (p. 222).

[12] *Philandinopolis, ou plus clairement les fidelles Amities, Contenons vue partie de ce qui estè & de ce qui peut estre, & de ce qui se peult dire & rapporter de la ville d'Angers, & pais d'Anjou*, Angers, Bibl. Mun. MS 994 [870], pp. 335–43.

to tolerate the people indulging in folly and making merry, for fear that holding them in too rigid a discipline will result in desperation.'[13] Natalie Zeman Davis reads these slanders as a kind of revolt unconnected with the season itself—simply an expression of frustration at being deprived of *charivari*.[14] However, such challenges to power occurred frequently at midsummer and, although Yves-Marie Bercé considers that it was the alcohol, at any season, which prompted riot,[15] at the Festival of St John the Baptist the alcohol appears to have given courage to express a perceived seasonal licence to abuse power. The nature of the liberties taken could explain why Renaissance historians preferred not to mention customs relating to St John the Baptist's day at all, particularly in Anjou where the social fabric had been destroyed by total anarchy during the English annexation.[16]

Another explanation could be the fact that solsticial games in medieval Europe involved belief in Fortune. The midsummer solar crisis is so-called because the sun is at a moment of change, and games often reflected the belief that such dramatic reversals were caused by Chance Fortune. Popular perception of this, in the Middle Ages, did not differ very much from that in Ancient Rome where Fors Fortuna had governed the day, and it appears that the early Church had been well able to accommodate observances to Fortune under the aegis of St John the Baptist. Evidence shows that, during the Middle Ages, midsummer in fact symbolized the validity of such beliefs, and rituals commemorating change were sanctioned provided the Saint's name replaced that of Fortune: a requirement which was not always observed. However, it seems the reason for present-day lack of knowledge about these traditions is that

---

[13] '...le peuple au lieu de cela renuoyé aux tavernes, ou apres auoir bien beu, ils comencent à cacqueter les pieds branslants soubs la table... dechiffrer le Roy, les princes, le Gouuerneur, l'Estat & la Iustice, & minuter des Cartels scandaleux & diffamatoires, qu'ils vont puis afficha[n]ts par les carrefours, ou sema[n]ts par les rues.' '...suiuant l'enseigneme[n]t qu'en a donné ce grand Politicque Theodorie Amatus.... Il disoit qu'il estoit quelque fois expedient de tolerer que le peuple face le fol, & se resiouïsse, de peur que en luy tenant trop gra[n]d rigeur, on ne le mette en desespoir.' Claude de Rubys, *Histoire véritable de la ville de Lyon* (Lyon, 1604). pp. 501, 499–500 respectively. See Appendix D.

[14] N. Z. Davis, 'The Reasons of Misrule', in *Society and Culture in Early Modern France* (London: Duckworth, 1975), pp. 97–123 (p. 106).

[15] Y.-M. Bercé, *Histoire des croquants: étude des soulèvements populaires au XVIIe siècle dans le sud-ouest de la France* (Geneva: Droz, 1974), vol. 1, p. 213.

[16] See Billington, 'Social Disorder', pp. 217–22.

scholars of folklore have improved on the Church's work. At the Renaissance, and again in the nineteenth century, a strong bias emerged against any perception of Fortune's ambivalence in popular customs. From the nineteenth century on, there has even been a denial of a dangerous aspect to Fortune in perceptions of her during the pagan era, in Ancient Rome, and this has reinforced how we now interpret Fortune in the Middle Ages.[17]

The seminal work for the twentieth century has been that of Kurt Latte who asserted that Fors Fortuna was seen in Rome as a positive force and was referred to as such by all the major Roman writers. He writes that the impersonal and incalculable nature personified in the Greek Tyche was 'neutralised in that optimistic assumption which characterizes Roman religion in general'.[18] Therefore, it is not surprising that Rome's river festival to Chance Fortune, the *Tiberina Descensio*, and held on 24 June, has recently been interpreted as a decayed water purification ceremony,[19] when the evidence from Ovid, Cicero, and others show that floating down the Tiber and rowing back was a rite commemorating change, mutability, and the passing of time.[20] A similar misunderstanding has been applied to Rome's sister city of Lyons which, among numerous midsummer festivals, enjoyed a boat combat on the Saône called the *Fête des Merveilles*. In 1573 the local historian, Guillaume Paradin, had associated this festival with observances to the death and resurrection of Saint Pothin, a first-century martyr whose life story was adapted by the Church, it seems, in order to Christianize a custom which already existed. Fourteenth-century records show that the intention to hold the festival on the day commemorating St Pothin's martyrdom—2 June—usually gave way to

[17] (Translation by Betty Knott-Sharpe.) By 1900 discussions about Fors Fortuna's influence on the Roman Republic had developed into two opposed views. R. Peter and W. Warde Fowler deduced that she was seen as inconstant, while G. Wissowa stressed a lucky goddess, protectress of peasants. See J. Champeaux, *Fortvna* (Rome: École française de Rome, 1982), p. 225.

[18] K. Latte, *Römische Religionsgeschichte* (Munich: C. H. Beck'sche Verlag, 1960), pp. 179–80. A study of Roman literature and records supports Warde Fowler's quite opposite view that Fors Fortuna 'represented chance, that inexplicable power which appealed so strongly to the later sceptical and Graecized Romans'. W. Warde Fowler, *The Roman Festivals of the Period of the Republic* (London, 1899), p. 165. See Billington, 'Fors Fortuna in Ancient Rome', in *The Concept of the Goddess*, ed. by S. Billington and M. Green (London: Routledge, 1996), pp. 129–40.

[19] J. Champeaux, p. 243.

[20] Billington, 'Fors Fortuna in Ancient Rome', pp. 129–40.

holding it on the Tuesday before the Nativity of St John and, in practice, St Pothin's day also moved to the same Tuesday. This, and other evidence, led M. C. Guigue to conclude that the foundation of the *Fête des Merveilles* had been by the people, not by the Cathedral Chapter, and that the festival had a Roman origin, celebrating the inconstancies of Chance Fortune at midsummer, similar to the *Tiberina Descensio*.[21] However, once again, twentieth-century scholars have removed the dangerous mutability, replacing it with purification.[22] This insistence on removing half of the meaning of Fors Fortuna in Folklore Studies is in curious opposition to our understanding of Fortune in early medieval literature and art, in which her ambivalence and changeability are perceived as essential to her role.[23] Present-day misunderstandings and gaps in our knowledge of medieval midsummer customs originate in this distortion of the goddess's function. The missing link is Chance Fortune, and some proof is needed of her survival from the classical to the Christian world.

Fors Fortuna had not been indigenous to Rome but, like the cuckoo in the nest, she not only found a home among the Roman gods, she also subsumed them when the Empire declined between 100 and 300 CE. As many recognized, the abstract concept of Chance was dangerous because it undermined all other beliefs. Pliny wrote: 'We are so much at the mercy of chance that Chance, by whom God is proved uncertain, takes the place of God'.[24] However, the doubt she cast on claimed power in the world was seen as a reason for hope by persecuted Christians. In Tertullian's address *To the Nations*, (Carthage 200 CE), he borrowed from the classical writer, Cicero, to send the following warning: 'Nations in general have had rule in their [due] time—whether Assyrian, Medes, Persian or Egyptian. The lottery of the time thus wills it'.[25] His

---

[21] M. C. Guigue, *Recherches sur les Merveilles* (Lyon, 1887), pp. 8–15 and 30–36.

[22] Champeaux, *Fortvna*, p. 220.

[23] See H. R. Patch, *Fortuna in Old French Literature* (Northampton, MA: Smith College, 1923), and Pierre Courcelle, *La Consolation de philosophie dans la tradition littéraire: antécédents et postérité de Boèce* (Paris: Études Augustiniennes, 1967).

[24] Pliny, *Natural History*, vol. 1, trans. by H. Rackham, LCL (London/Cambridge, MA: Heinemann, 1938), pp. 183–85.

[25] 'Regnum uniuersae nationes [*suis quae*]q[*ue te*]mporibus habuerunt, ut Assyrii, ut Medi, ut Persæ, ut Aegyp[*tii; est adh*]uc penes quosdam, et tamen qui amiserunt, non sine religionibus et cultu et †depropitiorum deorum moranban[*tur, donec Romanis*] cessit uniuersa paene dominatio. Sors temporum ita uolut....' *Ad Nationes* II. 18. *Corpus Christianorum*, Series Latina, vol. 1, *Tertulliani Opera*, Pt 1 (Turnhout: Brepols, 1954), p.

8

conclusion even adds the game of chance: the phrase *sors temporum ita uolut* is not in Cicero's original and, in this way, Tertullian derided the apparent permanence of pagan rule. The martyr, Cyprian, mocked pagan authority in the same way: 'kingdoms do not rise to supremacy through merit but are varied by lot'.[26]

After 312 CE, when Christianity became the established Roman religion, belief in the chance variation of power inevitably threatened its own stability. Fortune switched from being an ally to becoming a greater danger than any other pagan religion, and the tracts of Lactantius and Augustine aimed to extirpate her. This was carried through in many respects—shrines and images were destroyed, worship banned, sacrifice punished by death. When one of her temples was turned into an ale-house the poet, Palladias, bewailed: 'Fortune, fortune maker/breaker: Human nature cocktail shaker: Goddess once, and now a barmaid'.[27] Despite this, it is now well known that Fortune, again, did not disappear:

> The usual brief characterization of the Church Fathers as relentless foes of *fortuna* seems on the basis of a general examination of their writings, to be less than a complete assessment of the evidence. It is certainly true that theologians deny the existence of Fortuna and sometimes even proscribe the use of the word in the sense 'luck'. But this condemnation does not deter them from using the word whenever it is called for in their own writings.[28]

Verbal slips—as in Augustine's *Contra Academicos*[29]—were not the

---

75. Cicero wrote: 'I had learned from Plato [*Rep.* viii.2. 545] that certain revolutions in government are to be expected; so that states are now under a monarchy, now under a democracy, and now under a tyranny.' *De senectute; De amicitia; De divinatione* II. ii. 6–7, trans. by W. A. Falconer, LCL (London/New York: Heinemann, 1923). Plato himself makes less of the point.

[26] 'Regna autem non merito accidunt, sed sorte variantur'. *On the vanity of Idols,* 5, *Patrologiæ Cursus Completus* Series Latina, *S. Cypriani Operum Pars II* (Paris: Migne, 1865), vol. 4, col. 591. One of Cyprian's correspondents was the martyr Fortunatus (i.e. born by Caesarian after the death of his mother). The name was given, one assumes, before his conversion but it seems not to have been at odds with the Christian creed. For other classical borrowings by early Christians, see H. Chadwick, *The Early Church* (Harmondsworth: Pelican, 1967), p. 78.

[27] *Palladias: Poems: A Selection,* trans. by Tony Harrison, Poetica, 5 (London: Anvil Press, 1975), p. 63.

[28] J. C. Frakes, *The Fate of Fortune in the Early Middle Ages* (Leiden: Brill, 1988), p. 25.

[29] The *Contra Academicos* was written soon after Augustine's conversion, partly to refute, but partly to support Cicero's New Academy, and to explain to Augustine's friend,

only evidence of her survival in the thinking of the authorities. In some contexts and in adapted forms, 'fortune' remained 'a perfectly valid Christian concept'.[30] Pickering sees these adaptations as post-Boethian, but an example can be found surprisingly early, in the fourth century, for it was decided that the fairest way to pick judges in some criminal cases was by lot. One Code appeared in 376 and applied to provincial courts: 'it shall be allowable to adjoin such men, drawn by lot and not chosen by selection'. Another, in 423, applied to trials of senators: 'We believe it to be very easy to choose the best men from the highest ranking men, nevertheless, they shall be called by lot to act in this court.'[31] The absorption of *sors* into Christian thinking later proved hard to control,[32] but these early instructions allowed for a positive role to some rituals of chance. Other parts of the Code, too, show that after a repressive start, the more harmless aspects of pagan customs, such as the entertainment they provided and their value in the traditions of the people, were protected. There is, for example, the instruction of 399: 'Just as we have already abolished profane rites...so we do not allow the festal assemblies of citizens and the common pleasure of all to be abolished. Hence we decree that, according to ancient custom, amusements shall be furnished to the people, but without any sacrifice or any accursed superstition, and they shall be allowed to attend festal banquets, whenever public desires so demand.'[33] The tortuous opening syntax here indicates the pressure of

---

Romianus, the virtues of philosophy. Book 1 opens: 'I wish, Romianus, that Virtue, who never allows fortune to take anyone away from her, could, for her part, snatch from fortune, resist as she might, the man that is suited for her purpose. If that could be she certainly would already have placed her hands on you.' *St. Augustine: Against the Academics*, trans. and ed. by J. J. O'Meara (Westminster, MD: Newman Press, 1950), pp. 14–17. See Migne, Series Latina, vol. 32, Sancti Aurelii Augustini, col. 905. In Augustine's *Retractationes* composed at the end of his life, he denied he had referred 'to any goddess, but rather to the fortuitous outcome of events for good or evil affecting our own bodies or things external', and he regretted having mentioned fortune in such a way. O'Meara, p. 168.

[30] F. P. Pickering, *Literature and Art in the Middle Ages* (London: Macmillan, 1970), p. 168. Cf. V. Flint, *The Rise of Magic in Early Medieval Europe* (Oxford: Clarendon Press, 1991).

[31] *The Theodosian Code and Novels and the Sirmondian Constitutions*, trans. by C. Pharr (Princeton: Princeton University Press, 1952), Nos 9.1.13, p. 226 and 2.1.12, p. 39 respectively.

[32] V. Flint, pp. 68 and 217–225.

[33] *The Theodosian Code*, no. 16.10.17, p. 475.

public opinion, for 'the urban poor exercised an influence [beyond] their numbers and economic importance.'[34]

Midsummer remained their annual proof of the power of Fortune's changeability and, in the fourth century, the Church was highly ingenious, brilliant even, in the way it accommodated the indisputable reality of the solar crisis without casting doubt on Christianity. It is common knowledge that the Church did Christianize pagan festivals, but what is important here is how the original meaning of both solstices was adapted, for pagan understanding of seasonal growth and decline was harnessed in favour of the new Christian certainties. Augustine wrote that the festival of Christ's birth itself caused the darkest nights of the year to shorten: 'When we were living without faith, we were night. And, because this same lack of faith...had to be lessened by the growth of faith, so on the birthday of our Lord Jesus Christ the nights begin to be shorter.'[35] A causal connection is implied: Christ's birth makes the improvement at the mid-winter solstice.

As far as 24 June is concerned, one passage in the New Testament (Luke 1. 26) says that St John was born six months before Christ; therefore the opposite solstice was automatically right to celebrate his birth. However, Christ's nativity had been given solsticial significance and a parallel significance was found for the Baptist. It is a remarkable coincidence that John was reported to have said of himself in relation to Christ: 'He shall increase but I shall decrease' (John 3. 30). *Crescere* and *minui* are the words used in the Latin translation, and they suggest an original lunar metaphor.[36] It is also more likely that the statement originated from John the Evangelist than from John the Baptist. Maurice Casey and others consider that from verse 3. 31, there is a Johannine argument to persuade the Baptist's followers to accept Christ as the 'Christ', instead of John, as they had up until then. It seems most likely, therefore, that the previous line was never actually said by the Baptist but was the Evangelist's way

[34] A. H. M. Jones, 'The Social Background of the Struggle between Paganism and Christianity', in *The Conflict between Paganism and Christianity in the Fourth Century*, ed. by A. Momigliano (Oxford: Clarendon Press, 1963), pp. 17–37 (p. 23).

[35] *St Augustine: Sermons for Christmas and Epiphany*, trans. by T. C. Lawler (Westminster, MD: Newman Press, 1952), p. 102.

[36] For solar and lunar calendar computation at the time see D. K. Falk, *Daily, Sabbath and Festival Prayers in the Dead Sea Scrolls* (Leiden: Brill, 1998), p. 190, and R. T. Beckwith, *Calendar and Chronology, Jewish and Christian* (Leiden: Brill, 1996), pp. 276–78.

of making the prophet subordinate himself.[37] However, the metaphor of waxing and waning fitted later theology for the June solstice perfectly. St Augustine wrote: '[Christ] sent before Him a man John, to be born at the time when days begin to grow shorter, while He Himself was born when they begin to grow longer. This was to be a prefigurement of what the same John says: he must increase, but I must decrease'.[38] In the Middle Ages the births of Christ and John were the only Nativities celebrated in the Christian calendar, 'for their coming into the world had Christian meaning.'[39] Christ's birth is the first point of light in a faithless existence, whereas John's mortality represented the end of the pagan era. The cyclic nature of life from weakness to strength, and then to decline, was not only perceived but creatively incorporated into the Christian calendar since, as a pre-Christian, John the Baptist diverted scepticism away from Christianity and pointed instead towards the decline of the previous era, much as Tertullian had anticipated. As the last of the pre-Christian prophets, the celebration of John's nativity could retain the fundamental solsticial message that the day symbolized a brief and mortal zenith of power, which was to be superseded by the non-material religion.[40] In some places St John's *decollatio* was also commemorated on 29 August, further accentuating a pre-Christian fall from temporary power at the end of summer.

It is this perception of mutability in the midsummer solstice which is missing from current studies of folklore and medieval literature. Medieval writers dwell on the instability of material good fortune, yet, today, this

---

[37] Maurice Casey, *Is John's Gospel True?* (London: Routledge, 1995), p. 77. Cf. *La Vie St. Jean Baptiste: A Critical Edition of an Old French Poem of the Early Fourteenth Century*, ed. by R. L. Gieber (Tübingen: Max Niemeyer, 1978), p. xi.

[38] Lawler, ed., *St Augustine: Sermons for Christmas and Epiphany*, p. 121.

[39] Abbé Sachet, *Le pardon annuel de la Saint-Jean et de la Saint-Pierre à Saint-Jean de Lyon 1392–1790*, vol. 1 (Lyon: P. Grange, 1914), p. 221; Cf. Henri Gaidoz, *Le Dieu gaulois du soleil, et le symbolisme de la roue*, Études de mythologie gauloise, Extrait de la *Revue Archéologique* (Paris, 1886), pp. 15–16.

[40] In the twelfth century, John Beleth deviated from Augustine's reading. He noted the placing of the two nativities just after, not on, the days of the absolute lowest and highest points of the sun: 'finally, the days wane before the feast of St John and wax before the birth of our Lord' (aliquando dies ante festum sancti I- decrescant, & ante natale Domini crescant). According to this, festivities on 25 December celebrated an improvement already begun, those on St John's Day contained an awareness that the peak had been passed. See *Rationale Diuinorum Officiorum Ionne Beletho Theologo Parisiense authore* (Antwerp, 1562), p. 303.

12

tends to slip from view. In J. Cerquiglini's very interesting study of Guillaume de Machaut's *Voir Dit*, she sees a structural harmony in patterns of rise and fall, in terms of progression and balance: 'the lady [Fortune] cannot lie; the lady cannot betray'.[41] So, too, Cerquiglini's view of seasons is limited to the fateful, inevitable, yet ultimately harmonious, march of time. But, as I hope to show, medieval literature also put forward a more challenging view.

The omission of an ambivalent side to Fortune and the midsummer season is more explicit in folklore studies. In 1865 J. J. Clément Mullet considered all water festivals on St John's Day to be ancient purification rites, Christianized and made appropriate to 24 June, through John's baptising of Christ.[42] A case can be made for this in relation to festivals of immersion, as in Florence or Egypt, but not for boating customs, where the purpose was not physical contact with the water. Nor is Mullet's explanation the one given by Augustine, in his exegesis on how the early Fathers themselves interpreted the solstices in the Church calendar. The concern of the Church was to deflect mutability into channels which did not threaten it, and this was achieved by directing the symbolism of 24 June towards the medieval understanding of secular power, and away from Christian belief. The disruptive powers of Fortune could still be seen to threaten the individual's material life.

The scholarly view which ignores this misses fifty per cent of the customs which actually went on at the summer solstice, and the most dynamic of them: those which interacted with political life. For traditions on St John's Day which have not fitted the dominant theory have been overlooked, and are therefore missing from Muchambled's *Popular Culture and Elite culture in France 1400–1750.*[43] They are missing, too, from Philippe Walter's extensive and erudite work, *La Mémoire du temps: fêtes et calendriers de Chrétien de Troyes à la morte Artu,*[44] where almost nothing is said about the festival of St John the Baptist, although

---

[41] '... la dame ne peut mentir, la dame ne peut trahir'. J. Cerquiglini, '*Un engin si soutil': Guillaume de Machaut et l'écriture au XIVᵉ siècle* (Geneva/Paris: Slatkine, 1985), p. 62.

[42] 'Feux de Saint-Jean', *Revue Orientale et Américaine,* Société d'Ethnographie (Paris, 1865), pp. 12–13.

[43] Trans. by L. Cochrane, (Baton Rouge: Louisiana State University Press, 1985), pp. 50–83. (Even leaping over bonfires could have had a more dangerous, solstitial meaning than the one given.)

[44] P. Walter (Paris: Champion, 1989).

'this date occurs frequently in Arthurian romances'.[45] John Darrah's equally fascinating work on *Paganism in Arthurian Romance* also omits medieval associations with St John's Day which came from contemporary popular culture, rather than from the traditions of myth. And Ronald Hutton, too, gives no examples of games of ambivalence in his extensive cultural study, *The Stations of the Sun*.[46] Jean-Claude Aubailly confronts the fact of the limited information on midsummer, in his study of seasonal play-performance: 'Avec le cycle de mai notre revue se termine. En effet, le cycle de la Saint-Jean ne semble pas avoir été marqué par des motifs ou des coutumes spécifiques aussi nettement que les autres cycles, excepté toutefois les feux et les bûchers et les récoltes d'herbes investies de pouvoirs magiques.' He poses the unresolved question: 'Faut-il supposer une période de festivités (qui serait à raccrocher au cycle de Saint-Jean) vers la mi-juin?'[47] Other authors have fallen back on observations that all activities at midsummer were the remnants of a half-remembered fertility belief, as in the title, *The Summer Solstice Games: a study of English Fertility Religion*.[48]

However, as Natalie Zemon Davis says of *charivari*, the most vital popular celebrations in the Middle Ages were not 'a mere playing with primitive and magical customs of forgotten meaning. Rather they were a carnival treatment of reality'.[49] At midsummer, the central feature of such burlesque was the perception that no worldly power was invulnerable. Despite the rigour of the feudal system, or because of it, one of the most common St John's Day liberties was that of verbally attacking the authority of those in power above you, graphically described by Claude de Rubys. Such wild behaviour was not incidental to the festivities; as I shall show, hotheadedness was considered integral to men in their midsummer years, and was exercised by them at the midsummer of the solar year, when the symbol of power was seen to fall. The midsummer

---

[45] *Guillaume le Clerc: The Romance of Fergus*, ed. by W. Frescoln (Philadelphia: William H. Allen, 1983), p. 249.

[46] J. Darrah, *Paganism in Arthurian Romance* (Woodbridge: Boydell, 1994) and R. Hutton, *The Stations of the Sun* (Oxford: Oxford University Press, 1996).

[47] J.-C. Aubailly, 'Théâtre Médiéval et Fêtes Calendaires ou l'Histoire d'une Subversion', in *Between Folk and Liturgy*, ed. by Alan J. Fletcher & Wim Hüsken, Ludus, 3 (Amsterdam: Rodopi, 1997), pp. 31–64 (pp. 56–57).

[48] (Bexleyheath: Privately printed, 1985). Peter Burke accepts a similar view in *Popular Culture in Early Modern Europe* (London: Temple Smith, 1978), pp. 180–81.

[49] *Society and Culture in Early Modern France*, p. 106.

14

festive season appears to have been the one when the greatest liberties were taken in terms of breaking censorship, and this inevitably affects our perception of the pre-Lent carnival. The evidence shows that the first challenges to the hegemonic world view, in life and in literature, were in fact perceived to be appropriate to midsummer and Rabelais himself, the father of the carnivalesque, may well have combined midsummer elements with carnival traditions in his own parodies of power. In the case of twelfth-century romances, a festive principle is yet to be perceived in them at all. Yet the evidence shows that Chrétien was the first to have used a saturnalian perspective in his writing, one which was based on interpretations of beliefs and customs at the midsummer solstice. It is these which which form the matrix for the ironic view cast on the valour of the Arthurian court. Midsummer wildness, and other St John's Day traditions, were fully developed by writers such as Chrétien and Jean Renaut into critiques of events, plots, and people.

For belief in seasonal mutability did not have to be destroyed—it was a fact of life which could not be denied—and under the careful umbrella provided by the saint, solsticial customs continued in medieval traditions, and proved highly seminal in its literature. The development also involved other subjects. The solstice maintained connections with fortune, and with pride; it could be associated with either, or with both at the same time. A tapestry of ideas was available, from which authors wove individual designs. It is essential to know some of the metaphors which developed and, as they are tangential to the main argument, I have provided two appendices: one on the use of the wheel and the hill to symbolize fortune's power over people, and the other on the relation of horses to pride.

There is also evidence in the French literature to suggest that feast days during the whole period between May and August could be given over to developments on the theme of summer, midsummer, and the end of summer as a rise to an apex, followed by decline and death. Similarly, material in texts sometimes leads to the conclusion that traditions more specific to midsummer could spread into the weeks before and after 24 June. Precise evidence can be found in English records where, on the last Sunday in August 1601, the men of South Kyme in Lincolnshire played 'the death of the Lord of Kyme, because the same day should make an end of the summer lord game in South Kyme for that year.'[50] And, in

---

[50] C. L. Barber, *Shakespeare's Festive Comedy*, pp. 40–45.

1600, a king-ale held in Wotton St Lawrence spread over nearly a month from mid-June to early July. The first gathering was made on the 'sonday senight before midsomer', the second on the Sunday before midsummer, the third on that Monday, the fourth on the Sunday after midsummer (29 June) and the last on the following Sunday (6 July). Continuity between each gathering is indicated by payments for 'Ladyes Lyueries' and 'Lordes Lyveries' for some sort of festivity which belonged to the whole of the king-ale.[51]

As the 'Contents' page to this book indicates, solsticial customs permeated several areas of medieval life. Cultural, political, literary, and theatrical activities all might draw from the ethos of midsummer as well as from its events. Because of the diversity I have divided the book into those sections which contain chapters related to each other and between sections comes a shift from one genre or social context to another. Section I is a single, extended chapter covering all aspects of the available evidence on customs which occurred on and around St John's Day from the twelfth to the sixteenth century, with my interpretation of them. Section II then returns to the twelfth century to begin a largely chronological survey of more literary usage of these customs, and beginning with Chrétien's seminal midsummer tale of Yvain. Section II also includes studies of *Erec and Enide* and of *Lancelot*, where much of the action takes place between early and late summer. And this section ends with the Arthurian romances written after Chrétien in which references to the day of St John's Nativity provide the key to deciphering the plot. These are less well-known works, such as the *Perlesvaus, Fergus*, the Didot *Perceval*, and *Li chevaliers as deus espees.* Jean Renaut's *Galeran* was contemporaneous with some of these, but Renaut's differs in being non-Arthurian. Its context is, rather, urban, with the city of Metz a key location, therefore this tale is dealt with in Section III after a study of how St John's Day was incorporated into the civic culture of Metz, and also of Louvain, where a thirteenth-century interlude provides useful information. Following *Galeran* comes an examination of some later bourgeois plays which also pick up on themes and behaviour related to St John's Day, some of which can be related to the work of Renaut as well as further back to that of Chrétien. The final shift in the book (Section IV) is to a moral and satiric view of the traditions themselves, as found in

---

[51] P. H. Greenfield, 'Parish Drama in Four Counties Bordering the Thames Watershed', *English Parish Drama,* ed. by A. F. Johnston and W. Hüsken, Ludus, 1 (Amsterdam & Atlanta: Rodopi, 1996), pp. 107–18 (p. 111).

Jacquemart Giélée's *Renart le Nouvel,* Huon de Mery's *Le Tournoi de l'Antéchrist,* and Jehan de la Mote's *Voie d'Enfer et de Paradis.* These form the substance of one chapter, and Jean Michel's religious play, *Mistere de la Passion JesusCrist,* is the main focus of the last chapter.

I consider only French and Flemish material because of limitations of time, space, and this researcher's linguistic skills. Within this remit, though, the potential choice of texts is vast and some time has been invested in discovering which were in fact written with an interest in St John's Day in summer. Perhaps it is not so surprising, therefore, that some, such as *Perlesvaus* and *Renart le Nouvel* are not very well known today, since the tools for understanding them are, so far, missing. Therefore, as well as bringing the culture of St John's Day into scholarly debate and showing its relevance to the understanding of some major works, this book aims to reveal the value of other works previously neglected because they were developments in a now neglected tradition.

SECTION I

CHAPTER 1

Power Games at Midsummer

Le temps d'este approche/ Donnons des esveillons/ Faisons sonner la cloche .../ Allarmes et allassault .../ Faisons maintenant raige,/ Menons l'artillerie/ Pour dancer à plaisir./ Arras ... Avant que Sainct-Jehan vienne/ Tu seras trespassé.

from 'La Sommation d'Arras', 1543.

T he one midsummer tradition we know most about, apart from the lighting of fires, is that of rolling a wheel down a mountain on the eve of St John. The ritual was observed throughout Europe, recorded in Germany, France, and England and, like many popular customs, it straddled pagan and Christian belief. In the fourth-century Acts of St Vincent it is seen as a pagan practice[1] but in 1162, when the Parisian theologian, John Beleth, first gave details about traditional behaviour on the eve and the day of John's Nativity, he made the surprisingly objective comment: 'St John's eve is celebrated by both Christians and pagans because it holds allegorical and ritualistic significance.'[2]

His *Rationale of the Divine Offices* was also the first to explain that wheel-rolling was customary

> because John was a burning light who prepared the way of the Lord. But as the wheel [down the hill] is turned thus, [the people] think it is like the Sun

---

[1]   R. Hutton, *Stations of the Sun*, p. 311. J. Zwicker, *Fontes Historiæ Religionis Celticæ* (Berlin: Walter de Gruyter, 1934–35), I. 302–03; J. J. Hart, 'Rota Flammis Circumspecta', *Review Archéologique de l'Est et du Centre-Est,* vol. 2 (1951), pp. 82–87.

[2]   '(...multi in Nativitate eius gaudebunt quod observa[n]t Christiani & pagani) tu[m] propter allegoria[m] & mysteriu[m].' 'De Vigilia Sancti Ioannis', *Rationale*, pp. 302–03.

in its orbit which will descend when it can progress no further so that little by little it will descend. In the same way common belief has it that the blessed John came before Christ and arrived at the summit, for he was thought the Christ; and afterwards he descended and was diminished, as his own words say: 'I will decrease, but he will become great'.[3]

The concept of John as a burning light expresses anticipation of positive change at midsummer, and remains the Church's metaphor for the prophet who brought the world the first news of Christ.[4] In the thirteenth century it even led William Durand, Bishop of Mende, to use the adjective *lucifer* to describe him: 'John is called light-bringing because he illumines a new period/season...because his birth was like the dawn aurora, the birth of the true Christ was like the sunrise itself.'[5] This was somewhat risky verbal play by 1260, made possible, it would appear, because of the Baptist's pre-Christian role, and Durand, like Beleth, pointed to the magnitude of the Baptist's fall: 'thus was the fame of John, who had been thought the Christ, but he descended and was secondary'.[6] John's life was the example of the greatest possible rise and fall: the promise of fame at a celestial level, only to be followed by death, and dependence on Christ for salvation.

The custom of wheel-rolling during the night of St John's eve appears to have continued, unchanged, until the Reformation, when it comes as no surprise to find it attacked as superstition. Thomas Kirchmeyer's 1553 rejection of its solsticial nature[7] was translated into English in 1570 by Barnabe Googe:

---

[3] '...Ioannes fuerit ardens lucerna, & qui vias Domini præparauerit. Sed quod etiam rota vertatur hinc esse putant, quia in eum circulum tunc Sol descenderit vltra quem progredi nequit, à quo cogitur paulatim descendere, quemadmodum vulgi rumor de beato Ioanne Christo adueniente ad summum peruenit, quum Christus putabatur, posteaque descendit ac fuit diminutus, vt vel ipse de se testis est: Me, inquiens, opportet minui, illum autem crescere'. Ibid., pp. 304–05.

[4] In Lyon the presence of the *prévot* and *échevins* at the St John's eve bonfire was justified by the 'public rejoicing of the good news John brought'. Claude de Rubys, *Histoire véritable de la ville de Lyon* (Lyon, 1604), p. 500. See Appendix D.

[5] ...Joannes dictus est *lucifer*, quia obtulit novum tempus... quia nativitas fuit quasi aurora; nativitas vero Christi fuit quasi ortus solis. Guilelmus Durandus, *Rationale divinorum officiorum*, ch. XIV, para. 2, ed. by V. d'Avino (Naples 1859), p. 681.

[6] '...sic et fama Joannis, quod putabatur Christus, descendit, secundum...', Ibid., chap. XIV, para. 13.

[7] 'Inde diem magni Baptistæ solstitium fert', Thomas Kirchmeyer, *Regnum Papisticum* (Basle, 1553), p. 156.

Some others get a rotten wheele, all worne and cast aside,
Which couered round about with strawe. and towe, they closely hide:
And caryed to some mountaines top, being all with fire light,
They hurle it downe with violence, when dark appears the night:
Resembling much the Sunne, that from the heauens downe should fal,
A straunge and monstrous sight it seemes and fearefull to them all:
But they suppose their mischiefes all are likewise throwne to hell,
And that from harmes and daungers now, in safetie here they dwell.[8]

The Roman Catholic Church used the custom as a reminder of the decline inevitable in any worldly success, stressing that only Christ's power is permanent and, like John the Baptist, no-one, not even kings ruling by divine right, could avoid descending. Despite this, evidence shows that people remembered the changes attributed to fortune as much as they did the meaning of the saint's life. As the last two lines above show, if the falling wheel had an unobstructed run it was thought to carry away bad luck[9] and, in Lorraine in 1565, the Abbess of the Chapter of Épinal noted that the wheel rolled annually with straw was called *la roue de fortune*.[10] This association between the midsummer crisis and a fall from fortune is something which recurs in French customs, chronicles and literature, while reminders of the correct view came in vernacular translations of the *Divine Offices;* William Durand's explanation was reprinted regularly between 1473 and the seventeenth century.

Googe's translation of Kirchmeyer captures the dread and danger associated with the event—the heavy burning wheel plunging down a mountainside produced a supernatural awe, 'as if it were the sun'. The wheel is the most ancient solar symbol connected with Fortune, and wheels of fortune hung in some medieval French churches. It is also possible that rose windows in churches were designed as solar wheels.[11] Yet, despite this ancient association, medieval writers more often expressed a fall from fortune through an analogy with the mountain (see Appendix A). The phrase, *du mont aval* meant a fall in fame, status, or power as, for

---

[8] *Popular and Popish Superstitions and Customs...in Germany and other Papist Lands*, ll.781–88, trans. by Barnabe Googe, London 1570, in P. Stubbes, *Anatomie of Abuses*, ed. by F. J. Furnivall (London, 1877–82), p. 339.

[9] More clearly expressed in the original: 'In præceps, tutosq[ue], à cunctis se esse periclis', *Regnum Papisticum*, p. 156. Cf. Gaidoz, *Le Dieu Gaulois du soleil*, p. 19.

[10] Gaidoz, p. 20.

[11] Ibid., pp. 40–41, and Pierre Courcelle, *La Consolation de philosophie dans la tradition littéraire* (Paris: Études Augustiniennes, 1967), figs. 69 and 70.

example, at the opening of the romance *Meraugis de Porlesguez*, where
Arthur is challenged in his court by a dwarf who says the king's banish-
ment of Gawain has reduced his own fame: 'Rois, tu descentz aval du
mont'.[12] Froissart used the phrase to describe rowing up and down a river,
where a fall in fortune threatened.[13] And, sometimes, the direct solar
meaning was retained. Froissart wrote at the end of summer, 1378: 'The
season was descending to the valley and winter approached' ('la saison
s'en alloit aval et l'iver approchoit')[14] while, in *Li Tournamenz antecrit*
the sun at the end of the day's battle is said to have moved to the 'val
d'occident'.[15] *Aval et mont* was a commonplace phrase meaning all
classes of society.[16] *Mont* used alone could mean personal elevation or
hauteur, in terms of class, dignity, or success in life; and *aval* could also
be used alone to describe the most lowly.[17] The phrase, and variations of
it, were more common than were allusions to Fortune's wheel, possibly
because it provided a way of expressing a fall from fortune without
having to mention her by name, therefore without offending Christian
principles. The metaphor could also acquire Christian significance, as in
Le Panthère d'Amour, where the valley in which the Panther is found is
said to signify humility.[18] And the persistence of wheel-rolling throughout
Europe on St John's eve, with both its Christian and pre-Christian
resonances, could well have helped maintain the significance of the
phrase.

At the time Barnabe Googe translated Kirchmeyer's attack, another
hilltop custom was in evidence in English rural life. This was held on the
day of 24 June, and it incorporated an un-Christianized view of Fortune's
power. Since the Church ignored it totally in the Middle Ages, direct

---

[12] Raoul de Houdenc, *Meraugis de Portlesguez*, ed. by H. Michelant (Paris: Tross, 1869),
p. 56.

[13] The boat Richard II used to approach the rebels of June 1381 was described as travelling: 'amont (en haut) et aval (en bas) sur la rivière' Froissart, *Chroniques,* vol. 8, ed.
Buchon, *CNF,* vol. 18 (Paris, 1827), p. 32.

[14] Froissart, *Chroniques,* vol. 7, ed. Buchon, *CNF,* vol. 17 (Paris, 1824), p. 130.

[15] *Huon de Méry: le Tournoi de l'Antéchrist,* l. 2995, ed. and trans. by S. Orgeur
(Orleans: Paradigme, 1994), p. 226.

[16] For example in *Renart le Nouvel par Jacquemart Gielee,* l. 754, ed. by H. Roussel,
SATF (Paris: Picard, 1961), p. 41.

[17] *Dictionnaire historique de la langue française*, Académie Française (Paris, 1894).

[18] Nicole de Margivale, *Le Dit de la Panthère d'Amours,* ll. 629–30, ed. by H. A. Todd,
SATF (Paris: Didot, 1883), p. 24.

accounts did not appear until Robert Dover's Cotswold revival about 1630. The publication *Annalia Dubrensia* tells us that there were sporting competitions close to midsummer and Fortune's winner was crowned king at the top of Dover's hill.[19] The first scripted, theatrical example appears in the 1575 text of the *Chester Mystery Cycle*, which was performed on 24 June.[20] In the 'Shepherds' Play' a rebellious boy, Trowle, behaves like a fool-king[21] enthroned on a hilltop; he insults the Pope and his shepherd companions, whom he then defeats in a wrestling match. He throws the other shepherds down his hill as though he were Fortune turning her wheel. One of the shepherds says: 'Ofte wee may bee in thought wee be now under/ God amend hit with his makinge' (ll. 298–99), and Trowle's arbitrary behaviour is only cured by the birth of Christ. As is found in *Perlesvaus* (see Chapter 4), Christ is, here, shown as Fortune's natural controller, and the setting for both religious allegories was midsummer.

I have already noted that, in England, the death of the summer lord might be played out at the end of August near the time of the commemoration of the beheading of John the Baptist, or *decollatio*. The Lincolnshire example comes from a legal defence of 1601, where it was claimed as traditional practice by Talboys Dymoke. Dymoke was charged with lese-majesty done to the Earl of Lincoln and argued, as quoted, that on the last Sunday in August, they played 'the death of the Lord of Kyme, because the same day should make an end of the summer lord game in South Kyme for that year.'[22] Since the issue was events enacted at the end of summer, there are no details about the election of this lord but, in England in the sixteenth century, the understanding that temporary, midsummer lordship began at the top of Fortune's hill dominated literature and the theatre. *Annalia Dubrensia*, honouring Robert Dover, provides the only factual record. But one poem in it establishes the strength of the original custom, with the claim that Dover had revived the real tradition and an improvement on literary and theatrical pastiche: 'things there done

---

[19] *Annalia Dubrensia*, ed. by M. Walbancke London, 1636 (Menston: Scolar Press, 1973).

[20] L. M. Clopper, 'The History and Development of the Chester Mystery Cycle', *Modern Philology*, 75 (1978), 219–46 (p. 234).

[21] Richard Axton, *European Drama of the Early Middle Ages* (London: Hutchinson, 1974), pp. 186–87.

[22] C. L. Barber, *Shakespeare's Festive Comedy*, pp. 40–45.

in fact,/ Which Poets did but fayne and Players act'.[23]

There is evidence that, in France too, there was a continuation of hilltop games from the eve into midsummer day, and that these focused on a lord given temporary honours while mocked at the same time. If twentieth-century material were allowed then the proof would be over-whelming.[24] However, there is one example, from Laon in 1587, which in fact provides an earlier, and more precise, record than that from England.

Laon is spectacularly seated on a rock which rises out of the north French plain (Fig. 1) and on 24 June 1587, its geography provided a stage. A rebellion, which lasted for six years, began in February of that year and, during 1587, the rebels considered the political significance of three seasons, incorporating it where they could into their assumption of power. They first intended to depose the King's deputy, Prévôt Martin, at Shrovetide, but changed their minds in case the extra wine drunk by the people at this season led to his murder. (In Romans, seven years earlier, of course, the Shrovetide insurrection had led to homicide.) By contrast, in Laon, the rebels were still in control by the end of the first year, when they freed all the prisoners they could not afford to feed on Innocents Day and, in between on midsummer day, they returned Prévôt Martin to Paris. By then he had been in prison for three months, but the rebels waited until the early hours of 24 June for their gesture. Martin was brought out just after one a.m., dressed up in the furred gown of his former office, legs garotted under the horse he was place on, and a fairground rope was bound round his robes. Extra torches and lanterns were brought out so that the citizens could witness his discomfort. Townspeople given prefer-ence were those who provided evidence of the failings of the former

---

[23] *Annalia Dubrensia,* fo. I. 2ᵛ. See S. Billington, *Mock Kings in Medieval Society and Renaissance Drama* (Oxford: Clarendon Press, 1991), pp. 55–85.

[24] In the 1930s Arnoul van Gennep found customs still practised in Dauphiné for which he had no explanation and which included competition, a hilltop, and a festive mock lord on the day of St John. In several villages the herdsmen took part in a race to the highest pasture, arriving before dawn. The last to arrive was called the *litchbirrier,* butter-licker. Various forms of mockery might be applied; in some places he was crowned with a stinking weed and in the evening led on an ass—riding facing the tail—down to the village where he was treated to a mocking *charivari.* A. van Gennep, *Le Folklore du Dauphiné,* vol. 2 (Paris: Librairie Orientale et Americaine, 1933), pp. 338–46. The *litchbirrier* was mocked for coming last in a race, which is an appropriate St John's day reason and different from the motives behind the domestic *charivaris* de Rubys said were popular in Lyon in the same season. However, there are elements in common with the mockery of Christ in the *Passion* plays of Arnoul Gréban and Jean Michel (Chapter 9).

Figure 1: Laon. c. *1594.* Topographia Galliae. *Not paginated.*

regime—priests' mistresses and their children. As Prévôt Martin and six others were led away downhill, the audience shouted their curses and 'enjoyed the reversal in estate to which he was reduced on leaving them'.[25]

The Prévôt's fall from Fortune was down her hill. He was dressed as a surrogate king, which had been his role as Henri III's deputy; over his

[25] '...en ceste sorte conduictz par la cavallerie et infanterie hors les portes de la ville a la clerté de plus de deux cens tant torches fallotz flambeaux que lanternes afin destre mieulx et plus manifestement veuz et contemplez par les seditieux, car il y en avoit peu daultres nayant esté permis a chacun de sortir hors leurs maisons, trop bien a infiniz garses de prebtres et moynes filz et filles de putains macquereaux et macquerelles, pour en recepvoir la joie et le contentement de leur souhaict de veoir le prevost de la ville leur partie adverse en lestat ou il estoit reduict, car oultre ce quil estoit lyé et garotté comme les aultres par les jambes, il estoit encores lié par le corps sur sa robbe fourree dune grosse corde que Regnault Chastellain avoit voluntairement fourni, de laquelle il se servoit a garrotter ses ballotz de draps allant aux foires. En cest equipaige avec forces execrations et male-dictions donnez par ces bons assistans catholicques, ces sept prisonniers furent menez par dedans le faulxbourg de St. Marcel.' A. Richart, *Mémoires sur la Ligue dans le Laonnois* (Laon and Paris, 1869), pp. 162–63.

robes he was tied in a painful and ridiculous manner, and he was mocked.
His metaphoric descent was played out literally, by descending the rock
as the sun was rising on the day which marked the solar change. Summer
king games in England were based on imagined situations only, often
concerned with issues of power yet unable to influence them, as the South
Kyme incident shows. By contrast, this incident in Laon was the apotheosis of play. It staged the political realities of the moment: a change in the
town's power system, and one which also reflected the declining fortunes
of the king of France, Henri III.[26] While the 'violent jeering and curses'
directed at the main protagonist, the Prévôt, also make the event a political *charivari*.[27]

Other Traditions

Such a large area as France is bound to produce widely divergent forms
of seasonal customs and, although literature and chronicles from France
make more use of Fortune's hill than they do of her wheel, the rest of the
evidence for games played on St John's Day does not. In Verdun, records

---

[26] See *Henri III et son temps*, ed. R. Sauzet, 'De Pétrarche à Descartes', no. 56 (Paris: J. Vrin, 1992). The execution of Mary, Queen of Scots, in February 1587 was the likely immediate encouragement for the rebels.

[27] In 1833 Georges Peignot concluded that, until the French revolution, there were only domestic *charivari:* all political kinds were post-1789. (*Histoire morale, civile politique et littéraire du Charivari depuis son origine, vers le IVᵉ siècle* (Paris, 1833)). This view has been accepted, yet political *charivari* are recorded in Europe from the ninth century when, in Byzantium (*c.* 820), the usurper Thomas was mutilated and paraded publicly in the Hippodrome, on an ass. (See R. Guilland, 'Étude sur l'Hippodrome de Byzance', *Byzantinoslavica,* no. 27 (1966), pp. 288–307 (p. 303).) In Rome, in 997, a man, interestingly known as Crescentius, usurped Gregory V, and placed an ambitious monk, Philagathos, in the pontiff's seat. Gregory recovered power, Crescentius was killed, but Philagathos was horribly mutilated, and paraded through the streets of Rome facing the tail of an ass, repeating the words: 'here you see the punishment of one who wanted to remove the Roman pope'. A letter published at the time sees the monk's fate in terms of a rise and fall for the arrogant, and includes solsticial overtones: 'ce pape-là, aux mains sanglantes, ce pape arrogant et hautain (ò Dieu! ò Justice ò Soleil!) a trébuché; il est tombé'. G. Schlumberger, *L'Épopée Byzantine à la fin du dixième siècle,* vol. 2 (Paris: Hachette, 1905), p. 282. The incident at Laon and some others occurring at midsummer (see below p. 41) provide further evidence for such political *charivari* in the late medieval period. Cf. J. J. McGavin, 'Robert III's "Rough Music": Charivari and Diplomacy in a Medieval Scottish Court', *Scottish Historical Review,* 74 (1995), pp. 151–53.

survive giving information on its urban games—the Cathedral tradition known as the *feste de St Jean* (see Appendix B). Brief comments span a hundred years from 1447, when three francs were donated by the Chapter towards its expenses, to the revival of 'the good ancient custom' in 1532, celebrating a year free from plague and war. In 1485 two *maistres d'ostel* were mentioned, which suggests that a mock court was set up and, in 1502, the Chapter did not host the *feste* themselves but gave permission to certain gentlemen in the city: 'to put on the game that they wish to put on, on the day of St John the Baptist [agreeing to] lend them all that they could'.[28] There is no mention of geography nor elaboration on the properties or costumes loaned, nor mention of a midsummer lord, nor any mention of fortune.

For, in France, the election of midsummer lords only appears in the records when the festive custom had acquired either a rebellious purpose, as at Laon,[29] or civic value. For example, in Lyon, the *Fête des Merveilles* was abolished in 1400, and festivity focused instead on the midsummer fair. It was recorded that on the eve of St John's Nativity a *roi des coponiers* was elected who was to be the leader of twelve men for the policing of the fair. All *coponiers* were chosen from Lyon's watermen on the river Saône and Amadine Audin made the likely suggestion that before 1400, the title of *roi* was probably given to the man who had distinguished himself most during the river combat on midsummer day.[30] But there is no pre-1400 evidence to confirm this. Another civic incorporation occurred in Louvain, in 1267, when the election of its city leaders on 24 June was accompanied by a folk festival which appears to have had solsticial meaning. (See Chapter 5.)

The fragments of information so far known, from Lyon, Verdun, Laon, and Louvain, are so different that any attempt to rationalize them under a hilltop, midsummer, Fortune, and kingship pattern, as in the more compact island of Britain, only leads to confusion.

However, a curious coincidence can be observed in the differences between England and France. The English word for the hottest season is

---

[28] 27 Mai 1502: 'A la priere et requeste de Messieurs de la Cite, messieurs sont content et ont conclu que on leur permettre de faire le jeu quils veulent faire le jour de saint Jean, et leur prestera en tout ce qui pourra....' Verdun MS 183, fol. 45ᵛ.

[29] Also, Metz in 1405. See Chapter 5.

[30] A. Audin, 'Les Rites Solsticiaux et la Legende de St. Pothin', *Revue de l'Histoire de Religions*, 96 (1927), 147–74 (p. 166).

summer, from the Latin for summit, the highest point.[31] And, in English traditions, the highest place, the summit of a hill or mountain, is central to midsummer-king play. In France, although *du mont aval* was the commonplace expression for a man's decline in status, the term used to describe everyman in the midsummer kingship of his life was hot. And the French word for summer is *été* which derives from the Latin for hot. Philippe de Navarre in his *Quatre ages de l'homme,* written about 1260, made the first explicit analogy in the French language,[32] which can be summarized as follows: just as in the hot days of summer the corn ripens and the fruits of the earth are collected to see us through winter, so too, in the strength of youth man must work for his old age. His youthful heat enables him to work without need of good clothes, as in summer; (paras 74, 75)[33] and, to control their fires, 'youths must marry' (para. 77). The heat of youth results in many flaws. Young men suffer from error of judgement in their speech, they talk of their valour and prowess in love and speak ill of married men and fathers of women (para. 49). Young men believe they cannot die, and do not take care of themselves so that frequently they do die, in peril of their souls (para. 52). Although they have many good qualities, they are more joyful, courteous, generous, strong, vigorous, and valiant (para. 64), yet they are often too joyful and spendthrift (para. 56), particularly men of arms who squander their inheritances in play (para. 72). Instead, they must use their physical power, valour, and vigour for honour and profit. Knights, and other men of arms, must conquer with honour, for renown, and to gain temporal wealth and goods to make their lives honourable, and those of their children (para. 66); the valiant, however, can become cruel and proud (para. 67). Kingship at midsummer features in another caveat: men in their *été* years must not become proud of their cleverness and 'regnableté' (para. 65).[34]

---

[31] On 24 June in ancient Rome wheel-shaped cakes called *summanalia* were distributed. The word meant 'the supreme dawn' or 'the highest place'. M. York, *The Roman Calendar of Numa Pompilius* (New York: P. Lang, 1986), p. 134.

[32] Latin *Tractati,* based on the Greek concept of the four humours, and also attributing heat to youth, were known from the time of Bede. See J. A. Burrow, *The Ages of Man: A Study in Medieval Writing and Thought* (Oxford: Clarendon Press, 1986), pp. 12–25, and E. Sears, *The Ages of Man: Medieval Interpretations of the Life Cycle* (Princeton: Princeton University Press, 1986).

[33] *Les Quatre ages de l'homme,* ed. by Marcel de Fréville, SATF (Paris: Didot, 1888).

[34] 'Jones ne se doit fier dou tout en son senz por soutilleté ne por regnableté.' Ibid., p. 38.

The four seasons of the year had been perceived as a macrocosm, and the four stages of man's life its microcosm from antiquity. After the rise of Christianity the analogy continued, along with other methods of computing the ages of man, and often with a moral inflection.[35] Philippe finds that mixed qualities at the peak of life are inevitable; youths are composed of opposites: mentally they are children but physically adult, and the best they can do is to confess regularly so that if they do die suddenly they will not be damned (para. 53). He is not interested in either Fortune, or John the Baptist, only the moral constitution of man at his four seasons.[36]

References to a man's heat at the appropriate season are a commonplace in French literature throughout the Middle Ages and Renaissance. One of the most graphic examples is Michault Taillevent's calendrical poem, 'Le Passe Temps', in which it is stated that the hot time of youth ('jeunesse chault et boullant') rules all of a man's years ('se jeunesse domine ans').[37] This is further connected to Fortune's power over growth to heat and decline to cold, with St John's Day the moment of change. Taillevent wrote that, when he first became a youth at twelve years old: 'Ne Fortune ne me troubloit' (l. 44) and his hot or boiling years were spent outside all rule and compass, since his youthful expectations were to live in joy and wealth, always, but a new tune was heard at the St John: 'Je fus en jeunesse repeu/ D'espoir de toudis vivre en joye,/ Doubtant d'estre a l'arriere peu/ Mais avoir de biens grant monjoye,/ Ce propos jamais ne changoye./ Bains de joye ains ne vy sy flos:/ Nouvelle Saint Jehan, neuf siflos' (ll. 162–68). From here Taillevent regrets his folly as he declines into poverty and old age, able only to anticipate the release of death.[38] His error was to trust in his youthful good fortune instead of

---

[35] See E. Sears and J. A. Burrows

[36] William Durand endorsed Philippe's theories, about twenty years later in Chapter VIII of his *Rationale*, which he called, '*De Computo, et Calendario, et pertinentibus ad illa*', adding that this was a very beautiful chapter which clerics and laity needed to heed (*Pulcherrimus enim est liber iste, et clericis et laicis necessarius valde* (p. 725)). Durand said that the four seasons were easy to see in the life of man (p. 731) and he anthropomorphized the name of June itself, saying that it came from the Latin Junior, meaning 'in the prime of youth...in the flower of his or her age' (p. 733). Guilelmus Durandus, *Rationale divinorum officiorum*.

[37] 'Le Passe Temps de Michault Taillevent', ll. 386 and 550, *Un poète bourguignon du XVe siècle: Michault Taillevent,* ed. by R. Deschaux, Publications Romanes et Françaises CXXXII (Geneva: Droz, 1975), pp. 154–56.

[38] François Villon's *Testament* borrows something of this.

Figure 2: Wheel of Fortune, 1300 1400 added to the late 13th-century
Carmina Burana.

Figure 3: Wheel of Fortune, French, c. *1406.*

anticipating and preparing for the inevitable mid-life crisis.

Thus, Fortune's control over the wheel of life, which is clear in illustrations, might also be used in literary works.[39] Her circular movement
could be applied to these four inevitable seasons, as well as to a rise and
fall in fame within that cycle. Mottoes often appear at the four stages of
Fortune's wheel—*regnabo, regno, regnavi,* and *non regno,* or *sum sine
regno* (Figs 2 and 3). These make the moment of reigning in youth the
goal of life, first anticipated and, later, remembered. In Fig. 3 there is the
addition of mockery of such a temporary triumph; two of the figures on
the wheel carry either a bauble or a dagger, fool's insignia which reflect
on the value given to transient success (see Appendix A). Similarly, the
author of the 1494 *Calendrier nouvellement reffait* dismissed man's
perennial desire for summertime kingship: 'The twelve months outlined
with their qualities...show that each man has his reign, but not a very long
one'.[40] He further commented that men were hot and boiling varlets
during the great heat of June, that is between the ages of twenty-six and
thirty-six. Only then, it appears, did maturity begin, with reliability
achieved by the age of forty-two.[41] In Taillevent, and in other works, the
point is made that man's intemperate nature at his unstable summit
colludes with Fortune's plan for his decline.

In a more sympathetic vein, Pierre Ronsard, in his 'L'hynne de l'Este',
accepted even the anger, along with heat and kingship, during the mid-
summer of life. His poem features the personification of *Esté,* born of
Nature and the Sun: 'l'Esté fait masle entier, ardant, roux, et colere,/
Estincelant et chaud.../ Guerrier, prompt et hardi, tousjours en action,/
Vigoureux, genereux, plein de perfection,/ Ennemi de repos[.] Je te salue

---

[39] See J. Cerquiglini, *'Un engin si soutil': Guillaume de Machaut et l'écriture au XIVᵉ
siècle,* p. 73 and Burrows, *The Ages of Man.*

[40] 'par les douze moys figures/ Et leurs natures raportes/ Selon que chascun a son regne/
Tout homme na pas fort grant regne'. *Calendrier nouvellement reffait et autremet com-
pose... au quel sont adioustez plusieurs choses nouuelles* (Paris, 1494). BL Ephemerides
LR.41.d.2, fol. Miiiʳ.

[41] 'Juing[:] Vingt et six ans ne pls ne moing/ Cest .i. moys de gra[n]t chaleur plai[n]/ Et
aussi est qua trente six ans/ Deuient ly homs chault & bollans/ Et commen e fort a meurer/
A cueiller sens, et soy aduiser./ Juillet[:] Et quant vient regner en iuillet/ On ne lappelle
plus varlet/ Quil a des ans quarante deux/ Se moys.' Ibid., fol. Miir. Philippe de Navarre
said this dangerous time lasted sixteen years, between the ages of twenty and thirty-six.
Natalie Zeman Davis points out that youth groups which ran wild at festive seasons were
made up of unmarried men who might be quite advanced in years, though the late twenties
is the more realistic limit. *Society and Culture,* p. 104.

Esté le Prince de l'année[.]' ('Summer is completely male, ardent, red, and angry/ Fiery and hot, like his father [the sun]: warlike, hasty-tempered, and tough, always active. Vigorous, generous, full of perfection, and the enemy to rest... Prince of the year'.)[42] Ronsard is also explicit in connecting the etymology. The fact that *esté* means fire makes fire the meaning of the season: 'chanter l'Esté de flames reluisant,/ Et tout chargé de feu comme un masse ardante' (ll. 4–5). According to the macrocosm/microcosm parallel, the temperament of man's summer is inevitably similar. As Taillevent said: 'On y a si chault qu'on y sue;/ C'est Jeunesse car lors on bout' ('He is then so hot that he sweats. It is Youth, the time when a man boils').[43]

Midsummer Heat in Action

The above examples illustrate how common it was to associate the fire of *esté* with man's own summer condition. It is, therefore, either another coincidence or deliberately in keeping with this assessment that, in practice, at midsummer in France, it was not a hilltop but hot-headed rashness and ungoverned speech which featured in a young man's *été* behaviour. Claude de Rubys' account of slander in Lyon, around St John's day, is endorsed by records from neighbouring *comtés*.

For the only aspect of Verdun's *feste de St Jean* which is recorded with clarity is the Cathedral Chapter's concern over the content of performances. In 1498 two men were trusted to put on the game because they had entered into clerical training and undertook to do it 'honourablement sans faire esclaundre' (see Appendix B). Again, in 1501, clerics under orders were allowed to do the fête, on the promise that they would not include slander, and the fact that the injunction was repeated suggests that it was difficult to control. An example of what the slander might entail comes from the nearby town of Metz where, in 1512, on the eve of St John, a priest was thrown into the town hall jail for twenty-four hours, for calling lord Nicole Remiat a liar. The priest would have been released had he asked the lord's pardon, but he replied that he could do without his pardon.[44] The fact that he received such slight punishment for publicly

---

[42] *Ronsard: Œuvres complètes,* ed. by J. Céard et al., vol. 2 (Paris: Gallimard, 1993–94), p. 556–58, ll. 113–17 and 217.

[43] 'Le Passe Temps de Michault Taillevent', ll. 381–82.

[44] '...la surveille de la Sainct Jehan, fut prins ung prestre par deux sergens et mené en

defaming one of the nobility is surprising, so too his perseverance in the offence and the fact that de Vigneulles valued it for his diary. Together they suggest a liminal midsummer practice: a seasonal custom on the border of what was and was not allowed.

Louis XI attracted a substantial amount of midsummer abuse. In 1465 he was at war in Anjou and Brittany, against his brothers. Towards the Nativity of St John it looked as though he might lose and Philippe de Comines recounted the uncertainties in a letter dated 'le Lundy 24 Juin.' Immediately before the date, the letter ends with a reference to rumours being spread in the region that the king was about to fall from power. As De Comines put it: 'les estranges paroles que on disoit & semoit au préjudice du Roy, & contre son armée et puissance'.[45] A more striking example occurred at midsummer the following year in Lyon, where a written attack against the king became the centre of an unscripted drama. A man, whom the people called Fortune, although his name was Jean Le Doulx, was arrested on Sunday 29 June[46] and was charged with conspiracy in a plot to murder Louis because of a paper found on him with the alleged details. This sounds very like one of the leaflets the Lyonnais were fond of passing around in the streets and pinning up at crossroads. But, whether the assassination was intended, or whether the paper contained only a mocking boast, the people turned the scandal into a game by associating the assassination of a real king at midsummer with the most extreme fall from fortune, and with Jean Le Doulx her surrogate. He escaped from the king's prison at Roanne in early July and received the protection of the Bishop of Lyon, who had his own reasons for wishing to thwart Louis. For over two months Le Doulx was sheltered in

---

l'hostel de la ville. La cause fut pource qu'il avoit dementi seigneur Nicolle Remiat, seigneur eaigé et de justice, et y fut vingt quatre heures. Touttes-fois, à la requeste des ordinaires, fut mis à delivre par ainsy qu'il devoit demander pardon audit seigneur Nicolle, mais il luy quicta son pardon.' 'The Diary of Philippe de Vigneulles', in *Les Chroniques de la ville de Metz*, collected by J. F. Huguenin, ed. by S. Lamort (Metz, 1838), pp. 125–804 (p. 676).

[45] *Mémoires de Messire Philippe de Comines*, ed. by M. l'Abbé Lenglet du Fresnoy (Paris, 1747), vol. 2, p. 479.

[46] On 9 July le Doulx was reportedly arrested on the Sunday recently passed, rather than 'last Sunday'. Three days between arrest and the hearing would not have been long enough for the imprisonment, escape, and the exchange of letters between Louis, in Paris, and the authorities in Lyon. See L. Caillet, *Project d'empoisonnement de Louis XI en 1466: arrestation à Lyon de Jean Le Doux, dit Fortune* (Besançon: Jacques, *c.* 1909), p. 1, n. 2.

ⅩLyon Cathedral, appropriately consecrated to St John the Baptist. It is also recorded that he offered to give himself up on 28 August, the eve of the *decollatio* and, again, this looks like a playful gesture in keeping with the meaning of the day, for he was persuaded to return to the Cathedral just in time to avoid recapture.[47] The accounts do not say whether he was a young man, but his agility in evading the jailers in Roanne prison would suggest that he was. Instead, the written proceedings between July and September refer to him repeatedly as the man 'dit Fortune' and, as her agent, he enjoyed fame for a season, raised to eminence by his midsummer notoriety. This scandalous season lasted from the end of June to the end of August and the game status of the outrage against Louis's life appears as the main reason that Le Doulx escaped with his own.

The paper found on him concerned the death of the King, and the writing of epitaphs was a common aspect of these slanders. In 1465, the year when Louis had failed to acquire Anjou by force, the accounts of the Cathedral of Angers, begun on 24 June, contain a curious entry for the cost of a mass to the dead King Louis and his Mother Marie: 'missa defuncti Regis ludouici et Marie matris sue'.[48] Louis's mother was Marie of Anjou, but he did not die until 1483. And, at the end of June, 1471, it was reported that Louis was much displeased with the epitaphs and libellous defamations of the Lord Constable of Paris, and other men, which had appeared pinned up in the city slandering them.[49]

Lutheran upheavals in the following century produce evidence that licence, on the eve or day of St John, might still be taken to defame those in authority. On 21 June 1561 Philip of Spain had an order issued throughout Flanders preventing anonymous travel between towns and

---

[47] 'le 28 août, Fortune sortit de l'église Saint Jean et se rendit sur une place située dans l'intérieur du Cloître. Plusieurs sergents, conduits par Pierre Potier, se jetèrent sur lui, sous prétexte que ce lieu n'était pas protégé par les franchises du Chapitre; mais à ce moment, des gens d'église arrivèrent et le firent rentrer dans l'église.' Ibid., pp. 2–3. Cf. Archives Départementales Lyon: 10. G.585, fol. 1 and Archives Municipales, Lyon, MS BB10, fols 180ʳ-181ᵛ.

[48] Archives départementales de Maine-et-Loire, MS. 16. G. 9, fol. 127ᵛ.

[49] 'En ce temps dudit moys de juing mil IIIIᶜ LXXI le roy fut mal content des epytaphs et libelles diffamatoires qui ainsi avoient esté mis et atachez à Paris à l'esclande dudit monseigneur le connestable et d'autres.' *Journal de Jean de Roye ou Chronique Scandaleuse*, ed by B. de Mandrot, La Société de l'histoire de France (Paris, 1894), vol. 270.1, p. 260.

also: 'de faire ordannance de non mesdire ny mesfaire aux hommes d'église ou religion de jour ny de nuict... et la faire publyer lundy prochain', which was 'le 23 juin, veille de Saint-Jean-Baptiste'.[50] The prohibition was pinned up when the outrage was expected and, possibly, in one of the expected places. Five years later, attendance to hear a banned preacher in Tournai, in the last week of June precipitated the town's final rebellion against Philip. Crowds at this, and at other public meetings, were said to have grown from 11 June, and the climax was the evening of the 27th when, it was falsely alleged, a tumultuous and scandalous meeting by the preacher, took place outside the city walls. There were, 'many people of all ages, between five and six thousand, from the town and the neighbouring villages'. The jailing of some led to a larger meeting on the last day of June. Within a few weeks the widening split between the people's expressed wishes and those of their imposed *prévôt* and *jurés* resulted in Philip sending in his troops.[51]

Martin Luther

From a religious point of view, such assumption of free speech at, and around, the feast of the Nativity of St John could have received the sanction of the Baptist's own example in confronting King Herod. For example, on 24 June 1611, a fool was elected in Troyes to voice the town's opposition to an imposed Jesuit foundation. The man began his authorized, public speech with the statement, 'il n'est plus temps de dissimuler',[52] words which suggest that truthfulness was called for on the day of the Baptist's Nativity. Bearing this in mind, and how widespread the midsummer assumption of free speech was, perhaps it is not going too far to suggest that Martin Luther had the custom in mind when he wrote his first major reform treatise, 'To the Christian Nobility of the German Nation, Concerning the Reform of the Christian Estate', for he ends the

---

[50] Note by Charles Paillard, ed., *Collection de Mémoires relatifs à l'histoire de Belgique: XVIᵉ siècle, Histoire des Troubles Religieux de Valenciennes 1560–1567* (Brussels, 1874), vol. 1, 264–65.

[51] *Collection de Mémoires relatifs à l'histoire de Belgique: Memoire de Pasquier de la Barre et de Nicolas Soldoyer 1565–1570*, ed. by A. Pinchart (Brussels, 1859), pp. 47–65.

[52] The fool was, in fact, on the Jesuit side and delivered a speech like that of Mark Antony in Shakespeare's *Julius Caesar*. See *Siéges de Troyes par les Jésuites*, ed. by F. Pithou (Paris, 1826), pp. 49–54.

Preface with the date 23 June, 1520 and he begins it with a statement similar to that of the fool from Troyes: 'The time for silence is past'.[53] Luther's Treatise contains a frontal attack on the assumed worldly power of the Rome-centred papacy, exposing its tyranny, hypocrisy, and oppression of the peoples of Europe. Sometimes Luther draws from early Church teaching regarding material power:

> It is horrible and shocking to see the head of Christendom, who boasts that he is the vicar of Christ and successor of St. Peter, going about in such a worldly and ostentatious style.... He claims the title of 'most holy' and 'most spiritual', and yet he is more worldly than the world itself. He wears a triple crown, whereas the highest monarchs wear but one.... The Romanists say he is a lord of the earth. That is a lie! For Christ said... 'My kingdom is not of this world'... [the Pope should] leave the crown of pride to the Antichrist (pp. 139–40).

Like the anonymous priest from Metz, Luther accuses his adversary, as well as his adversary's agents, of lying: 'As pope he can tell lies, deceive, and make everybody look like a fool' (p. 153). The work is shocking because of the confrontational nature of the accusations, and what makes it likely that Luther drew encouragement from the liberties of the season, is his Preface to the Christian Nobility. In it he acknowledges he is 'a despised, inferior person', but makes no apologies for daring to address 'such high and great estates', calling himself God's Jester—derived from the Pauline concept of 'fools for Christ's sake'—and ending with the date written in full: 'At Wittenberg… on the eve of St. John Baptist in the year fifteen hundred and twenty' (pp. 123–24). This was Luther's first direct attack and it led to his excommunication. There was no way Pope Leo X would grant festive licence for this level of assault, but it is possible that the title of fool and the date were an appeal to the German nobility for their protection.

Relative Freedom on the Continent of Europe?

With the more usual eruptions of free speech on the eve and day of the Baptist's Nativity (and possibly lasting to the *decollatio)*, it is impossible to know whether young men took advantage of popular belief regarding

---

[53] *Luther's Works*, vol. 44, *The Christian in Society*, Pt I, trans. and ed. by J. Atkinson (Philadelphia: Fortress Press, 1966), p. 123.

their youthful hot-headedness or whether the moralizing was based on behaviour already established; but it is hard to believe that the two were disconnected since examples of slander and truculence in the *esté* season were so widespread. On the Continent, challenges to authority from the lower classes appear to have been legitimized by the date in a way which was inconceivable in Tudor England, as the South Kyme incident shows. There, Dymoke claimed that the death of the lord was part of a traditional game and did not express an attitude towards the Earl of Lincoln, but he and his companions were found guilty of lese-majesty. They were publicly whipped and ruinous fines imposed. The actual lord, whose death they mocked, was one elected within their own play but it does appear that extra text was added in 1601, so making the performance an analogy for their wishes regarding the demise of the Earl. One might use Philippe de Navarre's assessment, and say that this was rash of them, but rash because it was *not* licensed.[54] Claude de Rubys does not say whether the men of Lyon also had their own elected lord to mock within their game structure, but this is suggested elsewhere (see Chap. 1 p. 27, and Appendix D). All festive games were fluid: they could change from year to year and from place to place but, in view of the fact that French youth could get away with the liberty, it would not be surprising if powerful figures in the outside world became the more interesting targets. And, although it might be hard to credit that such aggressive, lawless behaviour could be considered game, Claude de Rubys did include it as such. He did not see the domestic *charivari* as a safety valve preventing actual insurrection. Instead, under the title of 'Real History of Lyon', his account of the alternatives included a festive form of temporary insurrection ('semances de sedition', see Appendix D). The records from Verdun show that similar behaviour in the *Feste de St Jean* was also classed as game and after a period of other difficulties, the festival was remembered simply as the 'good ancient custom'. The events in Laon on 24 June 1587 demonstrated open rebellion, but they were only one stage further advanced from the normal liberties of the season.

---

[54] Though there is evidence to suggest that in the fourteenth and fifteenth centuries, games of mockery on St John's eve, in England, were tolerated. See N. Davis, 'The *Tretise of Myraclis Pleyinge:* on Milieu and Authorship', *Medieval English Theatre,* 12 (1990), 130–32.

Chronicled Accounts

Chronicles not only provide examples of midsummer slander, they also reveal a philosophical attitude to the tradition, particularly to the association between the day of St John's Nativity and death. In the same way that Michault Taillevent placed his unpleasant change at the St Jean, a disastrous fall from power or strength to annihilation at midsummer appears to have held a curious fascination to chroniclers, as though it showed Fortune wielding her ultimate extremes at the appropriate season.[55] The English Edward III, who had been such a trial to France, died on 21 June 1377. Froissart recorded it as the evening of 23 June, and Buchon notes Froissart's inaccuracy.[56] A chronicle poem on Richard II's last and doomed venture into Ireland stated that it began: 'La veille droit de Saint-Jehan d'este/ Très bien matin',[57] while another fictional history on his fall, has him call on St John the Baptist at the moment of his realization.[58] In 1465 Jean de Roye found two real examples. Immediately prior to 24 June the secretary of the king's chamberlain was killed 'by ill fortune'. An archer was practising elaborate shots, when master Louis came out unexpectedly and 'the arrow went right through his body.... And, on the day of St John the Baptist, people bathing for pleasure in the Seine were all drowned, by ill fortune'.[59] (The second could have been an

---

[55] This is not to say that midsummer was the only time when fortune's apparent effects were recorded. Two autumnal comments on her changes for ill can be found in 1400 and in 1428: 'Mais fortune qui souvent tourne sa face aussi-bien contre ceux du plus haut état comme du moindre, lui montra de ses tours....' *Chroniques d'Enguerand de Monstrelet*, vol. 1, ed. Buchon, *CNF*, vol. 26 (Paris, 1826), p. 54. '[M]ais fortune, qui à nully n'est sure amie, lui monstra de son mestier...' 'Journal d'un Bourgeois de Paris', *Chroniques d'Enguerand de Monstrelet*, vol. 15, ed. Buchon, *CNF*, vol. 40 (Paris, 1827), p. 379.

[56] '...le roi d'Angleterre...trépassa de ce siècle en la vigile Saint Jean Baptiste....', *Chroniques de Froissart*, vol. 6, ed. Buchon, *CNF*, vol. 16 (Paris, 1824), p. 104.

[57] Froissart, *Chroniques*, vol. 14, ed. Buchon, *CNF*, vol. 24 (Paris, 1826), pp. 326–27.

[58] 'Si plaise à Dieu, et à St. Jehan Baptiste, que mauldits soyez-vous.' [Alone in his chamber] 'il dist piteusement: 'Dieu de paradis, ô vierge Marie, ô St. Jehan Baptiste… comment povez vous souffrir le grant tort et la grant trahison qu'on fait à moy.' *Chronique de Richard II*, in Froissart, *Chroniques*, vol. 15, ed. Buchon, *CNF*, vol. 25 (Paris, 1826), p. 28–29. A non-Christian example can be found in a French translation of a Turkish account of the fall of Constantinople. Although this happened on 29 May 1457, the taking of the 'proud city' was recorded as 27 June. '[L]a conquête n'eut lien que le 20 de *joumazi-ul-akir* 857 (27 juin 1453). La date de la prise de cette superbe cité.' *Chroniques de Monstrelet*, vol. 13, ed. Buchon, *CNF*, vol. 38 (Paris, 1826), p. 351.

unfortunate end to midsummer water purification.)

Summer was also the season for fighting, purely because of the good weather, but a seasonal perspective was sometimes added as, for example, in Jacques du Clerq's 1451 description of the French nobility ranged in their battle-splendour against the English on 24 June, to celebrate the day.

> Et pour estre à icelle journée de la Saint-Jehan, vindrent le compte de Nevers, de Clermont, de Chastres, de Vendosme, de Penthièvre, accompagniés de plusieurs autres chevaliers et escuyers; et feurent en bataille ce jour pour attendre leurs ennemis. Et fust la journée hautement et honnorablement tenue en riches et grands habillements.[60]

Fighting is described more as flyting in a chronicle 'Chanson' by Jean Molinet, which celebrates the Flemish victory at Guinegate on 7 August 1479. Here the French had the greater forces and Molinet indulges in a David over Goliath exultation on behalf of the young and humble Flemish prince who had overcome the pride of the French. His fustian density of insults prompts the comment 'sloppy' from the editor, but it appears as a pre-*decollatio* diatribe on the decline of an enemy.[61] And, in 1543, (as already quoted) the anticipation of taking Arras was turned into a poem exulting in the approach of midsummer combat: 'the time of *esté* is coming—ring the bell, summon up rage; Arras, you will be dead before the St John.'[62] Boasting, too, is found in the Count de Charollais's declaration, when fighting Louis XI in 1465. He sent the message ahead that he would be established in St Denis outside Paris by St John's Day,

---

[59] '...ung nommé maistre Loys de Tilleres...fut tué, par male fortune, d'un archer qui essaioit ung arc, duquel il tiroit une flesche contre ung huis qui estoit devant lui, à l'eure que ledit maistre Loys ouvroit, et lui vint passer la fleche tout au travers du corps... Et, le jour Saint Jehan Baptiste, XXIIIIe jour de juing, aucuns qui se baignoient à leurs plaisances en la riviere de Seine, par male fortune, se noierent.' *Journal de Jean de Roye,* ed. de Mandrot, vol. 270.1, pp. 48–49 (see p. 35 n. 49).

[60] *Chroniques d'Enguerrand de Monstrelet sur Jacques du Clerq: Mémoires,* vol. 12, ed. by J. A. Buchon, *CNF,* vol. 37 (Paris, 1826), p. 97.

[61] 'Ung jeune prince, humble et plain de vaillance [has defeated] L'orgueil de France.... Il a gaigné par sa chevallerie/ Le champ, le val, la mountaigne et la plaine.... Chantez comment François furent domptez/ Battuz, boutez/ pillez/ esparpillez,/ Desordonnez' etc., for twenty four lines, ending with 'un tel dance'. *Recueil de chants historiques français depuis le XIIe jusqu'au XVIIIe siècle,* ed. by L. de Lincy, Première Série (Paris, 1841), pp. 385–92.

[62] 'La sommation d'Arras', *Recueil de chants historiques,* ed. by L. de Lincy, Deuxième Série (Paris, 1842), pp. 438–40.

but events were to hold him up until July.[63]

One of the most telling examples of midsummer self-flaunting appears in Froissart's account of Edward III celebrating his maritime victory over the Normans, on the eve of St John, 1340:

> Quand cette victoire...fut avenue au roi Anglois, il demeura toute cette nuit, qui fut la veille saint Jean-Baptiste, sur mer en ses naves (vaisseaux) devant l'Écluse, en grand bruit et grand noise de trompes et de nacaires (timballes), tabours, cornets et de toutes manières de menestrandies telle-ment qu'on n'y ouït pas dieu tonnant.[64]

The final comment that the noise was so great 'one could not hear God's thunder' is taken from Chrétien's *Yvain*, where Chrétien included the din of accolade as a demonstration of midsummer arrogance by King Arthur. (See Chap. 2.) The difference in the chronicle account is that the caco-phony is directed against an enemy in a way reminiscent of *charivari*. Another example of such military derision occurred in 1372 when, after defeating the English, the Spanish sailed from la Rochelle on St John's Day. They too put on a triumphant performance, accompanied by strident music: 'horns, trumpets, muses, cornets, and tambourines', mocking the remnants of the English troops, who had to 'take their chance, as God or fortune sent.'[65]

These displays are examples of self-vaunting on the grand scale. It was suggested by Philippe de Navarre that, on the lesser scale, boasting was also one of a young man's errors in the high season of his life, and it

---

[63] *Mémoires de J. de Clerq,* vol. 15, ed. Buchon, *CNF,* vol. 40 (Paris, 1822), p. 7. A more curious example appears in a raid on a Luxembourg castle in 1521. Before it, the attackers claimed self-vaunting by the owner as their excuse to attack. The recorder wrote: 'Environ la sainct Jehan', a siege was made of the lord of Malbert, on the grounds that he had refused to pay homage to the Holy Roman Emperor or to be considered a Burgundian   so far a perfectly valid reason to attack him. However, the claim continues that Malbert had said that he 'estoit parfaict françois, et aussi le plus et le mieulx il se tenoit en France aupres du roy'. It seems likely that, here, midsummer boasting was invoked by the attackers, rather than being used by their opponent. See 'The Diary of Philippe de Vigneulles', in *Les Chroniques de la ville de Metz*, p. 759.

[64] Froissart, *Chroniques,* vol. 1, chap. 123, ed. Buchon, *CNF,* vol. 11 (Paris, 1824), pp. 340–41.

[65] '...les Espagnols...sachèrent les voiles à monte et se départirent, en demenant grand noise de trompes et de trompettes, de muses et de tambours'. '[L]e comte de Pembroke...et leurs gens se trouvèrent devant la Rochelle en ce jour devant nommé, il faut prendre l'aventure en gré telle que Dieu ou fortune lui envoie.' Froissart, *Chroniques,* vol. 5, ed. Buchon, *CNF,* vol. 15 (Paris, 1824), pp. 283 and 282.

certainly provides much of the comedy in French medieval literature. However, it is not as extensively reported in plebeian games in France as it was in England. For example, Robert of Brunne's *Handlying Synne* includes boasting in the English version of the text, though it is not in the French from which it originated.[66] It would appear that, on the Continent, mock boasting was not as popular as was the mockery of the genuine arrogance of the powerful, mockery which might itself turn into boasting, as in Molinet's poem.

St John's Day was also a traditional time for legal activities: courts were often held, and feudal loyalties, too, were sometimes expressed then. With these it is harder to perceive any significance in the date, except that in Chapter 5 I hope to show that the holding of some bourgeois elections on 24 June was not accidental. For, as with fighting, feudal acknowledgements made on St John the Baptist's day sometimes suggest an awareness of the date's implications. For example, in 1384 a declaration of vassal status, made on the day of St John's Nativity by Edmund de Endelsdorff chamberlain of the Duchy of Luxembourg, implied that Wenceslas had acted towards him as a surrogate Fortune in her positive mood: 'Edmund de Endelsdorff, chamberlain du duché de Luxembourg, l'a élevé à ladite dignité de chambellan et lui dit a donné à cet effet à lui et à ses heritiers le chateau de Rulant avec dépendences; en conséquance il lui jure fidelité, pour ce fief'.[67] It could simply be that, knowing the implications of the date, it is hard not to become aware of metaphors for, or against, power in declarations made with reference to St John the Baptist's Day. Similarly, it is hard to imagine that people writing then could fail to be aware of the implications of the date; and it is interesting to note that Louis XI, who was subject to so much Baptist day vilification, signed his own letters written on 24 June as 24 June only.[68]

For it has been said that before Christianity became the official Western religion Fortune had been an integral part of the thinking of the early Church fathers and, even when discarded, she had ways of reappearing. The same can be said for her perceived influence at the midsummer

[66] 'Hem were leuer here of a daunce,/ Of bost, and of olypraunce [pomp]/ [Th]an any gode of Gode of Heuene....' *Robert of Brunne's Handlying Synne: ad 1303,* ed. by F. J. Furnivall, EETS OS 119 (London: Trübner, 1901), p. 156.

[67] Trans. from the German by Fr.-X. Wuerth-Paquet, *Table chronologique des chartes et diplômes relatifs à l'histoire de l'ancien Comté de Luxembourg,* 2 vols in one (Luxembourg, 1868), vol. 2, p. 11.

[68] *Lettres de Louis XI, Roi de France,* ed. by J. de Vaesen and E. Charavoy (Paris, 1885).

solstice. The understanding that the day reflected on power, and on issues of life and death, permeated all levels of society, and through a range of meanings from the subversive to the affirmative. Sometimes events were staged in a semi-theatrical way, as at Verdun and in Jean Le Doulx's game against Louis. Power assertion by kings also had a theatrical aspect, used as a way of intimidating the enemy or, after battle, as a triumphant display. When these traditions are added to the midsummer customs already known, it becomes apparent that the season had its own richness and variety, with a more dubious moral pedigree than had other customs, such as the rolling of wheels, bonfires and bathing. One can understand why, at the Renaissance, details on self-flaunting and slanderous mockery might have been withheld.

Conclusion

It can be argued that, in fact, the wilder St John's day games were no more outrageous than those sanctioned by the Feast of Fools. However, in the lower strata of society, midsummer eruptions appear to have had a different rationale from that of other seasons used for subversion. As already said, carnival was a time which celebrated disorder as a concept: the governing concept of a separate and inverted world. This deliberate inversion of the norm was also the theme of the festival of the *Cheval Fol* of Lyon, which commemorated a failed rebellion of 1436, and was held at the earlier summer date of Pentecost—the season of the original rebellion. The stated attitude of the mutineers was that they had wished to replace order with disorder, as during the Christmas season. The rebels were reported to have said, 'we come from the woods and so we can make kings ourselves' ('Qu'ils estoyent du boys d'ou l'on faisoit les Roys').[69] In the licensed derision of this, one man dressed up as a king and danced inside a hobby horse along the route the rebels had taken, accompanied by cacophonous music and a crowd. A day of 'mad king' pranks ('faisant le Roy fol')[70] ended with a model of the *cheval fol* being burned and dropped into the river, to illustrate the end of: 'rebellious

[69] C. de Rubys, *Histoire véritable de la ville de Lyon*, p. 502.

[70] Ibid., p. 503. Amadine Audin considered that the five mock kings elected in summer at Lyon were all related to the midsummer solstice, despite their varying summer dates. See 'Les Rites Solsticiaux et la Legende de St. Pothin', *Revue de l'Histoire des Religions,* 96 (1927), 147–74.

fools/ Who, like crazy horses, run through the town/ Wanting to enrich themselves with goods plundered from the more able' ('fols mutinés,/ Qui, comme chevaux fols, couraient parmi la ville,/ Voulant à qui mieux paraitre plus habil,/ a s'enrichir des biens qu'ils avaient butinées').[71] This game was under the control of the authorities and it supported the hegemonic view that rebellion was an inversion of proper order.[72]

In contrast to this, midsummer revolt focused on the disorder of those in power: their arrogance and injustice—aspects which made them travesties of lordship. Although behaviour on 24 June was sometimes violent, midsummer rebels often had clear goals and tried to avoid physical conflict, as in Laon, where the season of violent disorder was rejected for the deposing of Martin, in favour of the season of satire on power. In Tournai, too, the thousands of people involved in the mass rebellion were careful to avoid violent disturbances.[73] The same applies to festive examples; the slander of the priest from Metz in 1512 involved invective only and, although Jean Le Doulx was accused of plotting murder, the circumstances of the charge suggest an over-sensitive reaction to a game of epitaphs.

In practice, the solsticial games were secular, whereas literature usually contained a moral view, critical of them. Hilltops, too, often not used in practice, feature in literature from about 1288, with the caveat that, at best, the heights achieved through successful ambition are unstable. At worst, personal ambition was seen as satanic, as in the archetypal story of Satan taking the youthful Christ to the top of the mountain and promising that he would be lord of all the world (see Appendix A). John the Baptist was often likened to Isaiah, for both prophesied that every valley would be exalted and every mountain and hill made low (Isaiah 40. 3–4). And, although the Church claimed the moral low ground, in practice St John's day could be a significant time for battles of power between it and the State over material issues. For example, the Bishop of Lyon, who supported Jean Le Doulx, also supported the House of Burgundy's opposition to Louis's centralization

---

[71] Count François Marie de Fortis, *Voyage pittoresque et historique à Lyon* (Paris, 1821), p. 153.

[72] The actual disorder of the imitation often went further than the authorities intended and led to the custom's suppression in the seventeenth century. See L'Abbaye J. Pernetti, *Les Lyonnois dignes de Mémoire* (Lyon, 1757), pp. 150–51.

[73] Pasquier de la Barre, *Collection de Mémoires relatifs à l'histoire de Belgique...*, pp. 59–60.

of state power in France. Figureheads representing secular power traditionally behaved with humility on St John's day—for example French
kings, such as Louis XI in 1471, personally lit the midsummer bonfire in
the streets of Paris.[74] The ethos of the season also supported struggles by
the aspiring classes against their masters. On the festive level, there was
the relief of airing perceived injustices, while more committed rebels had
cosmic and theological encouragement for an actual overthrow of power.

As far as literature and theatre are concerned, it would not be surprising if the various spectacles provided by the events of high summer
inspired the creative writing of Chrétien de Troyes, and others. One of the
most striking, and so far unexplained, features of the romances written
between 1170 and 1270, is the interest of their authors in the nativity of
St John the Baptist. Wilson Frescoln writes that in Guillaume le Clerc's
Fergus it 'is given unusual importance, recurring five times... this date
occurs frequently in Arthurian romances, as for example [in] Chrétien's
Yvain; li Chevaliers as deus espees, and [in] *Rigomer'.*[75] Frescoln omits
Renaut's *Galeran,* since this is not Arthurian, but here too there are
several references to the same date. In these texts, and others, the mention
of St John's day is a sign that complex meanings are used, drawn from
beliefs and traditions of the season, to 'deride' their heroes as much as to
'celebrate' them.[76] Many of the oppositions and contradictions in young
men, which were to be theorized about 1260 in *Les Quatre ages de
l'homme,* appear for comic effect in these tales. It becomes possible to
suggest that Chrétien de Troyes was the first European writer to conceive
a festive literary matrix.

---

[74] Jean de Roye, *Chroniques Scandaleuses,* vol. 1, p. 260.

[75] Frescoln, ed., *Guillaume le Clerc: the Romance of Fergus,* p. 249. See J. Darrah for a
more complete list of events taking place on this date in Arthurian Romance.

[76] M. Bakhtin, *Rabelais and his World,* pp. 11–12.

SECTION II:

Arthurian Romance

CHAPTER 2

Chrétien de Troyes:
Yvain

Chrétien a donc voulu nous donner dans la première partie de son roman
l'image d'une prouesse triomphante, juvénilement triomphante....

Jean Frappier

Romance literature was an innovation of the second half of the
twelfth century, initially written in verse as were the heroic
chansons de geste which preceded them. Romances, however,
with their imaginative plots became popular entertainment for aristocratic
readers. We have only a few biographical details for Chrétien de Troyes,
the first known writer of romance, yet the numerous extant manuscript
copies of his works testify to their wide readership. As far as his life is
concerned the key available details are his association with the town of
Troyes in Champagne, where he was supported by the patronage of
Countess Marie after her marriage to Henri le Libéral de Champagne in
1164. There is evidence, too, in Chrétien's *Perceval (Le Conte del Graal)*
that another patron was Philippe d'Alsace, Count of Flanders.[1] But the
dating of Chrétien's romances largely depends on internal, textual
evidence which now places the order of his major works as *Erec et Enide*,
in about 1170, *Cligés,* 1176, *Lancelot* and *Yvain* 1177 or 1178, and

---

[1] See *Yvain: le chevalier au lion: the Critical Text of Wendelin Foerster*, ed. by T. B. W.
Reid, French Classics (Manchester: Manchester University Press, 7th edition, 1984), p. ix,
and *Arthurian Romances: Chrétien de Troyes*, trans. by D. D. R. Owen, Everyman's
Library (London: Dent, 1993), p. xi.

Perceval about 1182.[2]

It is nothing new to argue for an ironic perspective in all these works; the debate began at least as early as 1968, with Peter Haidu's publication, *Aesthetic Distance in Chrétien de Troyes*, and soon followed by Philippe Ménard's *Rire et Sourire*.[3] Since then the simple theory that Arthur's court was presented as a place of ideal behaviour, and an example to the nobility who read Chrétien's works, cannot be sustained, although some elements such as the idealization of women—whose actual life was more usually one of neglect—could well have been introduced as a form of compensation.[4] Other moments of once-claimed idealization have been perceptively re-addressed through the concept of the *écart*: a deliberate gap between the ideal invoked by symbols in Chrétien's writing, and the reality of their relationship to protagonists in it.[5] Haidu's most striking example is the description of Lancelot's wounds, achieved in pursuit of his night with Guinevere. The fact that they remind the reader of the wounds of Christ on the cross only serves to accentuate the impossibility of comparing the two men.[6]

Two critics who have developed such perceptions into a more complete reading of the *Yvain* are Tony Hunt and Joan T. Grimbert.[7] Their analyses consider the realities of character behaviour without trying to explain it in

---

[2] For the dating, see D. D. R. Owen, p. xii, and *Chrétien de Troyes: Lancelot ou le chevalier de la charrette*, ed. by J.-C. Aubailly (Paris: Flammarion, 1991), p. 461. I have used the most recent editions by Flammarion for quotations from *Erec and Enide, Lancelot*, and *Perceval* and, for *Yvain*, the Flammarion edition of Wendelin Foerster's text. Here I have also used the more accessible printing in T. B. W. Reid's edition of the same text. Another edition, still highly respected, is Mario Roques, *Le chevalier au lion (Yvain)*, CFMA, no. 4 (Paris: Champion, 1960). Interestingly, the manuscript Roques has used is one in which midsummer antagonism has been reduced. For example, line 97 in the Foerster edition reads: "teisiez vos an!' while in the Roques edition this is, 'teisons nos an'.

[3] P. Haidu, *Aesthetic Distance in Chrétien de Troyes: Irony and Comedy in* Cligés *and* Perceval (Geneva: Droz, 1968); P. Ménard, *Le Rire et le sourire dans le roman courtois en France au Moyen Age (1150–1250)* (Geneva: Droz, 1969).

[4] T. Hunt, *Chrétien de Troyes: Yvain (le Chevalier au Lion)*, Critical Guides to French Texts (London: Grant and Cutler, 1986), p. 12.

[5] Peter Haidu, *Lion Queue-coupée* (Geneva: Droz, 1972), p. 21.

[6] Ibid., pp. 31–32.

[7] T. Hunt, *Chrétien de Troyes: Yvain*, and J. T. Grimbert, *'Yvain' dans le Miroir*, Purdue University Monographs in Romance Languages (Amsterdam and Philadelphia: John Benjamins, 1988).

terms of courtly ideals. For example, Grimbert states that Kay's attitude is that of a savage or *vilain*, the opposite to what is required by courtly etiquette;[8] and Hunt notes that 'Arthur's erotic retreat to the bedchamber' during the Ascension-day festivities at the opening of the story is a further indisputable breach of etiquette.[9] Two of Arthur's knights also fail in courtly expectation: Calogrenant is a poor courtly narrator, and Gawain is always absent when ladies need him.[10]

The question which arises is, what could be the rationale for this sustained ironic humour? So far, no explanation has been found which adequately takes into account Chrétien's contemporary readership. Hunt acknowledges the need to account for the sense of 'play' in the *Yvain* and attributes it to the spirit of intellectual enquiry in France's new universities (p. 11). Yet, rather more telling is the example of actual play in French society. For, in the same period when the churchman, John Beleth, showed objective interest in the customs of St John's day, the leading secular writer explored their thematic possibilities. Chrétien establishes the context of St John's Day at the opening of the *Yvain* and reaffirms it half-way through, so creating for the reader an expectation of midsummer behaviour which will explain the inversions, unite the different themes in the story, and provide a complete plot structure.

The tale begins in Arthur's court at Pentecost when, 'to the astonishment of his guests, Arthur gets up from table, discourteously abandons his knights, and joins Guinevere in bed',[11] causing shocked comment because 'onques mes nel virent/ A si grant feste an chanbre antrer/ Por dormir' ('never before had his court seen him retire at such a great festival').[12] One needs to go further than observe the breach of etiquette and note that Arthur's behaviour desecrates a day dedicated to God. Soon after returning into the hall, Arthur asserts that he will keep 'la voille/ Mon seignor saint Jehan Batiste' ('the vigil of my lord, saint John the Baptist', ll. 669–70). The declaration sets the parameters for folly in the king's court and places Arthur's initial libidinous action in a recognizable

---

[8] Grimbert, p. 83.

[9] Hunt, p. 24.

[10] Ibid., p. 23–24.

[11] K. D. Uitti and M. A. Freeman, *Chrétien de Troyes Revisited* (New York: Twayne, 1995), p. 76.

[12] Chrétien de Troyes, *Yvain: ou le chevalier au lion*, ll. 45–48, ed. by M. Rousse (Paris: Flammarion, 1990).

context. The festival celebrating Christ's spiritual power has been trav-
estied, and the semi-pagan festival, concerning worldly, transient power,
is to be observed: a fact emphasized by the inappropriate address of
seigneur for the Baptist.

During the king's absence the behaviour of those left in the hall had
continued with other parodic inversions: of courtly ideals, of courtly
manners, and even of the smooth narration. For after Arthur and
Guinevere retire, a group of knights gathers outside the bedroom door and
a reluctant Calogrenant begins the story which will result in the further
action, a story which is not to Calogrenant's honour but to his shame (ll.
59–60). The queen overhears, leaves the now sleeping Arthur, and comes
outside so quietly that etiquette is further prevented. Only Calogrenant
sees her and he responds by jumping abruptly to his feet. This provokes
Kay's ill-mannered sarcasm, which is not passed over but develops into
squabbling between him and the Queen, and culminates in Kay telling her
to shut up: 'teisiez vos an!' (l. 97) so that Calogrenant can continue with
his interrupted story.

The travesty of courtly behaviour in this section is more than a playful
application of irony: it comes from the tradition of seasonal inversion,
which appears to be hinted at during the quarrel. Kay's remarks to the
Queen contain the line: 'ne l'an nel doit plus haut monter' (l. 101). The
literal translation is 'one should not raise it (the quarrel) any higher', but
there could well be an intended pun in the spelling of *'l'an'*, meaning that
the year cannot climb any higher: time is passing therefore Guinevere
should not waste it by bickering. If so, then Chrétien suggests the festive
context before making it explicit on Arthur's return. Since the midsummer season was the time for abuse and flytings, including licence by
the lower classes to slander their betters, Kay's abuse to the Queen
becomes seasonally appropriate. Nor is Calogrenant slow in offering his
own insults to Kay, when he reminds the court that, 'Toz jorz doit puïr li
fumiers' ('the dunghill will always stink', l. 116).

It is Kay's abuse of Yvain which provokes him into leaving secretly at
night, so as to reach the spring alone before Arthur's St John's eve vigil,
and clear his cousin's and his own name by challenging the guardian,
Esclados. Yet Yvain's later dialogue reveals that his departure from
Arthur's court was not chivalric. Once in the castle in Broceliande, he
protests to Lunete: 'Soiiez certainne,/ Je n'istrai de ceste semainne/ An
larrecin ne an anblee... je ne feroie nuitantre' ('You may be certain I shall
never steal away from here like a thief... in the night', l. 1571–78). The

disorder which had reigned in the court during Arthur's absence is only superficially removed when he reappears, since his aspirations and those of the whole court are awry.

Pentecost can fall on any date between 10 May and 13 June, and Arthur swears that before a fortnight has passed he will go to the spring in order to arrive on the Eve of St John. Yvain leaves immediately and travels many days to reach the country where the spring is found: 'over mountains and through valleys and extensive forests and outlandish wild places'.[13] Vagueness over distance helps accommodate any of the possible Pentecost dates, since the journey to the midsummer adventure can be as short or as long as is needed to fill the time until the solstice. The indeterminate time period gives the sensation of leaving the known world; it is part of the *avanture* into the Celtic otherworld where fountains can cause storms.

Yvain arrives at the spring about a week before St John's Eve. This is known because he mortally wounds Esclados, pursues him back to his castle, is concealed there, thanks to Lunete's ring, falls in love with the widow, Laudine, and watches her grieving at the burial all in the same afternoon. Either that evening or the following day, Lunete speaks in his favour to Laudine, reminding her that the following week King Arthur is due to arrive at the spring and a defender is needed to prevent not just it, but all her lands from falling into Arthur's hands (thus throwing further doubt on Arthur's own chivalry). It would be particularly neat if Yvain had defeated the lord of the spring on the actual longest day of the year, 21 June, but this is not said. Yet, in these few days around the solstice, Esclados is toppled, Yvain takes over his role, and has to defend the spring again from the challenge of Arthur's champion, Kay. The worldly status of three leading knights is determined, Arthur is fêted, and Yvain marries Laudine.

During this period, Yvain is not alone in undergoing a reversal of attitude. The most dramatic character inconsistency is Laudine's change from grief and anger at the death of her lord to remarriage with his murderer. (The Jocastan resonances are clear.)[14] Yvain, contemplating her from his window on his first night in Broceliande, says, 'he is a fool to think of it' ('Por fol me puis tenir', l. 1428) yet he encourages himself with the conventional thought that all women are changeable. He can

---

[13] *Arthurian Romances: Chrétien de Troyes*, trans. by D. D. R. Owen, p. 291, ll. 760–70.

[14] Ibid. pp. 516–17.

hope, therefore, that Laudine, too 'changera ele ancore -/ Ainz le chen-
gera sanz espoir' (ll. 1438–39). Midsummer is about change, and a
change in men rather than in women, particularly abrupt reversals in male
status, with those in high and low positions changing places. This is
precisely the argument Lunete puts forward to win Laudine for him:
'When two knights have come together, armed for battle, and one has
defeated the other, which do you think the more worthy? For my part I
give the honour to the victor' (Owen, p. 303). Laudine replies that this is
'the greatest nonsense' and calls Lunete a 'foolish, tiresome, hussy' (ll.
1710–13). Laudine appears to be in the right, yet the season rules and she
does change, won over by the argument of the necessity of repelling
Arthur. Chrétien's adoption of inversion for the rationale is emphasized
by the comic lengths to which he takes it, creating, in this romance, an
upside-down world. Laudine not only accepts Lunete's argument but
apologizes to her for her previous harsh words. The lady humbles herself
to her servant and then asks to be taught by her. Further, the lesson is that
Laudine will have the noblest and handsomest lord from Abel's line ('Qui
onques fust del ling Abel', l. 1814)—an impossibility, since Abel never
reached marriage due to suffering the fate of Laudine's first husband. It
seems unlikely that Chrétien's audience would not have perceived the
joke. In the Old Testament the good man died and mankind was the issue
of the murderer. This appears as another *écart,* an anomaly in Lunete's
argument which brings the reality to the reader's mind. And its saturnalian context removes the problems that Hunt has found in Laudine's
change of heart.[15] Yet there is a moral underlying the comedy. Throughout the story, this appears to be that man, rather than woman, is still as
flawed as was Cain.

   For when Calogrenant and Yvain arrive separately in Broceliande, they
first encounter a grotesque figure. Calogrenant had asked whether he was
a good thing or not ('me di/ Si tu es buene chose ou non!' ll. 328–29) and
the creature had replied 'Je sui un hon' (l. 330). From this moment, it
would appear that we are to ask whether man is a good thing or not, and
when Yvain passes the same lout he is amazed: 'Comant Nature feire sot/
Oevre si leide et si vilainne' (ll. 798–99), words which contrast with his
wonder, on seeing Laudine, that Nature could make such a beautiful
creature (ll. 1493–99). The churl is guardian of a pack of fighting bulls of
'tel fierté et tel orguel' (l. 283), a description often used of knights; and

---

[15] Hunt, pp. 57–58.

the twelfth-century *Book of Beasts* describes bulls as 'endowed with such a ferocious wildness that, when somebody catches them, they lose their minds with rage'.[16] Similarly, when Yvain and Esclados attack each other, their actions derive more from the instincts of two violent animals than from rational men. Identical, armour-clad figures rush together full of mortal hatred, or midsummer rage, with lances which tear each other like horns. Paradoxically, Lunete could be right in her outrageous advice to Laudine: possibly neither knight in this part of the story is morally superior, or worthy of loyalty after death. Both are little more than fighting automata. Despite the fact that Yvain is constantly called lord and prince, son of King Urien, he is at the same time a midsummer lord only, as was the previous knight of the spring.

Lunete treats Yvain with the only courteous respect and love seen in the first part of the story but, when about to meet Laudine, she reduces him to fear of Laudine's temper and 'the imprisonment he will suffer' (Owen, p. 307). The conventional love-metaphor has an original resonance in relation to St John's day because, despite being the victor, Yvain also suffers downward reversals and, metaphorically, his worst wound comes from seeing Laudine: 'The effect of this thrust lasts longer than one from any lance or sword. A sword-blow is cured and heals very quickly once a doctor attends to it: Love's wound, though, grows worse the nearer it is to its doctor' (Owen, p. 299). He is speechless with fear in her presence, falls to his knees, a suppliant rather than conqueror and, later in the story, it is only in love that he is vulnerable.

They marry a day or two before St John's Day, and celebrate up until the eve, when they need to respond to Arthur's challenge at the spring. This combat, between Yvain and Kay, takes place on St John's day but, unlike the previous one, the battle provides direct comedy, fulfilling midsummer expectations that a fall will follow pride. Kay's vainglory, elevating himself through the mockery of others is crushed in a most satisfying way: he is knocked off his horse flat onto the ground, and his horse is removed; he is in fact humiliated in the same way that Calogrenant was (Hunt, p. 48). When asked, Yvain can speak his own name with the satisfaction of knowing it is now clear of all Kay's taunts: glory comes to him and ignominy to Kay in deserved measure.

But this is the sum of Yvain's midsummer elevation. It is not he who is feasted as champion and king, but Arthur; and moral judgement of Arthur

---

[16] *The Book of Beasts,* trans. by T. H. White, 3rd edn (Stroud: Alan Sutton, 1992), p. 77.

is implied, on a more serious level, by another gap between language and reality. The description of the courtly entourage entering the town is an inversion of Christ's entry into Jerusalem. The party rides great Spanish horses and is received with the town's acclamations, and with silk sheets, rather than palms, thrown under their horses' feet. Arthur is greeted with words which are partly reminiscent of those to Christ and partly of Satan's, claiming power over the world: 'Welcome to the king, lord of kings and of all the lords in the world' ('Bien vaingne li rois et li sire/ Des rois et des seignors del monde!' ll. 2370–01). Awnings over the streets, against the great heat of the sun, remind us, if reminder were needed, that these are midsummer lords, full of worldly pomp, pride, and arrogance. 'Bells, horns, trumpets', and even the church bells play so loudly that 'one could not have heard God's thunder' ('Li sain, li cor et les buisines/ Font le chastel si ressoner,/ Que l'an n'i oïst De toner.' ll. 2348–50)—a warning against such self-glorification.[17] Arthur compounds his neglect of Pentecost with self-aggrandizement at the solstice, as kings sometimes did in fact. King Arthur becomes a potential Antichrist and it is possible that, earlier, when he swore to see the spring on the Eve of St John, his oath was another parody, this time of a vow to the holy family for Arthur swears: 'on the souls of Utherpendragon his father, of his son and his Mother' ('L'ame Uterpandragon son pere,/ Et la son fil et la sa mere', ll. 663–64). Since the son is Arthur himself, the reference is otherwise redundant; and works in which Antichrist parodied the Saviour were prevalent at the time.[18] The *Yvain* shows how Arthur could be used as a warning rather than as a model for kings, and Chrétien's saturnalian treatment of Arthur's court was to become direct satire in the following century.

Pride is central to the action, yet Chrétien only refers to it directly four times at lines 286–87, 2186, 3984, and 4137, and the first, in the description of the bulls, is the most notable. Yet the animal used most often in the Middle Ages as a metaphor for pride was the horse[19] and Chrétien introduces this strategically in Gawain's advice to Yvain to 'break the

---

[17] See Froissart, *Chroniques,* I. p. 340–41, (above, p. 41), and J. Giélée's *Renart le Nouvel,* ll. 2337, 3554, and 3919 (below, p. 176).

[18] B. McGinn, 'Portraying Antichrist in the Middle Ages', in *The Use and Abuse of Eschatology in the Middle Ages,* ed. by W. Verbeke et al. (Louvain: Leuven University Press, 1988), pp. 1–48.

[19] See Appendix C.

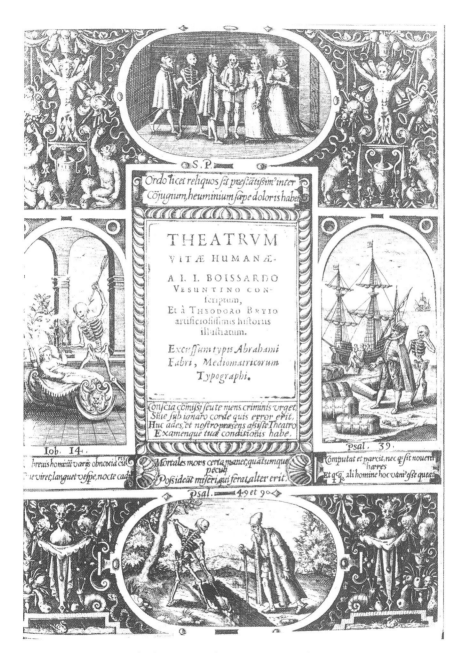

Figure 4: Boissard, Theatrum Vitae Humanae, *frontispiece, Frankfurt, 1596.*

bridle and halter' ('Ronper le frain et le chevoistre', l. 2500) immediately after Yvain's marriage.

Gawain is the third figure who should be beyond reproach. On his return to court Chrétien likens him to the sun ('solauz clamez', l. 2402), because he is lord of all knights ('des chevaliers fu sire', l. 2400). However it turns out that this sun/lordship equation is not a god-like comparison but rather a continuation of midsummer pride for, once Kay is shamed into silence, it is Gawain who takes up the mockery of Yvain, provoking him after his marriage into the second flawed ambition. Gawain's mockery relies on the theme of marriage as the topmost point of the wheel in the life of man, supplanting personal glory (Fig. 4), and Yvain's response to the provocation is as self-centred as before. So too is his method of getting his own way, since he does not persuade Laudine, but tricks her.

Midsummer imperatives still control the plot, for Laudine allows him to stay in Britain, taking part in jousts and tournaments, 'jusqu'a un an/ Huit jours aprés la saint Jehan' (ll. 2573–74). If he fails to return by the octave of St John the following year another reversal will result and 'l'amours devandra haïne' (l. 2564). Laudine also gives him a ring which will make him invincible in battle, a mistake no doubt, since, relishing his invincibility, the date for return slips by unnoticed. His honour in terms of prowess is increased but so too is his dishonour towards her and, it seems, also towards his king.

Fourteen months later, and still encouraged by Gawain, Yvain is curiously encamped on a hilltop outside Chester instead of staying in Arthur's court in the town below and it is the king who must come up the hill to see him. In terms of symbolism it serves to accentuate Yvain's arrogance; he has removed himself from a place where he is the vassal. More specifically, the symbolism is that of a hilltop king about to be brought low. We are told the date is mid-August ('miaost', l. 2679) which means a few days before the *decollatio* of St John and, when Yvain learns that Laudine's love has turned to hate, grief and shame destroy him. He falls in a matter of days from highest to lowest, from joy to despair, and the most renowned of knights becomes a naked madman roaming the woods.

If the story is to continue there must be a recovery, and references to God indicate the direction this will take. Yvain does hear God's thunder when Laudine's female ambassador delivers her message. She commends to God everyone in the camp except him, and in Yvain's mind it is as if he were in the pit of hell ('an abisme', l. 2789). After this, the seasonal imperatives are increasingly left behind as Yvain slowly discovers a Christian path, almost like the progress of Boethius in *The Consolation of Philosophy*, and beginning with the hermit in the forest praying to God to protect the distracted knight.

Laudine's gradual forgiveness comes after Yvain's last combat in the story,[20] a battle in which St John's Day expectations are reversed. In the narrative leading up to it, Chrétien also excludes any calendrical measurement: 'Jors avoit passez, ne sai quanz' ('the days passed, I do not know how many', l. 5872). Gawain reappears, after his long absence, having agreed to champion the opposing party in the dispute but, since neither knight knows the identity of his adversary, the combat begins with the blind animal aggression found in Yvain's first encounter. Both men 'strike with their pommels so hard on each other's helmets that they are quite dazed and almost knock out one another's brains. Their eyes blaze.... Their fists are large and powerful, their sinews strong and their bones hard; and they exchange vicious blows to the face' (Owen, p. 364). This reverses instantly when each learns the other's identity; competition for success becomes competition for failure as each man claims 'to have been defeated' ('Que chascuns outrez ne se claint', ll. 6313–14). Yvain, in particular, humbles himself to the other's lordship: '"Dear good lord... let the king, my lord, be in no doubt that I was definitely vanquished and defeated in this combat!"—"No, I was."—"No, I," they exclaim.' (Owen, p. 367) Whereas, previously, each man strove for power, now they strive to give 'la victoire et la corone' (l. 6359) to the other. The change from midsummer aggression to the opposite in the one fight leads to both a comic and a happy ending, in which Yvain is almost a changed man. But the word 'almost' has to be added because, despite the improvement in the second half of the story, Chrétien shows that even good men are mortal and therefore flawed.[21]

The second half is, necessarily, more serious, and even appears less well structured as Yvain stumbles his way through the world. However, as mentioned, change itself is a solsticial phenomenon. More interestingly, it appears that the pattern in the second half is as carefully crafted as in the first, with its plot and design developing in ways opposite to that

---

[20] Hunt (pp. 33–34) argues that there is not a true reconciliation.

[21] Jean Frappier, however, considers that Yvain does perfect himself. See *Étude sur Yvain, ou, Le chevalier au lion de Chrétien de Troyes* (Paris: SEDES, 1969), pp. 201–02.

of the first. Wandering aimlessly in despair is the antithesis of Yvain's previous journeys motivated by ambition. And, during the later journeying, women are more influential than men. Apart from the hermit, and the father victimized by Harpin, the men Yvain now meets are adversaries. Male rivalry had driven him to his present state and he is healed by the generosity of women, healed physically and spiritually for, through defending them, he purges his dishonour (Owen, p. 519).

Other events reflect back to the first half. For example, Yvain's first act of atonement is to repel the Count threatening the castle and lands of the Lady of Noroison. This first quest is a temptation, inviting a return to his former ways. The first we hear of the castle is that the Lady climbed the tower to see his approach better from the height: 'Et la dame fu an la tor/ De son chastel montee an haut' (ll. 3184–85). Since this is the only such description in the tale, a parallel with Fortune's castle is suggested, especially since Yvain's prowess in defending it provokes enough praise from the people to reawaken his pride. They compare him to the sun (l. 3249) and believe that the woman he loved would be happy (l. 3243–44), which is ironic in the circumstances. But, this time, glorification of Yvain comes only from the outside. He himself remains anonymous—as he thinks—and humble, and he proceeds with his solitary, thoughtful wanderings, despite Lady Fortune offering herself and her castle to him under any conditions.

Also, when Yvain learns that his disloyalty to Laudine threatens Lunete's life, the least he can do is defend her in combat. But carrying this out proves problematic, in contrast to encounters in the first part of the story. There Yvain's quests had been motivated by self-glorification and he had arrived at combats cool and well-prepared. Now he is harassed and beset from all sides by pleas for help. After his promise to Lunete, another plea to defend the maiden from the giant, Harpin, jeopardizes his chances of arriving in time to save Lunete, which would result in a worse betrayal than that to Laudine since Lunete would lose her life. What is even more ironic about these two missions is that Yvain is not the first choice. Both Lunete and the maiden's father had lost time in a fruitless search for Gawain, and now at the last minute both turn to Yvain as second best. Therefore, as he rushes from engagement to engagement he hasn't even the satisfaction of being their preferred knight. There is, at least, no longer any chance for his self-esteem to become reinflated. In reputation, Yvain always comes second to Gawain, and coming second is another midsummer theme. There could also be a further touch of paradox in the way that Gawain does keep his high reputation to the end, despite the fact that Yvain has done all the work for him.

Another contrast which reflects back to the first half is the fact that the importance of seasons becomes the importance of the hour. Twice Yvain has to defend a woman's life or her future at a precise time, and obstructions are thrown in his way, as though his previous inability to remember a twenty-four-hour agreement can only be purged by super-human timekeeping.

Paradox and oppositions throughout the narration continue the matrix of inversion and link the first and second halves. For example, at Yvain's marriage feast, Gawain was likened to the sun, and was attracted to Lunete—the moon (ll. 2402–09), an obvious attraction of opposites, which Chrétien develops into a more complex paradox than already perceived. Gawain tells Lunete not to change him for another defender, but then he cannot be found when she needs him: the sun proves unreliable, as it is at midsummer, whereas Lunete is the most faithful character in the book. Also Laudine's love/hate reversal is recalled at the end of the story before the combat between Yvain and Gawain. Chrétien muses for a hundred lines on the paradox of 'Love and mortal Hatred in the one vessel... How can two so contrary things dwell in one single lodging' ('Qu'an a an un veissel trovee/ Amor et Haïne mortel./ ... deuz choses, qui sont contreires', ll. 6022–26). On the one hand the comments are about mortal combat between close friends, but Chrétien's digression provides a reminder of the state of mind in Laudine, who is present, and it anticipates the possibility that a happy resolution for the combat could be repeated in the question of love. In the second half of the story, there is also a reversal of Gawain's earlier advice on breaking the bridle and halter. When Yvain sees Laudine again he 'checks and restrains his heart with great effort/ as someone holds in a strongly pulling horse' ('met son cuer an tel esprueve,/ Qu'il le retient et si l'afrainne,/ Si con l'an retient a grant painne/ Au fort frain le cheval tirant', l. 4348–51). There is even inversion in verbal abuse when, towards the end of the second half, insult is used for a generous reason. Yvain returns for the final combat at the spring but has nowhere to sleep except at an unknown castle, where people outside greet him, not with 'welcome', but 'mal veigniez, sire, mal veigniez' (l. 5115). Yvain takes offence until he learns that this is a warning.

The most moral reversal lies in the contrasting motives for combat in the first and second halves. Calogrenant's opening adventure was done for a trivial reason—pouring water on the stone at the spring for the pleasure of creating mayhem on someone else's land. This serves as a metaphor for the devastation knights did wreak on their travels, and it is an act wilfully repeated by Yvain. In the second half, Yvain's opposition to such activities provides part of his means of redemption. His first encounter, defeating Count Alier as he ravages the lands of the Lady of Noroison, also reads as a more realistic depiction of Esclados's original defence of the spring. Alier is another example of a knight who lays waste to another's land (ll. 3313–14) and Yvain, on his quest to reform, forces him to rebuild what he has destroyed. The next famously realistic cause Yvain takes up is to rescue the three hundred maidens from working for poverty wages—a possible comment on the weaving industry in Champagne at the time (Owen, p. 519). And, finally, he champions a young woman oppressed by corrupt use of the law. These inversions suggest that, despite the apparent triumph in the earlier deeds of Yvain, in fact they illustrate the behaviour of a lord who was spoiled, proud, and wilful, and whose subsequent pilgrimage teaches him the realities of other people's lives.

The use of the word 'fool' also changes from secular to moral. At the opening, Yvain's cousin, Calogrenant calls himself 'fool' to express his humiliation. Yvain ostensibly champions him, but it appears that Yvain's real spur is his own pride, hurt by his cousin's defeat, for he calls Calogrenant 'fool' twice, in his defence of him. By contrast, at the end of the romance, Yvain appreciates that his betrayal of Laudine was a serious form of folly springing from such pride, and for which he has paid in full.

However, Yvain's continued wish for fame in the second half is allowed, once divorced from self-glory, a delicate balance achieved in stages for, after rescuing the maiden from the giant, Yvain still wants her uncle, Gawain, to know of his achievement: 'Car por neant fet la bonté,/ Qui ne viaut qu'ele soit seüe ' (ll. 4280–81). Yet, he does not want his name mentioned: paradoxically he wants both fame and anonymity. At the beginning of the last mission there are signs of a greater change when he says, 'No-one wins fame by inactivity', adding, 'with God's help'[22]

---

[22] References to God are found throughout the story but in the second part they are real prayers rather than casual oaths. And, as with the change in Yvain's perception of fame, so too, his inclusion of God happens by degrees. In the long section from lines 3972 to 4085, before Yvain fights the giant, Harpin, God's influence is acknowledged, but by Yvain's hosts, who believe that God's good chance (l. 3974) has brought him there. The next morning Yvain hears Mass only to fill in time while he waits for the giant to appear; and it

('Or me doint Des eür et grace', l. 5104). Fame, earned in service to others, is not itself an evil if the lord achieving it can see beyond his personal success. When these provisos are met, the end of the romance affirms self-worth. Yvain is made humble, but he is not humiliated, and when Laudine continues her punishment of him, he returns to the spring in Broceliande, to create one last and justified storm of protest.

It is interesting that the word 'fortune' is never used, although the concepts of her and her wheel are very much alive in the tale. When Calogrenant is asked his identity by the guardian of the bulls, he replies, 'a man looking for *avantures*' (l. 362), in other words, a man putting himself in the hands of chance.[23] More graphically, the result of Yvain confronting Esclados was for one man to fall from power to death and to be replaced by the victor, even in marriage to the widow; and Chrétien emphasizes the completeness of the exchange:

> Mes ore est mes sire Yvains sire,
> Et li morz est toz obliëz.
> Cil, qui l'ocist, est mariëz
> An sa fame, et ansanble gisent,
> Et les janz aimment plus et prisent
> Le vif, qu'onques le mort ne firent. (ll. 2164–69)

('Now is my lord Yvain the Lord and death is completely forgotten. He who killed him is married to his wife and the people love him better and hold the living as more important than the dead.')

This is as unsentimental, one might say as callous, as Philosophy's comments on the workings of Fortune's wheel in *The Consolation of Philosophy*. The two men have simply exchanged fortunes. Instead of references to her, the solsticial context of the first half itself provides the connection. Yvain and the other knights are seeking the midsummer height of worldly glory, or the top of Fortune's wheel, while Yvain's fall, the following year, happens towards the end of summer.[24] Lunete falls

---

is his hosts' continued pleas to him in the name of God and Mary, which keep him there. However, later, when defending Lunete, it is Yvain who expresses the certainty that 'God and justice will help' (l. 4333), and in all his subsequent missions he acknowledges he needs God's help to succeed, even including the last one, the reconciliation with Laudine, which, he says, is all he wants from God in this life.

[23] See Henri Roussel, *Alain de Lille, Gautier de Châtillon, Jakemart Giélée et leur temps*, Actes du Colloque de Lille, Octobre 1978 (Lille: Lille University Press, 1980), pp. 307–31 (p. 310).

[24] The Lion which accompanies Yvain during his fall could be connected to the

too, and she reminds Yvain that if he defends her, the result will be either life for them both, or death for them both. From the Fortune perspective two alternatives dominate: either to be in a state of raised *hauteur*[25] above others, or to be shamed and below them. Yet, a hint of the Christian resolution is anticipated at the opening, in the first house Calogrenant finds in Broceliande. Here the host and his daughter do not change in their respect for him, when he walks back defeated from his encounter at the spring. Fortune's bleak alternatives only apply if you believe in them. A different set of values can free the individual: a point of view which is found in works from Cicero to Jean Michel.[26]

Chrétien's method of developing a story towards a Christian, moral conclusion is always entertaining. Didacticism is avoided through the revelation, rather than explanation, of folly. Sometimes this is done through paradoxical juxtaposition, as, for example, in the mixing of grief and comedy. When Yvain's wanderings accidentally bring him back to the spring in Broceliande a suicidal despair breaks out. His laments in the chapel are echoed by those of another, but instead of commiserating he responds with a challenge: 'Tes, fole riens!/ Tes diaus est joie, tes maus biens/ Anvers le mien,', ('shut up you fool—your sorrow is joy, your ills happiness compared to mine', ll. 3575–77). When Yvain had been at the top of fortune's wheel he had had to prove he was best and his fall does not remove the urge for supremacy, even in grief. When he learns it is Lunete he is abusing, the grief from his past behaviour is compounded by the new shame as well as with the realization that he has brought her down too. Similarly, when Yvain, concealed in the castle at Broceliande,

---

astronomical sign, Leo, which governs most of August, the season of Yvain's change. In chap. VIII of his *Rationale,* (d'Avino edn, p. 728), William Durand emphasized the lion's cruelty, ferocity, and fiery nature—qualities suitable to the first half of the *Yvain.* Appropriate to the ethos of the second half, he is the inverse: sensitive, loving, and comically humble.

[25] The subject of dominance, lordship of one man over another, explains why, as critics have noted, characters appear to be so polite to each other. When they are not abusing each other the word 'lord' is constantly applied. The subject of lordship was so closely allied to midsummer, that Rutebeuf wrote in '*La Griesche d'été*', that every man was a lord above him, debased as he was by his addiction to gambling.

[26] 'Come now my dear Lucius, build in your imagination the lofty and towering structure of the Virtues; then you will feel no doubt that those who achieve them ... are always happy; realizing as they do that all the vicissitudes of fortune, the ebb and flow of time and circumstance, will be trifling and feeble.' Cicero, *De finibus bonorum et malorum,* trans. by H. Rackham, LCL (London and New York: Heinemann, 1914), p. 473.

sees the burial of the defender of the spring, his response is not sympathy but regret that the evidence of his victory was to be hidden, for Kay would mock him unless he had proof. Regretting the burial of a defeated opponent is another mean response, as Hunt says (p. 45) yet, coming as it does after Laudine's wild grief, the contrast is almost comic. The dexterity of Chrétien's writing maintains an oblique light even where the underlying comment is serious, and the last combat uses such obliqueness in the most saturnalian manner, through an inversion of the comedy of the opening. At Arthur's Pentecost court, the laughs were provided by aggression at odds with the holy day, while the story's action ends with a combat in which the submissiveness is at odds with the aggressive situation. At the end, Arthur, too, redeems himself without didacticism. The inconclusive ending to the combat between Yvain and Gawain forces him to judge the dispute between the sisters, which he does with Solomon-like wisdom and Marcolf-like wit, by provoking the sister at fault to admit it (ll. 6382–419).

In Chrétien's mosaic of interrelated themes and actions, it is hard to find any event or concept which does not have an opposition or its reflection elsewhere in the tale, and it is the traditions and inversions associated with the Nativity of St John which provide the matrix for these complexities. In Chrétien's undercutting of the chivalric ideal, he did not 'overturn audience expectations',[27] nor would they have been 'initially… confused'[28] by it. The 'subversion and dismantling of the chivalry topos'[29] would have been signalled as soon as the midsummer context was established. From this point, Chrétien's readers would have been alert to all the possibilities of St John's day satire.

Therefore, the first European literary work to employ a 'festive critique'[30] of events is the *Yvain,* and Chrétien's complex plot functions through reversals and paradoxes associated not with Carnival but with midsummer. Yvain, Gawain, Arthur, and Kay are portrayed as varieties of midsummer lords, in their boasting, mockery, flyting, ambition, falls from glory to dishonour or death, and involvement in a faulty midsummer marriage. Although written before Philippe de Navarre's *Quatre ages de l'homme,* the characters contain all the rashness and contradictions he

---

[27] Hunt, p. 30.

[28] Uitti and Freeman, p. 85.

[29] Hunt, p. 33.

[30] Peter Stallybrass and Allon White, *The Politics and Poetics of Transgression*, p. 6.

was to associate with the summertime of youth. Worldly themes associated with the solstice are explored and, subsequently, rejected or inverted into Christian alternatives. And because of Chrétien's playful invention in applying solsticial paradoxes, he reduces the level of attack in the original customs. Instead of one figure, or enemy, singled out for harsh exposure, the multiplicity of faulty heroes, and the comic oppositions, paradoxes, and inversions woven through the plot, create a saturnalia out of solsticial mockery. This is assisted by his forgiving attitude, and ultimate sympathy, rather than contempt, for his main heroes, thus making the *Yvain* a unique combination of comedy and morality.

CHAPTER 3

Summer v. Midsummer
in the Progress of Love:
Erec and Enide and *Lancelot*

Je fais dancer les amoureux
Et despandre dans un esté

Folie: La Folie des Gorriers

The twelfth-century *Chanson de Roland* relates how the King Marsilie assembled his forces 'en mai, al premier jur d'estéd',[1] so associating any day in the month with the start of the hot season; for, as Jehan de Preis was to explain, it was the month as a whole which symbolized summer:

> Apres fist Virgile IIII ymagines de chez XII ymagines et signes qui signi-
> fient les IIII temps; chu sont: fevrier por printemps, may por esteit, awost
> por waym ou autompne, et novembre por yvier.
>
> (As Virgil laid down, out of the twelve images, those which signified the
> four seasons were February for spring, May for summer, August for
> autumn, and November for winter.)[2]

In practice, the symbolic moment was the first day that May arrived, yet some romances begin with festivals prior to this, in April or March, and these are nevertheless invoked as the start of the *été* season. The most

---

[1] *La Chanson de Roland,* l. 2628, ed. by I. Short (Paris: Librairie Générale Française, 1990), p. 182.

[2] *Œuvres de Jehan des Preis,* vol. 1, ed. by A. Borgnet and S. Bormans (Brussels, 1864), p. 233.

obvious example is the opening to Raoul de Houdenc's *Messire Gawain.*
'Ce fut au tans noviel d'esté,/ Que li rois Artus ot esté/ Tot le Quaresme à
Rouvelant./ Et vint, à grant plenté de gent,/ A Pasques, por sa cort tenir,/
A Carlion' ('It was at the new season of summer, when King Arthur had
spent all Lent at Roulevent and came to Carlion at Easter to hold court
with a great host of followers').[3]

The result of this extension to the summer period is, as Philippe Walter
has said, for some poets to treat the year as though it divided into two,
between *été* and *hiver*.[4] However, it is interesting to find that such
polarization is more than arbitrary: it reflects, instead, the argument of the
poem. For it is works most concerned with extremes of behaviour and extremes of fortune—the highs and the lows—which use the summer/winter
opposition to signify these experiences. Such usage appears, for example,
in 'le Passetemps' of Taillevent, in the first part of Jehan de la Mote's,
'Vie d'Enfer et de Paradis' and, with a further development, in
Rutebeuf's 'Grische d'hiver' and 'Grische d'esté'.

A structured use of season can be found in other ways. May is the
traditional month for love and the many lyrics which concentrate solely
on its youthful pleasures are set in the cadre of May alone, while poems
and romances which project forward from May to June, and beyond,
include more dangerous elements: temperamental changeability, reversals
of fortune, and conflicts. This movement happens quite clearly in *Erec
and Enide*, and also in *Lancelot,* when Guinevere changes towards her
lover.[5] St John's day is not mentioned in either but, at the post-Pentecost
period, love experiences a midsummer crisis, with the behaviour of the
protagonists fluctuating in ways similar to those in *Yvain*. The changes
and the conflicts have serious consequences in *Erec and Enide*, while
they are burlesqued in *Lancelot.*

In *Erec and Enide* the action begins at Easter, moves to Pentecost and
ends the following Christmas, with the changing seasons triggering plot
and character development. Just as in Laon, in 1587, when the different

---

[3] *Messire Gauvain*, intro. C. Hippeau (Paris, 1862), ll. 1–6. Cf. See M.-L. Chênerie, *Le
Chevalier errant dans les romans arthuriens en vers des XIIe et XIIIe siècles* (Geneva:
Droz, 1986), p. 243.

[4] P. Walter, *La mémoire du temps: fêtes et calendriers de Chrétien de Troyes à la Morte
Artu*, p. 17.

[5] Chrétien, in fact, spends more time portraying changeability in his male characters,
such as Yvain and Erec, than on the more often discussed reputation which women have
for unreliability; as discussed in Hunt, *Chrétien de Troyes: Yvain*, pp. 57–58.

plans of the rebels were timed for their most appropriate festive days, so too in this early novel, action appears to have been created to match the season it occurred in. For example Erec and Enide meet soon after Easter; she is of lower rank, but she is reborn socially by his love for her. She leaves home with a shift on her back, to be recreated in Queen Guinevere's chamber by the royal clothes put on her. As Jean Renaut was to say: 'a Pasques, au novel temps'; which is, in modern French, 'à Pâques, au temps du renouveau'.[6] Soon after Easter, Kay makes one civil and helpful remark to Gawain and respectfully calls him 'Lord'.[7] Yet, some time after Pentecost, an arrogant Kay challenges Erec and is sent sprawling from his horse (ll. 3951–4074). The fact that the dates of the three great Church festivals are placed in sequence, invites us to consider not just them, but also the periods in between, particularly the time of the lovers' trials which happens after Pentecost and when Prince Erec, like Kay, quite clearly changes in his behaviour. The resulting confusions and paradoxes coincide with the hottest part of summer, and the disorders experienced by Erec and Enide are the same as those traditionally practised then.

A summary shows how clearly defined these changes are. At the opening, King Arthur is in control of his Easter court and no irony can be found in his choice of hunting the white stag. Some resistance is made to the idea because of the dissension it might cause among the ladies, but there is no indication of a failing in the king. Erec does not take part in the chase, but keeps the queen and her maiden company until the insult of the stranger-knight, Yder, draws him away in pursuit, followed by combat, for the prize of the sparrow-hawk. The battle is fierce but there are no bestial comparisons, and each combatant behaves honourably. Erec puts the outcome into the hands of God and, although Yder is in the wrong, he does not vaunt himself. In the fighting, both are unseated but, since this is at the same time, there is neither shame nor glory for either man (l. 873). Erec achieves his chivalric purpose to restore the honour of Queen Guinevere and Yder behaves nobly in defeat, agreeing to submit to the queen in Arthur's court. Further, since Erec has won the sparrow-hawk he can bestow it on Enide, so bringing her 'Enor [honour] et joie et seignorage' (l. 1311). In these opening events there is an elegance of

---

[6] *Jean Renart : Galeran de Bretagne,* l. 4823, ed. by L. Foulet (Paris: Champion, 1975); *Renaut: Galeran de Bretagne,* trans. by Jean Dufournet (Paris: Champion, 1996).

[7] *Chrétien de Troyes: Erec et Enide,* ll. 1097–1102, ed. by Michel Rousse (Paris: Flammarion, 1994).

behaviour, and a conviction that courtly ethics give order to the world. Later, at the reception of Erec and Enide in Arthur's court at Pentecost, this order is defined in the hierarchical arrangement of the knights (ll. 1691–750) and soon after (ll. 1793–1814) comes a discourse on model kingship, based on instructions to rulers found in the *Miroirs des Princes*.[8] Erec's meeting with Enide is also conceived as an ideal, for the couple are a perfect match, both externally handsome and internally refined (ll. 1500–16).

Once the chivalric pinnacle at Pentecost is over, perfection topples into excess. The combat Erec had had with Yder was for a disinterested purpose but, when a tournament is held a month after Pentecost, Erec takes part for reasons of self-glorification: 'a joster et a bien feire,/ Por ce que sa proesce apeire' ('to do well in the jousts, to make his prowess known', ll. 2217–18). Therefore, although it is his opponent who has the title of Arrogant Man of the Heath and Erec vanquishes him, Erec's motives, too, invite the title of Pride. By the end of the tournament his success is as complete as was Yvain's and his prowess recognized as fully as he could wish; his fame was so great that people spoke of him alone, comparing him with Absalom, Alexander, and Solomon (ll. 2266–70). With this, and his marriage to Enide, initial success and happiness are complete.

Unlike the *Yvain*, conflict between the marriage bed and prowess is not felt by Erec, who abandons his worldly career for the new life. Instead, his declining reputation, and the people's mockery of him, grieve Enide and provide her with her first paradoxical problem. As a wife and perfect lover it is her duty to obey Erec in everything;[9] to oppose him, even in his own interests, would be less than ideal and Enide is dutiful during the waking hours. However, when she thinks Erec is asleep she looks at him from head to toe or, as Chrétien puts it 'a mont et a val' (l. 2490), since he is now lower in people's esteem, because 'mout avoit changiee sa vie' (l. 2468). Enide's grief breaks out, and one has to accept that this is a failure in terms of courtly love.[10] She uses the word *honi* (l. 2505) and, though she blames herself for bringing him this shame, the word provokes

---

[8]   Owen, p. 501, note to l. 1793.

[9]   Ibid., p. 500, note to l. 1482.

[10]   Chrétien tells us that Enide as well as Erec was changed by the wedding night, when she became a '*dame novele*' (l. 2104). Though not itself criticism, the phrase indicates the possibility of ambivalences in her as well as in Erec, appropriate if the season is five to six weeks after Pentecost.

another change in Erec, an excessive reaction to abandon court and civilization in search of the most dangerous adventures to prove her wrong.

Uitti and Freeman write that 'a proud young prince might well be expected to react as Erec reacted to this perceived criticism',[11] yet perhaps understanding his behaviour is not the same as condoning it, for once back in his armour, Erec becomes tyrannical. Enide, thinking she is to be banished, perceives other dichotomies in life, again blaming herself for, as she sees it, her pride in her happiness having destroyed that happiness (ll. 2606–09). She concludes with the more optimistic thought that: 'Ne set qu'est biens qui mal n'essaie' ('no-one can appreciate good without experience of evil', l. 2610), a Christian Manichaean[12] expression which is eventually proved true. Before this her troubles deepen, and she lays the blame openly on: 'Fortune, qui m'avoit atreite,/ Tost a a li sa main retreite' ('Fortune, who had drawn me to her,/ Has pulled back her hand from everything', ll. 2785–86). For the adventures Erec embarks on not only strip her of all dignity and comfort, they put both their lives at risk. Although there is no reference to St John's Day, Erec pursues his wandering life a few weeks after Pentecost and Enide's reference to Fortune is like those by Taillevent, and by chroniclers who associate this downward turn with the midsummer solstice. Further, Erec's attitude is now full of bravado, his adventures are a series of combats to discover who is the greatest man, and, in contrast to the challenges faced between Easter and Pentecost, the situations the lovers now find themselves in are full of paradox.

In the first two encounters Erec is wildly unreasonable but, as Enide notes, both times he proves that he is the best of all knights in terms of prowess—but not of chivalry, for his love for her has turned to hate and she is forbidden from speaking to him. Since Erec has placed Enide in front, she sees the threats first and is tormented by conflicting demands on her loyalty. She must either obey him, stay silent, and risk his death, or disobey and warn him. Each time she is a disobedient wife which, in their inverted circumstances, proves to be the right course of action. Later, she is accused of arrogance by the arrogant Count Oringle, who aims to murder Erec and abduct her. Erec is ignorant of the Count's treachery, and only Enide's wits save him, yet he rewards her with more verbal

---

[11] Uitti and Freeman, p. 46.

[12] Billington, *Mock Kings*, p. 2.

abuse. Erec has become all brawn and no brain, which is reflected in the noise and tumult of their encounters with opponents. Erec's meeting with the changed Kay becomes a contest in bravado which Erec wins, yet he also wins the combat despite the fact that fights in these tales tend towards the discomfiting of the more arrogant. Later comes his magnanimous battle to rescue Cabroc of Tabriol from two giants. In succeeding, Erec reunites two lovers but, to accomplish this, he abandons his own wife.

Despite his neglect of Enide, this is the first selfless combat Erec has undertaken since fighting against Yder and, if a chronological passage through seasons is intended, it could be that at this point in the story the season is the *decollatio* of John the Baptist, a date which marks the end of *été* disorders. The date would also give meaning to the second and near catastrophic meeting with Count Oringle; for Erec's return to Enide marks the nadir to which Fortune lets them fall from their midsummer height of success in combat and marriage. Erec's wounds, earned in defence of Cabroc, cause him to fall into a death-like coma and Enide's laments, appealing to Death to take her too, bring instead the Count, whose argument to persuade her into another marriage includes the second reference to Fortune in the romance. Fortune is kind to Enide, he says, taking her in one instant from poverty—now that her lord and protector is dead—to riches, and the honour of a title ('Povre estiiez: or seroiz riche./ N'est pas Fortune anvers vos chiche,/ Qui tel enor vos a donee/ Qu'or seroiz contesse clamee', ll.4801–04). This pragmatic argument, which is proved valid at midsummer in *Yvain*, is disproved here by the resurrection of Erec. His revival from a mock death prevents a mock marriage and, from this moment on, he and Enide leave midsummer behaviour behind; both characters appear to have matured or, as Chrétien puts it, through their trials they have reinforced their love ('Or ont lor amor rafermee', l. 5257).

The one objection to the argument that a chronological time sequence is intended comes in line 4779, at the point of the forced marriage. Chrétien writes that this was 'un jor de mai', when it ought to be the end of August. However, at the moment when Chrétien mentions May, the love story is about to be resumed and the disorders of midsummer left behind. It seems not impossible that May is recalled in anticipation of the change from combativeness in all its aspects to a love which will be restored. Since the seasons are used metaphorically in relation to the condition of Chrétien's heroes, the addition of a non-chronological metaphor helps to illustrate an emotional change.

And, before the romance comes to its Christmas conclusion, there is one more adventure for Erec to undertake, that of the Joy of the Court. In a garden inside King Evrains's impregnable castle of Brandigant the knight, Mabonagrains, has been imprisoned many years by an oath made to his lady never to leave unless defeated in combat. His honour will not allow him to submit if he can win, and the heads of knights he has vanquished are displayed in the garden. The adventure, Joy of the Court, is the quest to release him, and Erec insists on undertaking it although ignorant of what it entails, and warned against it.

It has been thought that this coda was to show Erec on a quest with a social dimension, applying himself to other people's needs rather than to his own glory.[13] Yet, he had already shown such unselfishness, almost losing his life in the combat to release Cabroc. The Joy of the Court differs by its public nature. The entire town comes out to warn Erec with the word *honte* (ll. 5446, 5536). Uttered earlier in private by Enide, this word had so offended Erec's pride that it had prompted all his injured, irrational behaviour. But, in his maturity, he can even bear the threat of public humiliation. A second dishonourable word, *recreant* (l. 5846)[14] is further introduced by Erec, when he tells Enide not to despair for him until she sees him behave in this perfidious way. His speech to the opposing knight also shows how much Erec has grown in stature. Mabonagrains utters inflammatory insults, typical of Kay, but Erec side-steps the anticipated flyting, calling the knight 'friend' and saying that there is 'no wisdom in threats' (l. 5923). Therefore, when Erec releases Mabonagrains by defeating him, the joy is twofold, for both Erec's fear of shame and the shame of the imprisoned knight are defeated. This is achieved honourably through the Christian opposite of humility, rather than the worldly opposite of pride, and so provides an appropriate stepping-stone towards the Christmas apotheosis.

Since there is a suggestion of magic in the garden prison, where Mabonagrains spends many years without, it seems, getting any older, it would be pleasing if the final quest could be equated with the season of All Souls which would complete the chronological journey through the year's dangerous seasons before arriving at Christmas. However, incidents in the Joy of the Court adventure relate more surely to the

---

[13] Owen, p. 505, note to l. 6121.

[14] Ibid., p. 504, note to l. 4918.

decollatio of John the Baptist, for the garden in which Mabonagrains is imprisoned is decorated with decapitated heads, and his joy is in coming second in combat with another man—a pleasure found at the end of the *Yvain*, and in later romances (see Chapter 4). One can also observe that his predicament was brought about by the possessive love of a woman.

In contrast, Enide's true love is proved by enduring Erec's midsummer disorders, at the end of which, in a neat reversal of John the Baptist's fate, Erec does not die, but only suffers an apparent death, from which he too is reborn in love for his wife. As Enide had said, good cannot be appreciated without knowledge of evil, and the disordered behaviour of youth (explored in a section which begins and ends with a reference to Fortune) appears as a university of life, in which value is discovered for proper order. This is not unlike the later experience of characters in Shakespeare's festive comedies.[15]

Other aspects in this tale lead to the conclusion that, on one level, the romance is a story of everyman and everywoman, told through popular customs and in which the participants are not intended to be real kings, queens, and princes, but as characters pretending to be them. For Enide is presented as a beauty queen, and even Erec is judged by his looks. Before the midsummer trials, Enide's beauty is the only quality by which the reader knows her: she is introduced as unique, a perfect creature 'whom God and Nature could only succeed in making once' (Owen, p. 6). The prize for killing the white stag is to kiss the most beautiful lady in the court, and the prize of the sparrow-hawk is awarded to the knight with the most beautiful lady. In each case Enide is the winner. She wins the kiss against the competition of five hundred daughters of kings (ll. 50–52) while only, herself, the daughter of a vavasour. Later, Guivret thinks her so fair that Iseult is a serving girl by comparison (l. 4946). Yet, the fair Iseult was also the daughter of a king and Guivret's observation leads to the conclusion that Enide has the potential to become a queen by virtue of her beauty, but by that only. Bearing in mind the emphasis on order at the Pentecost gathering, the significance of Enide enduring Erec's irrational behaviour is that it shows the strength of her *fine amour* and so proves her innate nobility. Chrétien's romance is the story of a girl who was born in the lowest rung of courtly hierarchy but who crosses social boundaries and acquires royal virtues. It also relates to 'every(wo)man' travelling through the seasons of life, for after a hopeful, spring-beginning to

---

[15] See Barber, *Shakespeare's Festive Comedies*.

adulthood, comes the turbulent stage which is inevitable in any seasonal progression on the wheel of life. And, only by surviving midsummer's disturbances can love be proved. As Uitti and Freeman observe, Chrétien's claim of *mout bele conjunture* (p. 14) in his story not only refers to the skill of the narrative in his creating a new form of composition, it refers, too, to the final harmony of the marriage.[16]

Erec and Enide holds a special place in twelfth-century literature. Not only is it the first of Chrétien's romances, it is the first of any romance novels, as we know them, and it has been observed that this adventure is, of all Chrétien's work, most like the *chansons de geste* which preceded it.[17] Another striking quality is its delicacy in depicting the relationship between Erec and Enide in their early courtship, their trials, and in the final harmony. This structural elegance is supported, rather than negated, by seasonal development, since seasonal challenges mark the lovers' progress towards an eventual unity.

The romance is not itself difficult to follow; the subject of Enide proving herself after a moment of disloyalty is clear to see. *Lancelot,* however, is more baffling; it is 'heavy with multiple meanings',[18] apparent contradictions and unexplained paradoxes. As D. D. R. Owen says: 'the normal scales seem so strangely distorted that the charge of carelessness has often been levelled against him. This, however, is a romance so full of incongruities that one suspects them, far from being the result of negligence, to belong to some total and original artistic design.'[19] One of the difficulties is due to Chrétien not having finished the tale himself; the ideas which sustain it up until Lancelot and Guinevere's night together lose their coherence after this point. Yet, up until this point, seasonal expectations of behaviour provide some illumination.

There is one obvious contrast between this love story and that of Erec and Enide: the earlier love match is consummated in marriage, while the second concerns Lancelot's illicit liaison with Guinevere. Easter, when *Erec and Enide* begins, was the most innocent season. *Lancelot,* however,

---

[16] Uitti & Freeman, p. 39.

[17] *Chrétien de Troyes: Erec et Enide*, ed. by J.-M. Fritz (Paris: Librairie Générale Française, 1992), pp. 5–6, and E. J. Buckbee, '*Erec et Enide*', in *The Romances of Chrétien de Troyes,* ed. by D. Kelly, (Lexington, KY: French Forum, 1985), pp. 48–60 (p. 48).

[18] *Lancelot ou le chevalier de la charrette*, ed. by J.-C. Aubailly (Paris: Flammarion, 1991), p. 9.

[19] Owen, p. xv.

begins on Ascension day (between 30 April and 3 June), and Chrétien's opening reference to the warm winds of April and May, suggests a date coinciding with the beginning of *esté,* therefore a hotter season of love. Incidents suggest that, again, Chrétien developed the progress of Lancelot's quest for Guinevere in a linear time sequence from Ascension to St John's day and beyond. Within the linear sequence conflicting expectations are established: the disorders of love are set against those of midsummer, and the clash produces comedy.

Lancelot was written in the same year as *Yvain,* either 1177 or 1178,[20] and, had *Lancelot* been second, some points of comparison between the two would have provided humour for contemporary readers. For example, Arthur's court on Ascension day is kept with all due Christian reverence, but Arthur still succeeds in being an ineffective king. When Méléagant enters the hall and humiliates him by declaring he has captured many of his citizens, the king replies that, though this grieves him, he will have to accept it. What is wrong with his court this time is the love between Lancelot and Guinevere. The weakening power of love, which we are told so much about during Lancelot's quest for her, affects all three sides of the triangle so that instead of exhibiting *été* pride, they are enfeebled, either by the emotion of love, or the difficulties, even shame, associated with its illicit nature.

This reading is very much at odds with those in which Lancelot is perceived as the finest example of the courtly *chevalier,* and it was this romance which led Gaston Paris to create his definition of courtly love, 'in order to account for the utter devotion felt by Lancelot toward Guinevere'.[21] Yet, as D. D. R. Owen has noted, the romance has, since, raised conflicting questions: 'Is Chrétien wishing to give a serious and sympathetic illustration (some would say exaltation) of the adulterous form of courtly love? Or are the excesses of such a love soberly criticised with occasional flashes of humour? Or is the whole romance conceived as a burlesque designed to ridicule not only an uncontrolled passion, but the lover himself?'[22] I am arguing for the third category, and the argument for burlesque is supported by the fact that the concept of courtly love was not itself medieval. Yet the romance as a whole becomes more interesting if seen with greater complexity—if the comedy fulfils a purpose—and the

---

[20]   See above, Chap. 2, n. 2.

[21]   Uitti and Freeman, p. 73.

[22]   Owen, p. 511, note to l. 1.

comparison I am tempted to make is with Shakespeare's Antony in *Antony and Cleopatra*. Here, the protagonist is also shamed by his adulterous love, he becomes a fool in the eyes of the world, yet faithfulness to this shaming love gives both him and Cleopatra heroic stature which defeats conventional opinion. Shakespeare's tragedy, too, was constructed along festive lines.[23]

In Chrétien's romance, Guinevere's low spirits are revealed in the complexities of the challenge which Méléagant offers. He states that, if a knight jousts with him and wins, the prisoners will be freed; but, if the knight loses, Queen Guinevere will be added to the captives already taken. When Kay asks to take up the challenge his proposal is rightly dismissed as 'orguel, outrage et desreison' (l. 186). However, Kay has already tricked Arthur into letting him go and, during the trickery, as Owen notes, Guinevere too, is not the forthright woman she was in the *Yvain*. Instead of the proud flyting between her and Kay, she goes so far as to throw herself flat on the ground beseeching him to tell her what has angered him. Therefore, the opening shows, with some humour, both king and queen as the opposite of assertive. Lancelot's behaviour, too, as he begins his quest for Guinevere, is the opposite to the *été* pride of Yvain. Lancelot is absurdly debilitated by love yet, at each encounter, he accidentally succeeds, sometimes because of the confusions which arise from his enfeebled prowess. And his love-disordered state produces further humour when it collides with midsummer aggression in other men. In this Romance, the conflict between the early summer condition of man's mind, and his midsummer condition, is divided into the separate behaviour of different characters.

Lancelot's absent ego is clear at the opening, for although the tale is about him, his entry into it is oblique and he is not identified by name. This, it has been suggested, is for reasons of safety when travelling into the unknown[24] but it can also be observed that anonymity is the opposite to fame. Lancelot's lack of identity reflects a descent in renown, even before he rides in the cart. Also, the opening sequence of Lancelot's quest involves horses, which mirrored a knight's worldly status (see Appendix C), and which Lancelot rides to exhaustion and death, himself ending up on foot, while Gawain's pursuit of Lancelot's furious ride is said to lead them both 'avalé' (l. 304). The metaphor and descriptions are further

---

[23] Billington, *Mock Kings,* pp. 209–17.

[24] See M.-L. Chênerie, p. 686.

symbolic of a descent in worldly fame before the cart incident occurs; therefore they show that humiliation is integral to Lancelot's quest. The cart, which becomes his only means of transport, is the first nadir, making it a further comment on Lancelot's shameful behaviour, rather than the cause of it. Chrétien is at pains to let us know that climbing into it symbolizes the depths of degradation, since it was used for the public humiliation of criminals. The man in it had been stripped of all honour and could never again be accepted into society. 'It was at that time... the saying originated: 'Whenever you see a cart in your path, cross yourself and turn your thoughts to God, so that it does not bring you bad luck' (Owen, p. 189). Since the cart reflects on his relationship with Guinevere, this also accounts for her resentment of his moment's hesitation before climbing into it which tells her that, subconsciously, he acknowledges some degradation in their love. In terms of fidelity, this is as great a betrayal as was Enide's moment of complaint over Erec.

Later events suggest that Lancelot's ride is also a festive punishment: a marital *charivari* against those who had broken society's taboos.[25] Philippe Ménard notes the people's unanimity in hurling abuse at Lancelot as he travels in it (ll. 405–13).[26] Also, at Lancelot's first night's lodging, he is prohibited from sleeping in the best bed. The reason given is the shame of the cart but, since the subject of the taboo is a bed, and one which is rich and luxurious, it would appear to be an analogy with sleeping with Guinevere. The taboo against Lancelot sleeping there suggests that, despite nineteenth-century arguments for courtly love outside marriage, his liaison with Guinevere is not wholly accepted within Chrétien's story. Yet, paradoxically, after the ride in the cart, the only aspect of life for which Lancelot has no shame, is his love for Guinevere. When told of the taboo, his low spirits turn to defiance; a moment of high spirits which deprives him of a restful night.

Apart from this, everything Lancelot does during his search for Guinevere receives the comment of 'shame', even his eventual combat with Méléagant, for, when people in the crowd find themselves on Lancelot's side, this is expressed as running counter to their wish for his humiliation ('Mes a l'autre tuit se tenoient—nes cil qui volsissent sa honte', l. 3546–47). The insistent repetition is comic rather than moral,

---

[25] The thirteenth-century *Roman de Fauvel* first names this as *chalivali*. See *le Roman de Fauvel par Gervais du Bus*, A Text, ll. 682, 694 and 761, ed. by A. Langfors, SATF (Paris: Didot, 1929), glossary.

[26] *Le Rire et le sourire*, p. 298.

since it turns a serious issue into a running joke, just as the outcome of Lancelot's sleeping in the banned bed turns into a comic struggle against its lethal booby-traps. However, one cannot ignore the conflicting attitudes in the narrative towards Lancelot's motives for rescuing Guinevere—Gawain has no objection, but ordinary people do—and it would appear that different views on courtly love outside marriage are brought into conflict in the story, creating another set of thematic oppositions.

The 'bed' incident takes place in a tower on a rock, and during the stay come reminders of a sudden descent in fortune for both Lancelot and Guinevere. The following morning, from a high window, he sees Queen Guinevere below, now taken prisoner; he wishes to fall to her and to his death, but is saved by Gawain. The theme recurs when Gawain then separates from Lancelot to cross into Méléagant's lands by the underwater bridge.

As Lancelot travels alone, totally absorbed in his thoughts of love, and without Gawain's protection, his vulnerability is further cause of humour. He travels like 'a man without strength... against love's domination... so absorbed in thoughts of love he can't remember who he is, or even his own name' ('Et cil de la charrete panse/ con cil qui force ne desfanse/ n'a vers Amors qui le justice;/ et ses pansers est de tel guise/ que lui meïsmes en oublie;/ ne set s'il est... ne ne li manbre de son non', ll. 712–17). Arriving at a ford, he fails to hear three challenges from its guardian, nor does he feel the blow of the lance which hits him. His senses do not grasp the reality until he hits the water. Then he fights like an oaf, angry to have been brought out of his reverie. He insults the man challenging him and will only fight a chivalric joust when his own mistrustful conditions are met. He is also so weakened by love that the fight takes longer than it should, bringing him more shame. Chrétien writes that, if yesterday Lancelot had met a hundred such 'en un val' (l. 872) he would not have had this trouble. In the encounter, it is his opponent who shows courtly ethics and prowess yet, despite Lancelot's lack of them, he succeeds.

His next anti-heroic response is to the damsel who obliges him to lie with her against his will. Once he reluctantly agrees, the damsel surprises him with a test which is a parody of Guinevere's predicament: one which presents Lancelot with a paradox. If he obeys the chivalric code and attempts to rescue the girl, his life would be threatened, and this he has to protect in order to save Guinevere. His perplexity and cowardly attempts to help the girl without endangering himself result in more comedy, and yet again he succeeds.

Comic inversion of heroism continues the following day when Lancelot sets out once more, with the girl. He faints when they find the comb with Guinevere's yellow hair in it, and demonstrates further lack of *été* spirit when he fails to respond to a challenge from a knight seeking to abduct his companion. If time is passing chronologically through these adventures then midsummer's approach appears to be heralded in this encounter, for the previous challenge at the ford had had knightly justification, whereas this one is made in overweening arrogance. The context of midsummer is also suggested by the next adventure when Lancelot, the girl, and her unwelcome suitor stumble into a field of sports and dancing. The incident has been described as passing through dangerous fairy territory: an otherworld encounter, dangerous to the hero[27] and, here, Lancelot's lack of knightly prowess saves him. The witches, or fairies, stop their dances because a knight shamed by the cart is not fit to see them. Paradoxically, 'the evil he carries with him becomes a good'[28] and love's enfeeblement passes to these powerful figures of the otherworld. For, when Lancelot enters the scene they become passive spectators and the entertainment which fills the pause is the harmless one of the arrogant knight, confronting his father and declaring that marriage to Lancelot's companion would be a better prize than 'fet roi coroné' (l. 1682): another comment which suggests the approach of St John's day.

In this highly eclectic narrative Lancelot has yet to visit a cemetery underworld, to encounter rebellion, and to experience quarrels over hospitality. Through all, love saves him because he is paradoxically so inept.

On his arrival at the castle of Méléagant's father, King Bademagu, where Guinevere is held prisoner, the clash between the enfeeblement of love and the aggression of midsummer reaches its climax, for Méléagant is waiting full of rage — 'D'ire et de mautalant color/ en a Meleaganz changiee' (l. 3158) — as he watches Lancelot's arrival from the tower of the hilltop castle. Méléagant and the castle are set solidly in the tradition of the topmost point of fortune's hill, and he contains all the arrogant and changeable qualities of the St John's day of youth: opposite to Lancelot, geographically, and in mood. He is also opposite to his own father, with whom (like the previous arrogant knight) he now has a rebellious

---

[27]   A. Saly, in Aubailly, ed., *Lancelot*, p. 438, n. 44.

[28]   Saly, ibid.

exchange. King Bademagu advises his son to behave according to courtly ideals and warns against doing anything 'por fol ne por orguilleus ' (l. 3209). But Méléagant *is* an arrogant fool and replies that his father wants him to become Lancelot's vassal, to declare his lands in fief to him— another midsummer tradition. Then, in contradiction, he adds he would rather do this than give up the queen. He is rash, hot-tempered, unreasonable, and unstable. The King tries again, threatening to help Lancelot if Méléagant persists, but his son boasts that he can manage without his help, and admits that they are opposites: 'vos plest soiez prodon,/ et moi lessiez estre cruel!' ('Let you be the moral man and let me be cruel!' ll. 3294–95). Bademagu then goes to meet Lancelot, and appropriately descends *aval* twice on his way: once from the tower to the courtyard (l. 3303) and then down to the bridge (l. 3310).

The public nature of Lancelot's tournament against Méléagant is highlighted: it is a spectacle which draws all the people from the surrounding area. They ride through the night to be present the next day 'devant la tor' (l. 3498):

> Ausi con por oïr les ogres
> vont au mostier a feste anel
> a pantecoste ou a Noël
> les genz acostumemant
> tot autresi comunemant
> estoient la tuit aüné.

(Just as it was fitting for people to flock to Church at Pentecost or Christmas, so too by custom and communal wish, everyone gathered there (ll. 3518–23)).

If the seasonal fitness for events found in *Yvain,* and, later, at Laon and in the *Chronicles,* is considered, then custom expected the flaunting of lordly pride and its discomfiture around 24 June.

The two opposites, the egoist and the anonymous knight, are equally matched. They fall off their horses at the same time, therefore neither is shamed (ll. 3603–04) and both fight like wild boars (l. 3608). When Lancelot's wounds (from crossing the sword-bridge) tell on him, a maiden asks his name of Guinevere, who is watching from above in the tower-prison. Guinevere's cool reply—'Lanceloz del Lac a a non/ li chevaliers, mien esciant' (l. 3660)—is the first time his identity is revealed, which promises an upward turn in his fortune. The girl calls out his name and tells him to look at the window where Guinevere sits though, at first, the sight only debilitates him. Keeping his eyes fixed on

Guinevere, he attempts to fight Méléagant blindly, behind his back. Made to feel *honte* (l. 3704) again by the girl for this, he shifts the combat round so that Méléagant is between him and the window, and the lady in the hilltop tower now reverses his fortune. Lancelot fights so well that he spins Méléagant around two or three times—one might say like a top or a wheel. Inspired by the opposites, Love and Hate, he fights so fiercely that he is declared the winner by all but Méléagant, whose foolish boasting which will lead to his death (ll. 3866–67) continues while Bademagu has him removed by force—and still protesting—from the combat. It is hard to believe that these events could be told in any spirit other than absurd comedy.

Méléagant's prisoners are released: there is joy from them, but Lancelot has no reward. Guinevere *lowers* her head ('s'anbruncha', l. 3941) when he comes to speak to her, and she insults him. Because he hesitated to climb into the shameful cart, her love has turned to hate. He is split in two as she leaves—his heart goes with her and his eyes and body remain behind, but he has to leave to meet Gawain at the underwater bridge. However there are more reversals; the people, angry at the removal of the protection of the sword-bridge, take him prisoner and they shame him more by tying his feet under his horse, and returning him as a criminal. The rumour which reaches Guinevere is that Lancelot has been killed and at this she starves herself, nearly to death. As in *Erec and Enide*, both lovers experience a desperate decline in fortune, suggestive of the *decollatio;* for the rumour reaches Lancelot that Guinevere is dead and he attempts to strangle himself. For some reason, he does not do this from the branch of a tree but from his saddle pommel, hoping that the horse will drag him along the ground. The result is that when he is discovered and cut free in time to save his life, he is found 'a terre cheü' (l. 4295) or, at the lowest point of Fortune's wheel (see Fig. 2). This and the journey back to Bademagu's castle are the deepest valley Lancelot experiences; he returns, still thinking Guinevere is dead, and laments the destructive powers of Love and Death. Then comes the euphoric upward reversal when he hears that not only is she alive, but, crucially, she wishes to see him: 'devant, grant duel et fier et fort,/ encor fu bien cent mile tanz/ la joie de sa vie granz' ('before great grief, fierce and strong,/ now his joy is a hundred thousand times greater', ll. 4404–05). During their successful assignation Lancelot returns to being an impetuous and even boastful youth (l. 4597), but, subsequently, there is no more characterization or plot structure according to seasonal associations. The story, finished by Godefroi de Leigni, has a different form in which the breaking of social codes is reconciled by chivalric ethics. Lancelot returns Guinevere to Arthur, instead of eloping with her.[29]

Before this point it is as though Chrétien threw in as many midsummer associations as he could, using them to keep the jokes flowing, like balls kept in the air by a spout of water. There are oppositions, reversals, inversions, paradoxes, magical allusions, arrogant fools, boasters, mockers, hilltop castles and combat. The protagonists all experience falls from fortune to shame and near death, and Lancelot's forbidden love appears to set a troubled mood which is at odds with the usual triumphant tone of midsummer. Triumph is the one feature which is missing and, when Lancelot defeats Méléagant, all he experiences is another downward reversal in keeping with his downward progression from the beginning of the tale.

As Dante was to say of all Chrétien's romances, they are 'very lovely intricate tales',[30] yet they have had their critics, from the thirteenth-century Jean Bodel, who called all Arthurian tales 'frivolous and amusing',[31] to the twentieth-century Gustave Lanson, who found them lacking reason.[32] Yet it is possible to argue that Chrétien did devise an artistic design for them through the matrix of seasonal expectations. In this, they differ from *chansons de geste*, despite the promising quotation at the start of this chapter. For, in the *Chanson de Roland,* the references to May and summer are made in relation to the anti-Christian forces and their brief period of success. The Christian contenders are presented with an absence of seasonal qualities, which would undermine their serious, and non-material, aims. Bodel was correct when he said that, by comparison, the romances do not have the same weighty purpose—they are, as described, romances concerned with that interesting period on the

---

[29] Uitti and Freeman, pp. 72 and 74–76.

[30] J. Misrahi, 'Symbolism and Allegory in Arthurian Romance', *Romance Philology*, 17 (1963–64), 555–69 (p. 569).

[31] '...n'en sont que trois materes a nul home vivant:/ de France et de Bretaigne et de Ronme la grant/.... Li conte de Bretaigne si sont vain et plaisant/ Et cil de Ronme sage et de sens aprendant,/ Cil de France sont voir chascun jour aparant.' J. Bodel, *La chanson des Saisnes*, ll. 6–11, ed. by A. Brasseur (Geneva: Droz, 1989), vol. 1, p. 2.

[32] Lanson in fact hit on the truth of many plots without finding their explanation. He wrote that Chrétien placed 'les Yvain, les Erec et les Lancelot de péril en péril, les jetant sans raison dans d'impossibles entreprises dont ils sortaient vainqueurs contre la raison'. *Histoire de la littérature française* (Paris: Hachette, 1909), p. 58.

wheel of life when men and women (but mainly men) approach and reach
the *regno* position. Illustrations of the top of the wheel show this to be
either marriage or a man's personal fame. In such illustrations (Figs 2–4)
the two are inevitably mutually exclusive; in the romances they are
further presented as at odds with each other. In *Erec and Enide* the
summer period begins in love and harmony, but ends with a struggle
between the two antagonistic forms of personal fulfilment while, in
Lancelot, the discord comes largely from outside, with the added season-
ing of internal moral unease.

Jean Bodel's observation on romances was an aesthetic one which
nevertheless allowed them a place in the literary canon. Later came moral
condemnation in the Prologue to the prose version of the *Vies des Pères,*
where the advice was given:

> Dame, de ce n'avez vo cure:
> De mençonge qui cuers oscure,
> Corrompant la clarté de l'ame,
> N'en aiez cure, douce dame.
> Leissiez Cligés et Perceval,
> Qui les cuers tue et met a mal,
> Et les romanz de vanité.

> ('Don't concern yourself, dear lady, with lies that darken the heart, con-
> taminating the light of the soul. Put aside Cligés and Perceval, and
> romances on vain subjects, works that slay and corrupt the heart.')[33]

It should be noted, however, that this does not condemn all romances as
works of vanity, and it is not impossible that the moral critic, unlike
Bodel, perceived the underlying thoughtfulness in works such as *Erec
and Enide* and *Yvain.*

---

[33] *Vies des Pères,* ll. 30–35, trans. by D. Kelly, 'Chrétien de Troyes: the Narrator and his
Art', in *The Romances of Chrétien de Troyes: a Symposium,* ed. by D. Kelly, pp. 13–47
(p. 24).

CHAPTER 4

Midsummer Romances after Chrétien

[L]i jors de la Saint Jehan vint; li chevalier furent venu de totes parz, qi molt se merveilloient por coi li rois n'avoit cele grant cort tenue a la Pentecoste...

Perlesvaus

O nce Chrétien gave his unique shape to the Arthurian legends, it is inevitable that romance writers after him 'had to come to terms with the great poet's legacy'[1] and, to some extent, they are derivative. Yet many later works have qualities of their own which have led to a reassessment of their individual merits; and a study of the St John's day traditions in them further reveals how authors rearranged 'the limited number of elements' that romances are composed of.[2] Festive fantasies, such as Guillaume le Clerc's *Fergus* and the anonymous *Li Chevaliers as deus espees,* stand at one end of the spectrum, with the serious religious allegory of the *Perlesvaus* at the other, while tales such as the Didot *Perceval* lie somewhere in between.

Fergus

The author of this burlesque text is known to have been the Picard, Guillaume le Clerc, who, it is thought, went over to England with the

---

[1] R. Blumenfeld-Kosinski, 'Arthurian Heroes and Convention: *Meraugis de Portlesguez* and *Durmart le Galois*', in *The Legacy of Chrétien de Troyes*, ed. by N. J. Lacey et al., vol. 2 (Amsterdam: Rodopi, 1988), pp. 79–92 (p. 79).

[2] Ibid.

Balliol family which also came from Picardy, and le Clerc's tale is now dated at between 1230 and 1250.[3] There are two extant manuscripts: one known as the A text, MS, Chantilly 472, in the collection of the Duc d'Aumale, at the Musée Condé. The other manuscript, known as P, is in the Bibliothèque Nationale, Paris.[4]

Prior knowledge of Chrétien is often assumed by later romance writers, and this is particularly true of le Clerc, who does not even introduce Arthur or Yvain by name, merely calling them 'li rois' (l. 2) and 'li Chevaliers au Lion' (l. 1420). His description of Kay is limited to the seneschal's red, possibly fiery, hair ('Et Kex qui ot les cevels sors', l. 16), with Kay's character only mentioned as 'maint autre que je ne sai' (l. 17), although it matters to know, since Kay's behaviour is to be the spring-board for the action. But, as Beate Schmolke-Hasselmann says, '*Fergus* is a work for connoisseurs'.[5]

Similar shorthand is used in le Clerc's introduction of season, which comes in the first line: 'Ce fu a feste Saint Jahan/ Que li rois a Karadingan/ Ot cort tenue comme rois' ('It was at the feast of St John that the king held court like a king, at Karadingan', ll. 1–3). Frescoln notes that the festival of St John the Evangelist is unlikely, since four later references to St John's Day are tied to 24 June.[6] But, since the nativity of St John also features in the *Yvain*, le Clerc's opening reads as another appeal to the cognoscenti, relying on the fact that the bare mention of the saint's nativity was enough to indicate the season and the kind of story which would follow. *Fergus,* like the *Yvain*, contains an abundance of midsummer elements: irrationality, insults, mockery, sudden death and other reversals, free speech, and the theme of opposites in character and behaviour. The main difference from tales by Chrétien is that le Clerc

---

[3]   B. Schmolke-Hasselmann, *The Evolution of Arthurian Romance: The Verse Tradition from Chrétien to Froissart*, trans. by Margaret and Roger Middleton (Cambridge: Cambridge University Press, 1998), pp. 15–19 and 251–60.

[4]   *Guillaume le Clerc: the Romance of Fergus*, ed. by W. Frescoln, pp. 2–6. A modern English translation has also been made by D. D. R. Owen, published in 1991 by Dent, and a modern French translation, by Romaine Wolf-Bonvin, was published in 1990 under the title of *La Chevalerie des sots*. Frescoln's edition of the A text is the basis for the present study, with my translations taken from D. D. R. Owen.

[5]   B. Schmolke-Hasselmann, p. 159.

[6]   Frescoln, p. 249. There are six references in all, some explicit—'Saint Jahan en esté' (l. 6944), 'Saint Jahan Baptiste' (l. 6965)—, others, in ll. 6388 and 6885, relate to l. 6965, and the other is in l. 3473.

ends with an endorsement of the festive ethos: the failings are part of a seasonal fantasy which is enjoyable as a parodic exaggeration of Chrétien's work,[7] and as a parody of the expectations raised by the mention of St John's day.

The promising youth, Fergus, discovered in the Scottish countryside, is given the hazardous quest of defeating the Black Knight, by Kay. The romance follows the progress of this and of Fergus's encounter with his wife-to-be, Galiene. All Fergus thinks of her at the opening is that she is 'a young woman "Qui bien peüst estre roïne"' ('who could well be queen', l. 1698), a possible borrowing from comments about Enide. And at the end of the tale, Galiene appears as a model of convention which may well discourage current interest in her.[8] Yet, when she first enters the romance, it is her lack of convention—a parodic inversion of the reader's expectations of a courtly maiden—which provides most of the comedy. Surprisingly, for a tale of heroic male adventures, it is she who is the more original character. Chrétien's heroines are largely passive,[9] but Galiene is the active one and the fiery temper and rashness of youth's midsummer erupt in her rather than in Fergus. It is she who goes to his bed when Fergus arrives at Lidel Castle, and when he laughs at love, the rejection provokes a histrionic display of wounded pride. She swoons, then 'leaps up like a mad woman, goes back to her room and falls onto her bed wanting to die' ('Saut sus com[me] feme dervee;/ En sa canbre s'en est entree,/ Si se laist chaoir en son lit... Or se het, or covoite mort;' ll. 1993–97).

Her proactive nature and extreme reactions have something in common with women in *fabliaux* where, it has been noted:

> ...sexual difference in itself is not a central concern.... The principal preoccupation of the genre is, rather, an impulse to overturn perceived hierarchical structures of all kinds.... Hierarchies, in the *fabliaux*, are shown to be constructs, to derive from convention, not nature. In showing gender to be a construct, a category which clever men and women can manipulate, the *fabliaux* unwittingly anticipate modern theories of gender

---

[7] Owen, p. 85.

[8] Galiene is not included in R. L. Krueger, *Women Readers and the Ideology of Gender* (Cambridge: Cambridge University Press, 1993), nor in S. Gaunt, *Gender and Genre in Medieval French Literature* (Cambridge: Cambridge University Press, 1995).

[9] There are active and seductive women in *Lancelot* and *Yvain*, but these are not the heroines.

and create a space in which female characters are empowered.[10]

Festive seasons, of course, were times for an inversion of roles in practice which might also include the empowerment of women, as on 24 June 1587 in Laon, where the mistresses of priests were invited to speak their minds to the departing *prévot*, or, as in Holland, where a village tradition survived at least until 1570 in which, on St John's Eve, 'women were free to choose partners and men were bound to comply.'[11] This custom helps account for the curious fact that in *Fergus* it is Galiene who takes the sexual initiative. And, since it appears that le Clerc wrote *Fergus* after 1220, then his literary model for an independently-minded woman may well have been Jean Renaut's equally determined female protagonist, Fresne. (See Chapter 6.)

When Fergus leaves Lidel Castle, Galiene leaves too and disappears into Lothian, where we next hear of her as owner of the Castle of Rocebourc under siege from another king, whose braggart nephew, Arthofilaus, is sent to negotiate surrender. The castle is a metaphor for herself who must surrender to a rival in love. Impulsiveness is still part of her character, for she promises Arthofilaus that if she fails to find a defender in eight days, to fight both him and his uncle, she will give in and marry this king. Then she bewails her 'rash boast [uttered] in an amazing fit of temper',[12] sends her maid, Arondele, to Arthur's court for help, while she weeps day and night in the castle. All her joy and beauty are laid waste and she cannot recover them, 'no matter how much she might prosper during one of the longest days of summer' ('Tant eüst grant prosperité,/ En un des plus lons jors d'esté', ll. 5623–24).

The story then follows a complex sequence of accidents and near-disasters, with midsummer ingredients following fast and furiously. Arondele does not find a champion at Arthur's court as all are away searching for Fergus but, on her return, she meets Fergus unknown to her. He assures her that a knight with a radiant shield will rescue Galiene, but Galiene's next fainting fit prevents Arondele from giving her the message and, when Galiene comes round, what she does hear is her nobles saying it would not be so bad if the other king married her. Her midsummer rage

---

[10]   Gaunt, pp. 235–36.

[11]   Simon Schama, *Rembrandt's Eyes* (London: Allen Lane, 1999), p. 62. The Dutch custom of sexual obligation is also that exacted of Chrétien's Lancelot: ll. 943–45, 1035–45, 1074.

[12]   Owen, p. 85.

bursts out again: 'Taisiés vous, pugnais gengleors' ('shut up, you stinking slanderers', ll. 5640) with the addition of a malevolent and paradoxical wish: 'Mal aventure et mal tormen/ Vos puisse Jesus Cris donner! ('may Jesus Christ bring you ill fortune and sorrow!' ll. 5642–43). Conflicting emotions run through her, and 'tote la nuit jusqu'al matin/ la pucele se dementa,' ('all night she drove herself mad', ll. 5704–05). Although she attends mass next morning, Galiene has resolved on the unforgivable sin of suicide, intending to jump to her death from the top of a tower: 'defeated, sorrowing, and angry' ('mate et dolante et courecie,' l. 5714) she hears the attacking king's mocking call, 'Dame, dormés vo matinee?/ Avés vo bataille oublïee?' ('Lady are you asleep? Have you forgotten this morning's battle?' ll. 5727–28). Galiene is in the highest tower; she, paradoxically, commends herself to God and puts her head through the window to let herself fall *aval* (l. 5771). But God would not let this happen and, instead, she sees a knight's blazing shield as Fergus rides towards the castle. The rays of the rising sun catch on his armour and, with splendid, positive midsummer irony, this sign renews her hope and so prevents her fall. Insulting challenges from the combatants follow, after which Fergus easily overcomes the impossible odds. Arthofilaus is killed, and the king experiences that decisive fall off his horse onto the ground. As death approaches in the person of Fergus, the king sees no choice but to humble himself and give in. At this point Fergus does not reveal himself to Galiene; he sends the enemy king to admit defeat to her, and Fergus disappears once more.

Arthur announces a post-Pentecost tournament to entice Fergus back, which Galiene also attends. Fergus's quest is to earn knightly fame while hers is to win him in marriage and, at the tournament, she surprises us with behaviour opposite to her previous headstrong actions and un-governed speech. Convinced that Fergus was the knight with the radiant shield, she goes humbly to Arthur and spins the tale of herself as a poor, fatherless woman in need of a husband, whom she begs to be none other than the *bel escu* (l. 6700). Galiene had approached Fergus arrogantly; she now goes to the opposite extreme and le Clerc draws this to the reader's attention in a line which grates today: 'La pucele molt s'umelie' ('the maiden humiliates herself, greatly', l. 6737). However, the point of this is that it is in stark contrast to her previous behaviour, and it is done for a purpose. The fact that she is on a quest for a husband remains a reversal of the lady's role, while her active, and fluctuating, behaviour throughout, are explained by the midsummer rationale.

Half-way through *Fergus* comes the reminder of this seasonal context
in an unexplained conversation about dubbing knights 'L'autre ier après
le saint Jahan' ('after St John's Day the other year', l. 3473). The
comment reminds the reader of the festive setting for the story, which
then continues with insults. The scene is a council chamber in Arthur's
court, where war is discussed against the Black Knight, whom Arthur
believes has killed Fergus. When Arthur asks his knights for their opinion
on strategy, all remain silent except for Kay, who cannot resist a jibe at
Fergus, and Gawain responds by calling Kay a slanderer ('Vous parlés
trop pour gent deduire./ Vous par estes tant fort jaingleres', ll. 3435–36).
However, Arthur defends Kay and rebukes Gawain: 'Mesire Ques est
costumiers/ De tels coses dire et conter,/ C'autres ne saroit porpenser' ('it
is customary for my Lord Kay to say and recount certain things that
others are not able to consider', ll. 3489–91).

The recall of season mid-way through the story is also the point of
lowest fortune for Fergus and Galiene and, immediately after the council
scene, the reader returns to him searching for her, 'En tel dolor et en tel
cure' ('in great pain, care, and misadventure', ll. 3655–56), reminiscent
of Yvain at his lowest point.[13] Eventually, Fergus finds the waters of
healing, where his good fortune is foretold by a dwarf and, soon after,
comes the parallel hope of improvement for Galiene, when the light of the
rising sun saves her from death. The story then ends at 'Saint Jahan en
esté' (l. 6944), when both their fortunes receive a dramatic upward
reversal. On this final St John's day the couple also hear mass before both
are crowned; therefore their worldly good fortune is not shown to be at
odds with godliness. Le Clerc was almost unique in giving St John's Day
traditions such a final endorsement and, in so doing, the extremes become
aberrations which can be enjoyed rather than criticized.

The announcement for the fifteen-day tournament[14] included the
promise that the winner would receive a crown and a kingdom (ll. 6304–
05): an offer repeated to Fergus when the identity of the successful
stranger is known. But the scope of this kingship is limited. One finds
oneself asking, is he really to be king of Lothian, or something less?
Arthur informs Fergus that, if he wishes, he can marry Galiene, which
would bring him the rule of Lothian, and growth to his lands of the

---

[13] Schmolke-Hasselmann, p. 163.

[14] This is in fact over in a week at most. The jousts last from the Tuesday before St John's
Day to 24 June.

country of Tweeddale ('Se vos volés donrai le vos;/ S'arés de Lodien le regne,/ Et je croistrai vostre demainne/ De la contree de Tudiele', ll. 6878–81). Just as the 'young girl who might be queen' calls to mind game, so too does the title, King of Tweeddale; and the whole story could have been a celebration of local midsummer traditions. Fergus is well-born, yet a peasant, therefore an ordinary youth in his prime of life who sets out for fame, conquest in battle, and finally gains kingship through marriage. The fact that he becomes 'rich and a crowned king', 'A ceste feste Saint Jehein' (ll. 6883–86) means that the reader too would be likely to see this as part of a game pretence.

Therefore, on one level, the story reads as bucolic fantasy, yet it also has the most realistic geography of any of the romances. Protagonists do not explore otherworld lands but travel between Roxburgh, Edinburgh, and Carlisle, and this has given rise to a debate on its provenance. Could the romance have been commissioned by Alan of Galloway, whose family names appear in it, to honour his marriage or to support his claim to the Scottish throne (since Scotland was symbolized by the region of Lothian)? Or could it have been commissioned by le Clerc's patron, John Balliol, in support of his own claim, since he was Alan's rival for power in Scotland? Joan Greenberg and Beate Schmolke-Hasselmann have successfully disproved the first argument,[15] and yet the alternative, that John Balliol commissioned the work to enhance his own reputation also appears flawed in view of the reductive nature of the story. For example, the dwarf promises Fergus that Fortune wishes to lift him up as high as she can raise him, and it has been noted that this 'invokes in an extremely graphic form the hero's rise to the monarchy: *regnabo*'.[16] However, even without the midsummer context, Fortune's promises are at best dubious and with it, as here, a fall is implicit in any rise on her wheel, while the actual rise accomplished at the end of the romance has in it the possibility that Fergus is, in fact, only King of Tweeddale. The analogy with bucolic game mocks the validity of any serious claim. And yet there are other complexities, since elsewhere in *Fergus* we have seen the ironic perspective reversed into a positive one, when the rays of the dawn sun bring hope. The ambivalences of the midsummer season are burlesqued in such a way that it is difficult to ascertain just where any certainty might lie, and this brings to mind a third possibility: that it was commissioned by

---

[15] J. Greenberg, 'Guillaume le Clerc and Alan of Galloway', *PMLA*, 66 (1951), 524–33.

[16] Schmolke-Hasselmann, p. 265.

John Balliol to ridicule Alan of Galloway's claims to ascend the Scottish throne. If so, it would also accord with the tradition at this season of issuing a challenge to the would-be powerful through mockery. It would in fact appear that *Fergus* is the second extant example of contemporary political conflict aired in a midsummer context (the first being Renaut's *Galeran:* see Chapter 6.)

Li Chevaliers as deus espees

Until recently this work, also from the north of France, was only given passing acknowledgement. One manuscript copy survives (BnF fr. 12603), which Beate Schmolke-Hasselmann considers to have been written at about the same time as *Fergus,* but nothing is known of the author, and the sole printed edition is that made by Wendelin Foerster in 1877.[17] However, Schmolke-Hasselmann's recent study reveals innovatory features. For example, the author introduces the apparent death of Gawain, which leads to Gawain's poignant quest to recover, not just his fame but also his identity. This happens when a knight—later named as Brien—seeks combat with him at a time when Gawain is unarmed. Brien's quest is to kill him in order to win the hand of a girl who has rejected all lovers because of her devotion to Gawain. Only when Brien brings proof of Gawain's death will she agree to marry him instead. Gawain is seriously wounded and falls unconscious from his horse. But Brien does not kill him in case such uncourtly behaviour brings retribution, and Gawain's quest becomes that of repairing his personal obliteration: 'he becomes *cil sans nom'* (the nameless one), and even refers to himself in that way.'[18] As in the case of Chrétien's Lancelot, anonymity is the furthest one can be from fame and, while Lancelot is oblivious, Gawain is deeply concerned about recovering his status. He catches up with Brien in the town of Rades, on the feast-day of the nativity of St John the Baptist when Brien, like Fergus, is to be given the hand of the lady, which will bring with it the declaration of his kingship.

On the one hand there is, as Schmolke-Hasselmann shows, the identity crisis and Gawain's serious quest to repair it. On the other, and as she

---

[17] Ibid., p. 17. Foerster's edition of *Li Chevaliers as deus espees*, published by Niemeyer in Halle in 1877, was reprinted in Amsterdam in 1966.

[18] Schmolke-Hasselmann, p. 123. The text I have used in the 1877 edition.

suggests for *L'Atre périlleux*, there is also a comic element; for the image of courtliness in Arthur's court at the opening, and again at Rades, is undercut by the suggestion of king game. In the case of the confrontation between Gawain and Brien the game element is overt and the sequence of events is heralded by the line: 's'estoit ele des nuis d'este' (it was one of those nights of summer', l. 3862). The following morning Gawain sees Meriadeuc, Brien's messenger, approaching in great haste. Asked why, he replies:

> 'Si m'i enuoie uns siens parens
> Ki n'est pas ore en maus loiens
> Cest des Illes li rois Briens
> Ki de grant ioie est ore plains.'
> 'Comment?' dist mes sire Gauuains,
> 'Li rois Briens? onques mais dire
> Ne l'oi'—'Vous dites uoir, sire.
> Ie mespris, encor ne l'est mie.
> Mais em conuent li a s'amie,
> K'il l'ert, por ce ke il ocist
> Mon seigneur Gauuain, ce li dist,
> Et ele l'en croit mout tres bien.' (ll. 3888–99)

('He is on an errand for king Brien of the Islands, who is now full of joy, and is no longer in a state of ill luck.' 'What', says Gawain, 'King Brien? I've never heard him called that.' 'You say truly, lord, for it isn't done yet, but he's told his girlfriend that he will be, because he's killed Lord Gawain, as he says, and she believes it completely.')

This exchange comes across as local gossip, or dialogue from an improvised play, rather than serious politics. It stimulates Gawain's anger and prompts him to accompany Meriadeuc. As in *Yvain*, the journey to the midsummer adventure is long, though described more realistically. The first night they stay in a hotel where the talk is of the coronation and Gawain's alleged death. When asked, Gawain tells the host who he is, and receives the advice that he must attend: For 'Tu es mors sans aler auant' (l. 4122); his fame, which is more than his life, will be extinguished. Gawain sets off again, along 'Le chemin de uie u de mort' (l. 4590) and encounters another life or death incident appropriate to midsummer on his way, when he kills Guernemans on his 'mout grant chaual espaignois' (l. 4633) after each man had hurled crude 'fool' insults at the other ('Ne uous peussies entremettre,/ Ce cuicie, de greignor folie', ll. 4644–45, and 'Vous aues grant folie dite', l. 4658). St John's eve finds

Gawain still far from his goal, but his guide discovers a hotel and promises him that, tomorrow, Gawain will be there on the feast of St John, when Brien will really be king ('Car Briens ert rois uoirement/ Demain, s'ert feste saint Iehan', ll. 5260–61).

Rades is first described as the capital city of the kingdom with the 'queen, [archbishop and four bishops] holding court there, where my lord king would be acclaimed' ('La roine en tient les cites,/ S'en ert mes sire rois clames', ll. 5325–26). However, when Gawain arrives he is like a visitor for Rades's fête day who sees the celebration of a beauty queen and of the fighting champion of the region. A procession starts, with the queen in a dress of black samite, and a cape of gold set with rubies: 'Il n'ot ou monde sa pareille,/... Ne n'auoit pas xviij ans' ('there was not her equal in the world, [and] she was not yet eighteen', l. 5428). 'Et apres uoit Brien ki uient,/ Ki mout estoit nobles et fiers/ Et ot bien .ij.c. cheualiers/ Auoec lui contrement la rue;/ Et ot une reube uestue/ De samit bloi a oiseles/ D'or' ('Then Gawain saw Brien very noble and proud, with at least two hundred knights. He was dressed in blue samite decorated with golden birds.' ll. 5432–38): 'il fu biaus et avenans' ('he was a handsome, prepossessing young man', l. 5440). Gawain's reaction to this scene, with queen, archbishop, and bishops seated before Brien on ivory chairs, is that he had never before seen such a beautiful display of lordship, and so cleverly done ('Et lors se dist/ Mes sire Gauuains, k'en sa uie/ Ne uit mais, ki la seignorie/ Par raison de biaute eust,/ N'onques mais en liu u il fust,/ N'esgarda si tres biel adroit', ll. 5452–57). The visitor compliments a well staged performance of lordship which he finds misplaced in the honouring of Brien (ll. 5458–59). The author builds an initial picture of regal splendour, only to puncture it by revealing it as a form of play-acting. Yet the description of queen, archbishop, and bishops provides the most humiliating context for Brien's exposure on St John's Day, when his vainglory is overturned.

The seventeen-year-old beauty queen turns out to be the girlfriend mentioned earlier by the servant. She had agreed to take Brien 'a seignor' (l. 5497) for the most unlikely of reasons: 'Por ce k'il disoit ke mellor/ Cheualier u monde n'auoit' ('because he said that the world did not hold a better knight', ll. 5498–99). Her acceptance was made although 'ele sauoit/ Mout plus tres bel et mains uilain/ Et meillor, mon seigneur Gauuain' ('she knew my lord Gawain to be better and less base (or rustic)', ll. 5500–02). She is proudly aware of the aesthetic nobility her beauty gives her, claiming to be 'one of the most beautiful of women

[who] does not want to bestow her love on any but the most handsome and most nobly born of knights' (Schmolke-Hasselman, p. 125). Since this man, Gawain, is dead the queen would take Brien as lord and the match 'would make him king' ('ele le prendroit/ A seignor et roi le feroit', l. 5511). As in *Fergus*, the young man with most prowess on St John's day is to be rewarded with the most eligible girl of the region.

Before the coronation comes Brien's ludicrous claim: 'Gauuains est ocis uoirement./ Ie sui cil ki l'ocist sans faille,/ Si n'a cheualier ki me uaille/ En tout le mont, sage ne sot' ('Gawain is well and truly dead, and I am definitely the one who killed him. There is no knight, wise or idiot, who is as good as me in all the world [or mountain—see Appendix C] ll. 5522–25). After rather more of this, Gawain is provoked into intervening. He wins the combat, the queen is disillusioned, and Brien ridiculed: 'li rois poissans,/ Briens est fols et mesdisans,/... Cist haut homme, k'il uous espoust... . Mout a faite grant mespresure/ Et si a de ce mout grant tort,/ Quant il uous dit, ke il a mort/ Mon seigneur Gauuain et ocis' ('the powerful king Brien is foolish and a slanderer. This high man you have espoused does great wrong when he tells you that he has killed my Lord Gawain', ll. 5681–91). 'Ie di k'encore est uis et sains/ Li nies le roi Artu, Gauuains,/ Si sui pres de ce moustrer ci' ('I can say further that Gawain, the nephew of the king, is alive and well, since he himself shows himself here', ll. 5695–97). Brien protests as ludicrously as did Méléagant: 'Dame, c'est uoirs sans faille/ Que i'outrai d'armes en bataille/ Et ocis mon seigneur Gauuain' ('Lady, it is true without a doubt that I took arms against my lord Gawain and killed him', ll. 5707–09), before he backs down: 'Dame, ne deues pas quidier,/ Dist il, ke ie soie mentans' ('I cannot deny that I am a liar', ll. 5723–24). 'Honteus fu Briens et dolens/ Por la roine et por ses gens/ Et 's'esmerueille k'estre puet,/ Et dont a cel cheualier muet,/ Ki... afferme ucraicmcnt/ Que messire Gauuaiis est uis' ('Brien is shamed and cast down because the queen and her people could see that Lord Gawain is here', ll. 5753–59). He disarms, asks for mercy and is tormented with shame, 'Car tous iors li ramenberoit/ De l'onnor ke si ot perdue' ('for always he would remember the honour he had lost', ll. 5840–41). His punishment is to go, voluntarily, to Arthur's court, to be put in prison ('S'en ira por metre en prison/ A la cort le boin roi Artu', 5848–49), as though carrying out the penalty in a game of forfeits. As with the combat on St John's day between Yvain and Kay, Gawain recovers his fame completely from the man who had destroyed it and their positions, in terms of status, are reversed.

The issues in their encounter could have been serious, but the persistent elements of 'play' undercut it. Something similar occurs in Arthur's court which is established as the epitome of feudal rule, a place of 'superlatives and extremes',[19] and where Kay functions solely as steward, not as disturber of the peace. This perfect court is opposed by the absurd King Ris (King Laughter) whose objective against Arthur is expressed in terms of taking the king's beard. Therefore, Arthur's model kingliness is also threatened by a travesty and the manner of insult suggests that this power struggle, too, should be judged as game rather than as politics. The St John's day combat, half-way through, focuses on these elements of play, for the incident between Brien and Gawain only becomes intelligible in terms of midsummer game, and it provides a moment to reflect on the familiar pattern of self-aggrandizement and its fall. The author accentuates the absurdities and conscious role-playing by actors (in Brien's case by an inadequate actor) instead of disguising the play-acting origins of his material in a more complex narrative.

Li chevaliers is not great literature, but one can see the reason for contemporary interest in it, since popular culture is combined with the Arthurian legend, and this suggests that there was not necessarily a division between élite and popular cultures at this period. The readership for this romance, along with that for le Clerc's, would have had to agree with Bodel in finding such tales amusing, even if frivolous. In both romances there is the motif of a lowborn man becoming king through marriage, as all young men on the wheel of life might do in their midsummer season. This festive subject is affirmed in both stories, rather than challenged by a moral subtext. *Fergus* is written rather more skilfully. Its nonsense not only makes sense as a political jibe, or a witty skit on Chrétien's romances but, like *Lancelot*, it also makes sense as a parodic pot-pourri of every St John's day feature the author can cram in.

The Didot Perceval

This romance exists today in two versions, the E, or Modena manuscript, and the D manuscript, held in Paris. William Roach has thought that the tale in each was drawn from the work of the Burgundian, Robert de Boron, who wrote soon after Chrétien, thereby giving the Didot *Perceval*

---

[19]   Schmolke-Hasselmann, p. 59.

a relatively early date between 1190 and 1212.[20] Other scholars have placed it later in the thirteenth century and its value has been judged accordingly. 'To some critics it has been an important, early link in the chain of French Grail tradition, while to others it has seemed a late and feeble effort made by an untalented author to piece together a group of irreconcilable episodes borrowed from earlier sources'.[21] The tale contains three episodes: Merlin's establishment of Arthur as rightful king, Perceval's quest, and the final *Mort Artu.* Both manuscripts contain all three but there are striking variations between them and William Roach considers the D version to be the more important for critical purposes.[22] Yet, the shape of the compiled text as we have it in both the D and the E versions neatly divides into two contrasting adventures, not unlike the structure of some other romances. And, for this present study, it is only the E version, the Modena, which is relevant since only here is the day of St John's Nativity referred to. This text is strong in midsummer traditions, even suggesting an attack on the materialism of the Church as well as creating a telling irony in the fate of Arthur. And, through the rationale of the day of St John's Nativity, the combination of tales in it no longer appears arbitrary.

The longest part of the story is Perceval's quest to perfect himself, in which he eventually succeeds and becomes 'lord of the Grail' (l. 1911). The achievement comes immediately after Pentecost, when Perceval retires to a monastery, and Arthur's court prepares to disband, now that the miraculous adventures associated with Perceval are over. Arthur is downcast, so Kay suggests a venture to conquer Normandy and France, in order to hold the court together. A précis of the story which follows itself conveys the midsummer pattern, for Kay's post-Pentecost idea succeeds in every way. Arthur summons all the barons to his aid giving them rich

---

[20] *The Romance of Perceval in Prose: A Translation of the E Manuscript of the Didot Perceval*, ed. and trans. by D. Skeels (Seattle: University of Washington Press, 1961).

[21] *The Didot Perceval: According to the Manuscripts of Modena and Paris*, ed. by W. Roach (Philadelphia: University of Pennsylvania Press, 1941), pp. viii–ix. Because of the complex derivation exact provenance is not established.

[22] Ibid., pp. 8–9. Roach's edition, containing both manuscripts in their original, remains the most accessible and reliable transcript of them. The D text had previously been edited by Eugène Hucher as 'Perceval, ou la Quête du Saint Graal', *Le Saint-Graal ou le Joseph d'Arimathie*, vol. 1 (Le Mans and Paris: 1875–78) and the E text transcribed, with inaccuracies, by Jessie Weston as *The Legend of Sir Perceval*, vol. 2 (London: Nutt, 1906–09). I have used Skeels's authoritative 1961 translation.

gifts and they respond with the encouragement that they will make him 'lord of all the world' ('sire de tot le mont', ll. 1958–9) if only he has the courage and energy to proceed.[23] Arthur achieves his immediate goal without effort: after Normandy, Paris falls into his lap. There, he is crowned king of France, and his authority is accepted by the French lords. He returns to Britain with his Alexandrian mission to conquer the world half-achieved, and is received rapturously by both the common people and the nobility. The latter are then invited to join him at his court in Cardiff at the 'St John in summer', where Arthur will be magnificently generous: 'for there I would like to share out among you all my gains, all shared communally. I am not so poor that I can't make you all rich... .. When he left all talked about the good fortune Arthur had experienced which had raised him so much with his conquering of France' ('Car jou i volrai departir de mes avoirs partie tot communalement, ne ja n'i ara si povre que je ne face rice.... A tant.... parloient... que bele aventure li estoit avenue, qui estoit si amontés que il avoit France conquise', ll. 1262–66).

The emphasis, here, is on Arthur enjoying St John's day success at the top of a remarkable pinnacle of power and this continues in the wealth and honour displayed at the St John's Day festivities. All the high men of Britain come to Arthur's court, so many they could not all be counted. The Mass Arthur attends is chanted by the Archbishop, which enhances the king's reputation; then he, and the four greatest kings of Europe seat themselves on the highest dais. Inevitably, before they can eat there comes the challenge from outside: twelve white-haired men enter, finely dressed and, misleadingly, carrying olive branches. Any impression of modesty is quickly dispelled when they cross to Arthur's dais and one 'parla molt orguelleusement' (l. 2189) on behalf of the Emperor of Rome, to whom the lords of France had previously been in *fief*. The messengers' *orgueil* even includes the assumption that God is in Rome's pocket:

> Cil Dex qui sor tot le mont a poësté et en puet faire a son commandement, il garisse l'empereor de Rome en cief, et en après l'apostole et les senators de Rome qui le loi doivent garder et maintienant. Et cil Dex que vous m'oés ramentevoir, il confonde Artu et tos cels qui sont en son commande-ment, car il a mespris vers Diu et vers sainte yglyse... car il a recolpé et retaillié çou que sien devoit estre... le roi... qui se terre tenoit de Rome et en rendroit treü a Rome cascun an.
>
> (May God, who has power over all the world and can do all things by His

---

[23]   Lines 1952–59. Roach, ed., p. 245. Trans., Skeels, p. 71.

commandment protect above all the Emperor of Rome and after him the Pope and the senators of Rome who must guard and defend the law. And may God, upon whom you hear me call, bring ruin to Arthur and all those who are under his rule, for he has done wrong to God and to Holy Church... for he has lopped off and cut down that which ought to belong to it... the king... who held his lands of Rome and who gave tribute for them each year to Rome (ll. 2189–98, Skeels trans. pp. 78–79).)

The pomposity of his language increases in the final, splenetic insults:

Or saces que nos en mervellant nos desdagnons, et en desdagnant nos en mervellons, que si viels gens comme vos estes que tos li siecles vos doit despire, et estes serf de vos testes et tos jors l'avés esté, et li vostre ancestres autresi. Et or vos volés enfrancir et vivre sans servage ausi com autre gent.

(Now know that while we wonder at you we have contempt, and while we have contempt, we wonder at you, for you are such vile men that all the world must despise you, who have been slaves all the days of your life, and your ancestors before you. And now you wish to be free, and to live outside servitude as other men do (ll. 2198–202).)

He concludes with threats of a whipping for the king and the boiling alive of his followers. On the messengers' departure, Arthur and his supporting kings discuss this 'great shame', and take the legendary decision to confront the Emperor, Julius Caesar, on his own territory, leaving Britain in Mordred's care. Again, Arthur's overseas venture has phenomenal success, this time against the combined might of the rest of the known world. Arthur personally kills Caesar, after which the tripartite enemy falls into confusion. Arthur is now crowned, a second time, in Rome, and for a moment he can truly claim to be the greatest king in all the world.

At this point, of course, he learns that Mordred has usurped his own throne in Britain and has married Guinevere. The message received could not be more devastating:

Rois... saces que tes niés Mordrés a ouvré encontre toi comme traïtres, car il a te feme espousee, et porta corone dedens le premier mois que tu departis de ton païs, et a tous les cuers des gens. Et saces que tu n'as castel qui plains ne soit d'arbalestriers et de cevaliers et de serjans, et n'i a cevalier en le terre qui contre se volenté fust que il ne fesist ocire. Et saces que il a mandés les Saisnes qui furent del parenté Engis qui tant guerroia vostre pere, ne en toute le terre de Bretagne ne lait il canter ne messe ne matine; et bien te disons se tu ne le secors tu le perdras, et miels vos vient il vostre terre conquerre que l'autrui.

(King... know that your nephew has worked against you as a traitor, for he espoused your wife and bore away your crown in the first month after you departed from your country, and he has the hearts of all the people. And, in truth, you have not a castle that is not full of crossbowmen and knights and soldiers.' [All supporters of Arthur are slain and Mordred] has summoned up the Saxons born of Engis, who warred so greatly against your father... and we say to you that if you do not aid the land you will lose it. Better it becomes you to conquer your own land than another (ll. 2549–59, Skeels trans., p. 90).)

Arthur's rise to phenomenal height was effortless and just as swift and decisive is his fall; he is robbed not only of power but also of family and home. Up to this point, it had been the Emperor of Rome who had appeared at fault, but the perspective suddenly changes and Arthur's success is itself questioned as grandiose vainglory emanating from midsummer ambition. The charge is particularly true for the first foray into France since it had no purpose other than to keep the court united. Now, at the end of the second venture the curse by the messengers from Rome is realized. Arthur and his forces are obliged to return from Rome to challenge Mordred; Gawain, Kay, and King Lot of Orkney are killed as they land. Arthur eventually wins the first battle, then pursues Mordred to Ireland and succeeds in killing the mock king. But Arthur is also mortally wounded.he is taken to Avalon where he disappears into myth.

The message one might take from the story as a whole is that the example of Perceval is set against that of Arthur. The man on the road to Christian sanctity achieves his apotheosis—renown with humility—at the feast of Pentecost, whereas Arthur's worldly midsummer success leads to ultimate loss. His material splendours are hollow, badly motivated, and ephemeral. However, beyond this theological message, one has to take into account the role of Merlin, who prophesied Perceval's success and guided him to his goal, while it was his prophecies for Arthur, too, which inspired both of the king's worldly ventures. It is as though these diametrically opposite journeys are fated, and Perceval and Arthur simply fulfill their destinies. The tale, as we have it in the Modena manuscript, provides a simple demonstration of possibilities rather than a moral comparison. The only clear criticism is against the Pope in the challenge from Rome, which ostensibly comes from Julius Caesar. Yet, the words chosen reveal that the grievance is in fact felt by the Church: 'Arthur has done ill to God and the Holy Church and the law of Rome, for he has... taken the taxes which belong to it'. This seems too close to thirteenth-century disputes between Church and secular powers to be totally accidental and rather stronger comment on the same issue was to come in the *Roman de la Rose,* and *Renart le Nouvel.* The charges of power-seeking and materialism were still a large part of the issues which Luther was to raise in 1520.

Perlesvaus

The *Perlesvaus* differs from the others in that the subject of the whole Romance is a religious quest rather than one wholly, or partially, for personal self-glorification. William Nitze has concluded that it was written not very long after Chrétien's *Perceval,* 'after 1191 and before 1212, presumably soon after 1200'.[24] It appears therefore to have been roughly contemporaneous with the Didot *Perceval.* The original text was Flemish and Nitze has further established that it was written for 'Jean de Nesle II, lord of Nesle and castellan of Bruges'.[25] Several copies of the *Perlesvaus* were made and extant manuscripts can now by found in Brussels, Paris, Chantilly, Bern, and Oxford, while there is a Welsh Gaelic translation in Aberystwyth.[26]

In the *Perlesvaus* the central quest for the Holy Grail appears to be developed into a metaphor for the need to re-Christianize the world and, bearing in mind its probable early dating, the allegory could have been written in support of the last Crusades. As Bryant says, this is one Arthurian romance which cannot be dismissed as trivial[27] and, in 1946, J. N. Carman made a bold claim for it. He found the *Perlesvaus* 'a sort of symbolical New Testament, canonical and apocryphal, employing a system of knightly substitutions for Biblical characters'.[28] According to his

---

[24] *Le Haut Livre du Graal: Perlesvaus,* ed. by W. A. Nitze and T. A. Jenkins, vol. 2 (New York: Phaeton, 2nd edn, 1972), p. 89. For further discussion of the dating see *The High Book of the Grail, A Translation of the Thirteenth Century Romance of Perlesvaus,* ed. and trans. by N. Bryant (Cambridge: D. S. Brewer, 1978), p. 1.

[25] *Le Haut Livre du Graal,* vol. 2, p. 74.

[26] See Nitze, vol. 1, pp. 3–12. The manuscript Nitze reproduces is the Bodleian MS Hatton 82, a previous edition of which was published by Charles Potvin in Brussels, 1866. My quotations in English of ll. 697–98, 1187–88, and 1737–38 are Nigel Bryant's translations, *The High Book of the Grail,* pp. 36, 48, and 62.

[27] Bryant, p. 3.

[28] J. Neale Carman, 'The Symbolism of the Perlesvaus', *PMLA,* no. 61 (1946), 42–83 (p. 42).

analysis, Perceval represents Christ, and Gawain, St John the Baptist. Some of his conclusions have rightly been called over-ingenious[29] but the article does illustrate a fruitful approach to romances in general. Carman remarks on the criticism of obscurity, a flaw which, he argues, only appears because twentieth-century readers no longer enjoy the same cultural background. The author of the *Perlesvaus*, writing 'for the serious reader of his time' did make his concept clear. 'He has amply provided the hints necessary for a public skilled in exegesis, acquainted with the minutest legends of the life of Christ and his disciples.'[30] However, the analysis Carman then provides does not convince because he is engrossed by the biblical past, whereas the pivotal element is medieval perception of the season of St John's Nativity. Bryant notes, 'the mere substitution of knightly figures... for New Testament counterparts is not in itself terribly exciting'.[31] In fact, the author's skilful use of St John's Day traditions makes the *Perlesvaus* one of the most exciting religious manifestos of the time.

The story begins at Ascension when Arthur is chid by Guinevere for his laziness (which a maiden later says has turned him into the 'plus mauvés roi du mont').[32] The result of Guinevere's intervention is that Arthur visits the Chapel of Augustine, where he is inspired to change his behaviour. He returns to set up the holy quest for the Grail, so bringing in a new era 'de bien fere... d'oneur [et] de largesse' (l. 566) in his court. His knights are summoned to discuss this on St John the Baptist's Day, the festival which launched the worldly and highly flawed quest in the Didot (Modena) *Perceval*. The *in*appropriateness of the day for instigating a holy quest is remarked on in *Perlesvaus* by Arthur's knights, who '... furent venu de totes parz, qi molt se merveilloient por coi li rois n'avoit cele grant cort tenue a la Pentecoste; mes il ne savoient pas l'achoison' ('... came from all around, wondering much why the king had not held this great court at Pentecost, which none could understand', ll. 583–85). Carman notes the reaction without finding an explanation for it. Yet the author says that Arthur did not intend the meeting to be at midsummer. It had to be then because, on his return from the Chapel, time was too short for all his dispersed knights to reassemble in

---

[29] Bryant, p. 5.

[30] Carman, p. 42.

[31] Bryant, p. 5.

[32] *Perlesvaus*, l. 519, ed. Nitze, vol. 1, p. 44.

Pennevoiseuse by Pentecost. Therefore, the date of midsummer came about by chance, which provides a pleasing irony. But the fact that the knights question the date draws our attention to the clash between purpose and season. In a further paradox, since Arthur's court had been in decline before the holding of this feast (his knights had left him because of his inaction), the court's fame does begin to grow from midsummer (again similar to the Didot (Modena) *Perceval*). But, here, the author inverts secular romance expectations in a way appropriate to the Christian subject matter, for it is Christ's power, not Arthur's, which increases. The quests of Gawain and Perceval to bring about re-Christianization are not motivated by personal vainglory; therefore, in every way, despite their start at midsummer, the changes to Arthur's court are for the better.

The quests of Gawain/St John and Perceval/Christ follow in sequence, filling the first nine branches of the story, and the plot is one of the most complex written. For example, concern for re-Christianization applies to Christ's power over the material as well as over the spiritual world and the dual need is followed in two separate plots. The first is expressed as the struggle for Perceval's ancestral home, the Vales of Kamaalot, now under the control of the Lord of the Fens, while spiritual weakness is shown in the failing health—followed by death—of the Fisher King. The improvement in both material and spiritual aspects is gradual, and the mission only flourishes when Perceval, who had also been languishing at the beginning, recovers his vigour in Branch V.

During the gradual improvement, 'fall' associations with the mid-summer date are relevant to Gawain's quest, for his contribution to reviving Christian power is only as successful as was that of John the Baptist in redeeming the world. Gawain temporarily regains Kamaalot, but he fails spiritually, as he does not put the questions to the Grail in the Castle of the Fisher King. Yet, he still seeks the right path and his quest contains several inversions of secular midsummer expectations. Some are light-hearted and others catastrophic. The wife who gives him a separate bed for the night falls from honour to death at the hands of her jealous husband. Were it not for this end, one could see a humorous side to the situation, since Gawain's reputation, mentioned later by the Maidens in the Tent, is that he is a philanderer as in other romances. But the fact that an innocent dies a horrific death can be seen as an allegory for Christ on the cross. Another, more humorous piece of reversal, comes on Gawain's first entrance, which is: 'seur un megre cheval grant e descharné, e ses hauberz estoit enrooilliez' ('on a feeble horse, large, but all skin and bone

[and] his hauberk was all turned to rust', ll. 697–98). The comedy of this Don Quixote figure is still apparent today[33] and, in the Middle Ages, it would have been stronger, playing as it does with the tradition of mettle-some horses embodying the midsummer pride of their riders (see Appendix C). The inversion of midsummer expectations is different from that found in *Lancelot*. In *Perlesvaus*, the theme running counter is the humility inherent in a religious quest and, when a better horse for Gawain is offered, he replies: '... ge ne le puis amender... J'avré autre quant Dieu plera' ('There is nothing I can do about that—I will have another when it shall please God', ll. 1737–38).

Gawain's quest is to cure the Fisher King's ill health by putting unspecified questions to the Holy Grail, kept in the Fisher King's Chapel. His first attempt even to enter the land of the Fisher King is, however, refused until he wins the sword with which John the Baptist was beheaded. This begins a quest within the quest, through which Gawain will prove whether he is as pure as John the Baptist and so fit to be received. The discussion about his horse, and subsequent offers of love from the Maidens in the Tent, come during this inner quest and Gawain's courteous resistance to the two worldly temptations both proves his spirituality and helps strengthen it, so making him capable of overcoming the mountain-top giant who possesses the sword. The analogy between Gawain and the Baptist is close at this point, bearing in mind the Prophet's connections with mountain tops, and considering that Gawain's success results in not only winning the sword but also in baptizing its owner. The sword is said to bleed every day at noon, which is explained as the hour when the Baptist was beheaded. Yet this is the moment when the sun begins to fall in the sky, the daily reminder of the midsummer solstice, and a reminder of John's own limited function in the Christian world. Similarly, Gawain comes before, but is secondary to, Perceval and, after his failure in the Castle of the Fisher king, Gawain's fame declines. Other mishaps befall him: he incurs reproach and shame and, despite his earlier success at Kamaalot, many people think that he is dead. Midsummer traditions explain these experiences and, despite Arthur's reluctance to initiate a Christian quest on the semi-pagan day and his knights' bewilderment by it, the religious view of midsummer is exactly relevant to the Gawain/Baptist story.

---

[33] Ménard, *Le Rire et le sourire*, p. 308.

Regaining the sword is Gawain's only complete victory. But he does enjoy partial success in his battle with the Lord of the Fens, and the combat with him is reminiscent of that of the Virtues against the Vices in Prudentius's *Psychomachia* and in *Li Tournoimens Anticrist*, for the Virtues here are the protagonists. Also, when defeated, the Lord of the Fens does not, like defeated knights in *Erec and Enide, Perceval,* or *Fergus,* agree to surrender in Arthur's court. A moral method is mixed with romance and, instead of playing the game, the Lord behaves like an unregenerate Vice, while other knights decide that 'faut il a Monseigneur Gavain, dont avez vos la garde .i. en du chastel de Kamaalot' ('the castle of Kamaalot is in [Gawain's keeping only] for a twelvemonth', ll. 1187–88). Game laws do appear to apply to Gawain, for St John's day kings who had proved themselves the best for one year were usually secure until the following summer. At this point comes the real Christian challenge, when Perceval defeats the pagan Lord of the Fens for all time.

It is initially surprising to find that Fortune, disguised as the Bald Lady with the Cart, is a major player in this Christian story. Her entry is at the St John's Day meeting and it is she who initiates the quest, for only when the Fisher King recovers will she regain her hair. One of the ways to describe Fortune's duplicity was to say she had hair in front and was bald behind, appearing beautiful when she welcomed you, but ugly when she turned her back. In this story, her duplicity is a disfigurement she must suffer until a knight asks the right questions in the house of the Fisher King. Therefore, in *Perlesvaus*, Fortune is not at odds with Christianity, but is herself in search of God's control over her. And when her identity is later explained, in the Castle of Enquiry, we learn that the cart she rides in is like her wheel: 'Li chars qu'ele maine aprés li senefie sa roe, car tot autresi com li chars vet seur ses roes, demaine ele le siecle' ('just as the cart is borne by its wheels, so is the world controlled by thc whccl of Fortune', ll. 2194–95, Bryant, p. 74). Material well-being is acknowledged as her gift, but the actual goal in the story is not worldly goods or honour but the redemption of the world in which that honour is obtained. Fortune herself is unfortunate until this happens, and the repeated greeting by travellers throughout the adventures is to wish each other 'good fortune'. Though the maiden's cart, pulled by a mule, is magnificent, it is a cart of ill fortune, more aligned to the one Lancelot rode in than a place of honour, until the right spiritual forces control her and the world through her. In her cart are the heads of a hundred and fifty knights, all victims of the decline of the Fisher King, and beheaded, as was John the Baptist. And, just as Fortune's power at midsummer was put under the Baptist's control, this maiden accompanies Gawain on his quest, needing his protection and hoping he may succeed for her. Gawain finally leaves her with the declaration that he will always be at her service.

It also appears that Fortune is depicted in maidens other than her, for example in the girl who appears soon after the Bald Maiden disappears. She is also looking for the good knight, and has with her the head of a knight. Gawain's quest includes a sequence of unmarried women and, since Fortune is supportive of Christianity here, all could be images of her, even the priestesses carrying in the Grail and the ragged maidens who receive Gawain in the Poor Castle after his failure. Carman notes that the author has Perceval appear in disguised forms, under the names, Per-les-vaus and Per-lui-fet (Bryant, pp. 50 and 55). It is also possible that running parallel to the intangible, elusive, but ever-present promise of Christian redemption, is the equally elusive, but ever-present symbol of worldly issues.

It could even be that it was a disguised figure of Fortune who instructed Arthur when he sought inspiration at the Chapel of Augustine at the opening of the Romance. A maiden with a wounded arm appeared there and explained the name 'Per-les-vaus' as 'He Who Has Lost The Vales' of Kamaalot (p. 30). And, subsequently, the Lady with the Cart enters with her right arm in a sling. In *Branches* V to VIII, the Lady with the Cart also serves Perceval, bringing him news and acting as his hostage in the home of the Lady of the Pavilions. But she does not ask his assistance, and it would appear that the author did not see a close association between her and the controller she seeks. Finally, the action from Branches V to VIII ends just after midsummer the following year when Gawain's temporary control of Kamaalot comes to an end, and Perceval undertakes the bloodthirsty and mocking revenge on the Lord of the Fens: one which is appropriate to the pagan aspects of the season, but not to a figure of Christ, except perhaps in the context of the Crusades. Yet, through this, Perceval regains the valleys of Kamaalot, and the Grail reappears in the Chapel of the Fisher King.

As my attempts to negotiate its complexities show, this romance contains one of the most carefully crafted of midsummer plots, almost comparable to a modern thriller in its ingenuity and in the technique of dropping oblique clues. Thanks to the author's thoroughness in, for example, establishing the unsuitability of St John's Day for the start of a holy quest, he also helps confirm other evidence for midsummer as a day symbolic of worldly power. The midsummer content also provides one reason for suggesting that the author was engaged with contemporary issues, and intended to reawaken crusading zeal.

In other romances there are more peripheral allusions to St John's day as, for example, in *Les Merveilles de Rigomer* (ll. 14756–821) and in the vulgate *Merlin* where, on this date, Lancelot is dubbed knight before embarking on a quest and appropriate comments are made in the preceding week.[34] But, sometimes, even brief episodes contain original reworkings. In *Guiron le Courtois* Arthur builds a chapel dedicated to the Saint on the site of the combat between Ariohan and Meliadus, which had taken place on 24 June. Ariohan had undertaken the challenge out of pure chivalric ideals, to test Meliadus: 'ta force et ton merveilliux pooir'[35] and to see whether he was the best knight in the world. The proof leaves the contender close to death but, on recovery, he leaves Britain, marries, and becomes king of Denmark. Then Ariohan returns to the chapel, this time prepared to lose to the chivalric ideal, not his life, but his increased worldly honour. He makes the pledge that if he finds another knight as good as Meliadus he will take off his crown and place it on that man's head, and give him all honour ('Se ge trovasse ore un tel home com fui cestui, ge osteroie ma corone de ma teste et la metroie en la soie et leisseroie toute onor...').[36] On the chivalric level, Guiron is another John the Baptist figure, seeking the reverse to self-aggrandizement and finding satisfaction in being secondary to a greater man, as already noted for the reformed Yvain in his final combat. Something similar occurs with Loth's battle against Arthur's forces in Robert de Boron's *Merlin,* although this is portrayed as an honourable struggle for supremacy, with the alternatives for each side, power or death. Twelve kings are killed in the onslaught, after which Arthur feasts Loth's memory and has a church of St John erected on the battle site to keep Loth's renown alive through the

---

[34] *The Vulgate Version of the Arthurian Romances*, ed. by O. Summer (Washington: Carnegie Institution, 1909), vol. 3, pp. 118–23.

[35] *Guiron le Courtois*, ed. by R. Lathullière (Geneva: Droz, 1966), p. 234, para. 47. The text Lathullière uses comprises a number of manuscripts as the tales of Guiron were developed in several parts of Europe over several centuries. Emperor Frederick II is known to have read them in 1240 and they were also enjoyed by England's Edward I. Lathullière, p. 13.

[36] Ibid., p. 235, para. 48.

coming centuries.[37] Here, the warrior who came second is honoured by the victor with a Baptist's memorial. Although the errors of pride featured as typical midsummer behaviour, yet the figure of St John was an example of the opposite virtue, so extending the range of possible interpretations.

The fact that the stories of Chrétien preceded these romances was not necessarily a negative factor in their time. What might be seen as derivative can also be viewed as a deliberate play by their authors against readings already created, sometimes for comedy and sometimes to make a serious point. It also becomes hard to avoid the conclusion that St John's day was central to the conception of most Arthurian romances. Chrétien's *Yvain*, le Clerc's *Fergus,* and the anonymous *Perlesvaus,* can each be read as elaborate midsummer games: festive tradition in novel form. The *Yvain* and the first nine branches of *Perlesvaus* are the most elegant, subtly combining other lines of thought and so lifting the tales above simplistic narrative, whereas *Fergus* and the midsummer incident in *Li Chevaliers* rely on direct borrowing from popular culture, which, necessarily, reveals more of their festive origins. And, in this context, *Fergus* could be described as an apotheosis of festivity.

However, there is no wish to claim that the romances were the origin of all plots, characterization, or depiction of emotions—such as anger— essential to any later fiction. In the *Chanson de Roland*, young unmarried men are also said to be 'turbulent',[38] and as a result they play the ambiguous game of *escrime* (fencing or cruder forms of combat) rather than chess. The traditional association between youth and intemperance could, here, help our understanding of Ganelon. Further, it is obvious that both genres involve questions of chivalry, disputes, treachery, combat, and claims to supremacy. However, even though *chansons* were told by jongleurs in a semi-mimetic way,[39] there remained the underlying claim

---

[37] *Merlin: Roman en Prose du XIIIᵉ siècle*, ed. by G. Paris and J. Ulrich, SATF (Paris: Didot, 1886), vol. 1, p. 262. Another text worth consideration is Von Strassbourg's *Tristan*, where tribute from Britain is compelled by Rome, as in the *Didot Perceval*. The author says, 'at the solstice', and allusions to Fortune and political revolt make St John's day likely. See *Gottfried von Strassburg, Thomas: Tristan*, ed. and trans. by A. T. Hatto (Harmondsworth: Penguin, 1967), p. 122.

[38] P. Jonin's modern French translation of 'E as eschecs li plus daive e li veill,/ E escremissent cil bacheler leger', ll. 112–13. *Le Chanson de Roland*, ed. and trans. by P. Jonin (Paris: Gallimard, 1979), p. 60.

[39] Ibid., p. 41. There is, too, in *Roland*, an act of self-abasement (ll. 3092–97) by dismounting and lying prone on the earth. This reveals Charlemagne's humility in prayer, not

that the stories were true. In the *Chanson de Roland,* for example, pride and anger exist as facts of life. Ganelon becomes a traitor through his pride, but he is also depicted as brave, while Charlemagne's pride is justified *fierté.* And the disputes are between peers: no servant would dare address a king in the way that Kay speaks to Arthur. The claim to truth is found in other ways: hills and valleys exist purely on the geographical plane, and combats are realistic—men split open from head to navel tend to die.

And, as already said, seasons do not influence, or colour, the Christian action. At the opening it is prophesied that, once Charlemagne succeeds in Spain, he will baptize the captured pagans on the day dedicated to the invincible slayer of anti-Christian forces, St Michael. Yet, when Charlemagne does prevail, his success comes without a reminder of any season as though any such mention might undercut the seriousness of the issues. The purpose of the story is to promulgate a Christian 'truth' which may be heightened with symbolic acts, such as dropping the king's glove, prophetic dreams, and by techniques such as repetition, while God is even said to stop the movement of the sun to help the Christian emperor. But no matter how far-fetched, the incidents unfold as a factual documentary. By contrast, in romances, the fiction is established largely through the use of season, particularly a season subversive towards normal order, which, in the twelfth century, was midsummer rather than Shrovetide. The drama in the action is strengthened and maintained by those outrageous qualities associated with the season.

There is one work which has been said to stand on the cusp between *chansons de geste* and romances, that is, the twelfth-century *Roman d'Alexandre.* It is an extended calendrical survey of an extraordinary man, whose biography is divided into four parts from birth to death, very like the sequence on Fortune's four-part seasonal wheel from *regnabo* to *sum sine regno.* The pattern is, unintentionally, shown in Harf-Lancner's précis of the sections: *Branche* I: birth to Alexander's first major campaign; *Branche* II: a sequence of victorious battles ending with the greatest triumph, against the Persian king, Darius; *Branche* III: Alexander's exploratory ventures, under the sea, into the sky, and the prophecy of his death; *Branche* IV: his death.[40] As well as this there are

---

shame inflicted by a fellow knight. Afterwards his increased personal worth is reflected in his physical beauty (ll. 3114–19).

[40] *Alexandre de Paris: le Roman d'Alexandre,* ed. by L. Harf-Lancner, Le Livre de Poche (Paris: Librairie Générale Française, 1994), pp. 59–61.

Figure 5: King Alexander in state. Histoire d'Alexandre, *fol. 127ʳ*
Flemish, c. *1470.*

Figure 6: King Alexander, grotesque, lower left border.

features within individual *Branches* which also contribute to a seasonal perspective, particularly in Part III where, despite his aiming for the stars, Alexander is said to find himself in regions such as the Perilous Valley. This is in contrast to the end of *Branche* II, where he is *montés* (l. 2991), enriched by Darius's wealth, and his opponent loses everything, including his wife, who commits suicide. Alexander himself remains modest but others call him 'the conqueror of the world' (l. 3056). Alexander's extraordinary successes were achieved as a young man; therefore, they inevitably make him a youth reaching a pinnacle of uniquely vigorous years, and with no competitors to rival him. At the same time, not even he can escape the underlying cycle and he dies at the peak of his fame. Since Alexander had been a pagan warrior-king, it would not have been un-Christian to perceive his life as one ruled by Fortune's seasonal wheel, and a later illustrated manuscript of his exploits even includes a mocking inversion of his success at the summit of his achievements, half-way through the story of his life. Here he is shown as female, and clubbing a large helpless bird (Bodleian MS: Laud Misc. 751 fol. 127^r: Figs 5 and 6).

The question raised by accounts of Alexander's life is whether they were considered 'true' and written in his praise, or whether they were seen as semi-fiction with his exploits perceived ambiguously because his motives were not Christian. And the only other character in medieval culture famous for the claim to be 'lord of all the world' is Satan.

The *Roman d'Alexandre* is, however, not paradoxical in its construction and in this it is like *chansons de geste*, whereas the complexities in romances make them, today, more difficult to understand. Yet, as T. E. Kelly has observed, the argument that twentieth-century difficulties in understanding them lies in 'romance writers being little concerned with this aspect of their craft' is not sustainable.[41] Hunt and Grimbert have already shown that it is possible to understand *Yvain* in its entirety through the consistency of its ironic approach. An understanding of the midsummer context brings this irony into full focus and also makes other romances equally accessible. Carman's observation that the author of *Perlesvaus* made his argument clear for the readers of his time applies to this sub-genre of romance as a whole. Twists and turns in the narration and apparent contradictions were part of a characterization and plot structure based on expectations prompted by a contradictory and combative season.

---

[41] See T. E. Kelly, *Le Haut Livre du Graal: Perlesvaus, a Structural Study* (Geneva: Droz, 1974), p. 37.

SECTION III:

The Urban Setting

CHAPTER 5

Civic Power in Louvain and Metz

Tout d'abord le duc promet de renouveler les échevins chaque année à la Saint-Jean...

Joseph Cuvelier (Louvain)

Dimanche 23ᵉ juin, vigille de Sᵗ· Jean Baptiste furent esleus... des treizes... comme d'ancienté et non autrement.

la Hière (Metz)

Arthurian romances were obviously set in a world which was different from that of twelfth- and thirteenth-century society, even though analogies with contemporary life could be drawn. The difference between them and *Galeran,* written about 1216 by Jean Renaut, is that he based his analogies directly on the example of his contemporary society. While not entirely 'realistic',[1] Renaut's method was to place Galeran's pursuit of chivalry in a world where communities might be based in towns as well as in courts; where class differences are examined, and individuals from the bourgeoisie act as protagonists. The Nativity of St John the Baptist, and its octave, feature three times, once in such a way that it produces a social paradox. For the climax to Galeran's worldly success, halfway through the tale, is set during an aristocratic midsummer celebration in the city of Metz. The contemporary reality casts an ironic reflection on this description since, by 1216, there were new bourgeois customs in Metz for the day of 24 June, which had superseded the old feudal traditions.

---

[1] *Renaut: Galeran de Bretagne, traduit en français moderne*, ed. and trans. by Jean Dufornet (Paris: Champion, 1996), pp. 10–12.

For freedom of speech on 24 June was not limited to festive or
rebellious displays. Belief that the solstice demonstrated the inevitability
of change and the fall of the great appears, at times, to have been harnessed in support of the bourgeoisie, whose rise during the Middle Ages
created a continual challenge to those in power above them. In the twelfth
century the Church was particularly vulnerable, suffering as it was from
dwindling finances, internal disputes, and dissension between the Pope
and the Holy Roman Emperor.[2] Aristocratic power, on the other hand,
was organized on a regional basis, and often found the middle classes an
ally in its own disagreements with the Church. Counts, such as Henri II of
Champagne, improved their people's rights so as to weaken ecclesiastic
hold.[3] Their main concern was financial support and manpower for military campaigns: provided these were guaranteed on oath, many dukes and
counts were glad to give up the responsibility of civic organization, and
thriving towns were awarded franchises to elect their own internal
governments. As historians have said, the tendency was for the richest
bourgeoisie to form its own élite; and, often, the ordinary citizen perceived little change in a system where patrician *échevins* replaced counts,
dukes, or their appointed mayors.[4] Many such cities became autonomous
states and their success was commemorated in 1311 when Philippe le Bel
added to the mint a coin wittily called 'le bourgeois fort'.[5]

However, what is often omitted in the need to make European urban
history coherent, is the fact that there were periods when towns such as
Metz, Louvain, and Trondes not only held elections on 23–24 June, but
these elections were perceived by the citizens to give them a free choice,
even if, sometimes, the range of candidates for *jurés* had been partially
selected from the town's great families. In Metz the election of *jurés* on
24 June was established in about 1205 and, by 1216 when Jean Renaut
was writing, the ordinary bourgeoisie in Metz were enjoying an early
period of economy-led independence. Despite other more problematic

---

[2]   *The Oxford Dictionary of Popes* (Oxford: Oxford University Press, 1986) and *Lives of
the Popes in the Early Middle Ages*, ed. by H. K. Mann, 19 vols (London: Kegan Paul,
Trench, Trübner, 1925–32), XV (1929).

[3]   M. Boutiot, *Des institutions communales dans la Champagne Méridionale* (Troyes,
1865).

[4]   See J.-C. Rossiaud, 'Crises et Consolidations', in *Histoire de la France urbaine, II, La
Ville médiévale,* ed. by G. Duby (Paris: Seuil, 1980), p. 411.

[5]   *Œuvres complètes de Rutebeuf,* ed. by E. Faral and J. Bastin, 2 vols (Paris: Picard,
1959–60), I, p. 529, note to ll. 66–69.

times, Metz provides the longest-running success story, for its status as a
republic remained until the upheavals of the mid-sixteenth century, when
most of the information regarding 24 June appears. Fortunately, there is
evidence from Louvain closer to the date when *Galeran* was written. In
1267 the temporary success of its ordinary bourgeoisie produced a cameo
of the date's political significance.[6]

By 1210 Louvain's political masters were seven patrician *échevins,*
who each held office for ten to twelve years but, in 1213, permission was
granted by the Duke of Brabant for the citizens to elect their own *jurés.*
Although not itself universal suffrage it was the beginning of the concept
in the Netherlands. As Cuvelier puts it: 'Au lieu de venir d'en haut, les
pouvoirs, cette fois, viennent d'en bas'.[7] Citizens were clearly aware of
how delicate their foothold was: the entire voting bourgeoisie was obliged
to attend every meeting of the Communal Council. Those absent, without
good reason, were fined.[8] Decisions made thus represented the wishes of
all citizens: an important fact for *jurés* facing an entrenched power
structure.

Two generations later, and local democracy came closer. In 1267, the
Communal Council promised the Duke 'à ne l'élever aucune plainte au
sujet des torts que la duchesse, ses fils et ses partisans avaient occa-
sionnés à la ville' ('not to raise any complaint on the subject of the
wrongs done to the town by the Duchess, her sons, and their friends').[9]
By coincidence, or not by coincidence, in the same year the town won
from the Duke the huge concession that their immediate political masters
would in future be changed annually on 24 June. The document reads:
'Preterea promittimus eisdem de anno ad annum, ulterius et semper in
festo beati Johannis Baptiste, scabinos renovare' ('From henceforward
we promise that from year to year, for ever and always, on the Feast of

---

[6]   Nicholas mentions that *jurés* had a more active role in Louvain than in the rest of the
Low Countries, but he omits the evidence of more democratic control between 1267 to
1361. *The Growth of the Medieval City* (London: Longman, 1997), p. 230.

[7]   Joseph Cuvelier, 'Les institutions de la ville de Louvain au Moyen Age', *Mémoires de
l'Académie Royale de Belgique,* 2nd series, vol. 11 (Brussels: Palais des Académies,
1935), passim. See p. 118. This shows that David Nicholas is not correct in his observations that power always came from above. See his claim that *jurés* 'were assigned' to the
towns they protected, *The Growth of the Medieval City*, p. 231.

[8]   Cuvelier, p. 119.

[9]   Ibid., p. 122.

the Holy John the Baptist, the *échevins* will be changed').[10] This 'momentous reduction of *échevin* power'[11] lasted nearly a century, during which time the morning of midsummer day was occupied with swearing in both the *échevins* and the *jurés,* after which the town bell and band played from 11.30 a.m. to noon heralding the results. Although half an hour is a short period of time, it was nevertheless called a *kermesse,* or people's festival, by a contemporary recorder who wrote:

> Cette musique était composé de tymballes, trompettes, cors et hautbois. Pendant la *kermesse* ils étaient obligés de jouer sur l'estrade de la maison de ville aussi longtemps que jouait le carillon, c'est-à-dire depuis onze heures et demie à midi.
>
> ('This music combined timbals, trumpets, horns, and oboes. During *la kermesse* they had to play on the balcony of the Town Hall for as long as the bell rang, that is to say from 11.30 to midday.')[12]

The music marked the climax of the election of the town's great men at the peak of the day which celebrated the turning point of the sun. Bearing in mind how universal was the understanding of the meaning of St John's Day, such rejoicing reflects on the reduction of *échevin* power to a year at least as much as it celebrates all the men being given their temporary status as local lords, and Duke Wenceslas, who inaugurated the change, was reported to have said that the arrogance of the *échevins* wearied even himself.[13] Nine years after 1267, in Arras, a town where the *échevinage* held unbroken power, Adam de la Halle included satire on them in the *Jeu de la Feuillée,* commenting on the lack of decline of two *échevin* families despite their sitting at the top of Fortune's wheel.[14] His summer play reveals open antagonism and, in Louvain, the accompanying music from strident instruments could have been similarly antagonistic, displaying an element of triumphant *charivari,* against the unpopular, and

---

[10] 'Privilèges accordés à la ville de Louvain, par Jean I, duc de Brabant.—Louvain, 29 Juin, 1267.' Joseph Cuvelier, 'Documents inédits concernant les institutions de la ville de Louvain au Moyen Age', *Bulletin de la Commisssion royale d'Histoire,* vol. 99 (Brussels: Palais des Academies, 1935), passim. See p. 262.

[11] Cuvelier, 'Les institutions de la ville de Louvain au Moyen Age', p. 80.

[12] G. J. C. Piot, *Histoire de Louvain depuis son origins jusqu'aujourdhui,* Pt. 1 (Louvain, 1839), p. 131, n. 1.

[13] Piot, *Histoire de Louvain,* p. 128.

[14] *Le Jeu de la Feuillée,* ll. 789–93, 808–09. *Adam de la Halle: Œuvres complètes,* ed. by P.-Y. Badel (Paris: Librairie Générale Française, 1995), pp. 346–49.

defeated, patricians.

A century later the citizens of Louvain were outmanoeuvred and the then duke was obliged to respond to events by banishing his revolutionary mayor, Pierre Coutereel, whose last elections were held on 24 June 1361.[15] Subsequently, the *échevins* changed the date of civic appointments—no longer elections—delaying them until the feast of Peter and Paul.[16] They also removed all bourgeois representation in councils and infiltrated gilds with patrician overseers.[17] The non-cooperation which resulted caused economic decline, riots, and the duke's renewed attempts at reconciliation. His second in 1378, to remove 'the dissension, discord, and commotion',[18] was imaginatively thought out and included the election of three plebeian *échevins*.[19] There was not, though, a return to 24 June for the day of the investiture; 'for ever and always' went out of the window and the statute only mentions the day of elections in a subordinate clause:

> Et quod omnes boni Homines praedictorum Fratrem de Gilda & Opisicorum postero die post festum Sancti Joannis Baptistae ante prandium, dum campana Consilii sonatur....

> (and that all the good men of the aforesaid brotherhoods of gilds and artisans on the day after, the day following the feast of Saint[20] John the Baptist [will come together] before noon, when the council bell will be rung.)[21]

There is no mention here of the town band and the presence of the patricians does not seem to have been expected, yet a fine was included for any Gild member or artisan who failed to attend.[22] The twenty-fifth of

---

[15] *Les Quatorze livres sur l'histoire de la ville de Louvain du Jean Molanus,* ed. by P. F. X. de Ram, II (Brussels, 1861), p. 1270.

[16] This was confirmed in a Charter of 1373. See Aubertus Miræus, *Opera Diplomatica et Historica,* 2nd edn, II (Brussels, 1723), pp. 1024–25. Cf. Cuvelier, 'Les Institutions de la ville de Louvain au Moyen Age', p. 131.

[17] Miræus, *Opera Diplomatica et Historica,* p. 1025.

[18] Ibid., p. 1026.

[19] Piot, *Histoire de Louvain,* p. 128.

[20] The decree of 1267 had called him 'holy'. 'Saint' was the conventional, less reverent term.

[21] Miræus, *Opera Diplomatica et Historica,* p. 1028.

[22] '& si quis eò non venerit existens in Oppide incurret mulctam quinque solidorum grossorum....' Ibid.

June appears to have removed the *kermesse* aspect from the election results and, with it, popular support. Economically, however, Louvain continued to prosper under the 1378 system and perhaps with less acrimony, since the inflammatory politics had been removed.[23]

The reforms in Metz had begun with opposition to Church authority[24] and, by 1237, Bishops were banned from living inside the city walls[25] while, in the fourteenth century, they were forbidden from entering except with prior negotiated agreement.[26] This repudiation of ecclesiastic feudal power was architecturally demonstrated in 1315, with the building of a palace for the thirteen *jurés*, facing the bishopric which it had supplanted. The process of their election took place between the evening of 23 and the morning of 24 June in the parishes of Metz. Each *juré*, chosen locally, was then announced at the town hall, and the oath was taken by them on 24 June. Further reversal can be seen in the role of the mayors for, after 1250, these did not wield power, but were reinstituted as three civil servants who liaised between parishes and were responsible to the one *Maistre Échevin* and to the *Treize*.[27] Metz could get away with the

---

[23] Another example of challenge to the authorities through use of the date can be found in the small town of Herck, near to Liège. Unlike Louvain, Liège's *jurés* gained no civic autonomy from their *échevins*, but in Herck in 1325, the Guild of Weavers appears to have decided they were strong enough to go their own way regarding their internal organization. On November 17 they gave the local mayor and *échevins* seven months' warning of their intentions: 'seroient esleus par les tisserans, chascun an, le jour saint Jehan-Baptiste, IIII maistres et les juréz d'icellui mestier. Lesquelles ordonnances les maire et eschevins de ladicte ville porroient rapeller toutes les foiz qu'il leur sembleroit expediant.' *Chartes confisquées aux bonnes villes du pays de Liège et du Comté de Looz*, ed. by É. Fairon (Brussels: Palais des Academies, 1937), pp. 273–74.

[24] A charter of 1179 replaced the system of appointing a *Maistre Échevin* for life, with the one changed annually on 21 March. He was to be elected by monastic foundations and the chief canon of the Cathedral, not by clerics with territorial ambitions. Feu M. Girard, Baron de Hannoncelles, *Metz ancien*, 2 vols (Metz, 1856), I, p. vi.

[25] Ibid. This uncompromising stance resulted from the fact that, prior to 1179, Bishops had ruled Metz through their *échevins*, and the city had some twenty-eight religious foundations in it, ten more than in Lyon. See D. Nicholas, *The Growth of the Medieval City* (New York, Longman, 1997), pp. 28 and 143.

[26] Girard, Baron de Hannoncelles, *Metz Ancien*, I, p. iv.

[27] According to the 1256 declaration, these were chosen after the elections of the *treize*. *Histoire générale de Metz*, ed. by J. François (Metz, 1769–90), III, Part ii, *Preuves*, p. 211. The *Maistre Échevin* was supported by 26 other *Échevins*, who did not wield power. See de Hannoncelles, I, p. vi, and J. Schneider, *La ville de Metz aux XIIIe et XIVe siècles* (Nancy: Georges Thomas, 1950).

inversions because its banking strength made it a medieval Switzerland, economically stronger than either the Church or the *Comté* of Lorraine, both of which were in debt to it,[28] and their lands or property were acquired by bankers, in lieu of payment.

The twenty-fourth of June for the election of *jurés* could have been accidental, but its importance in the citizens' minds is made clear in a *Diary* kept by La Hière during 1551–57, when a bishop—Robert de Lenencourt—tried to bring the Messine Republic back into line. In 1551 he defied the ban against residing in the city and made the old bishopric habitable after centuries of disuse. He then ordered the gentry to present themselves to swear allegiance and, since the gentry could not decide whether or not they wanted to do this, they ordered the bourgeoisie to take the oath instead, and the bourgeoisie refused. In spring, 1553, when the citizens were occupied with skirmishes outside the city walls, Robert took his revenge. He claimed there were not enough *jurés* left in town to run the courts, and held his own elections three months early appointing his own men,[29] even putting elderly clerics into the Civic seats. His coup, reappointing his men each Easter to forestall the people's June elections, lasted three years, but after negotiations with the king of France, la Hière was able to record:

> Dimanche 23ᵉ juin 1555, vigille de Sᵗ˙ Jean-Baptiste furent esleus par les paroissiens des paroisses de la cité de Metz pour porter l'office des treizes de la justice temporelle, et firent le serment comme d'ancienté et non autrement: Le sʳ Jean le Braconnier, l'aisne, le sʳ Mᶜ Jean de Termonge, apoticaire: Sᵗ˙ Gergonne.—Le sire Mᶜ George de Laitre, le sire Henry Jeune, l'orfebvre, sʳ Michel Praillon, le sʳ Colignon Malgras, le sire Jean Hutin, l'escrivain: Sᵗ Jacques.—Le sire Mangin le Bachelle, l'orfebvre, le sʳ Jacomin Remion: Sᵗ˙ Vy—Ferry Fronay, le boucher de Porte-Mozelle: Sᵗᵉ˙ Seglaine.—Le sʳ Humbert le Raille, le marchant: Sᵗ˙ Victor.—Le sʳ Claude de Vallier: Sᵗ˙ Ferroy.—Le sʳ Matellin, le Febvre: Sᵗ˙ Gegoulf.[30]

Only seven parishes were involved—the next year the number increased to eleven—but this list of *jurés* includes a blacksmith, a butcher, and a writer, along with men from high-class trades such as the goldsmiths,

---

[28] François-Yves le Moigne, *Histoire de Metz* (Toulouse: Privat, 1986), pp. 142–44.

[29] La Hière, 'Annales de Metz', ed. G. Zeller, 'Fragments inédits de chroniques messines (1553–1557)', *Annuaire de la Société d'Histoire et d'Archéologie Lorraine*, vol. 34 (1924), pp. 221–63 (pp. 221–23).

[30] Ibid., pp. 243–44.

while the ceremony was held quietly on the eve, not the day, of St John. The following year, however, and in 1557, the last year of la Hière's diary, 'les noms et surnoms des treizes [furent] créés le jour de feste St. Jean-Baptiste 24e juin 1556'. In 1557 this was done in the presence of the King's representative,[31] cementing a change in allegiance and protection.

Had 24 June not held symbolic value to the Messine republicans, they could have played Bishop Robert's game and held further elections before his own. But the combined evidence from Louvain and Metz is that the day underlined the claim that these were democratic proceedings, or at least that they represented the will of the people. Interestingly, in 1551, la Hière recorded that the bishop 'vint à Metz entour la St. Jean-Baptiste'.[32] Whether he did in fact is, perhaps, not the point; the phrase reads as one proclaiming the Bishop's own challenge to the established power system since the local situation in Metz, in 1551, had turned the Church into the aspiring class.

A complicated situation arose in 1405, some fifty years after some of the wealthier bourgeoisie had opted to be vassals of princes, and had begun to live as minor lords on lands granted to them outside the town.[33] Their changed status led to a need to pay the costs of repelling an incursion onto these lands during a ducal struggle,[34] and their attempt to pass the expense on to the citizens in Metz resulted in a blunt rejection by the remaining bourgeoisie and artisans, which erupted on 24 June:

'Faut il que pour eulx et pour raichetter et gardeir leurs terres, que nous soyons taillies? Ces quatre seigneurs avec leurs gens n'eussent mie prins la cité; nous estions bien pour la deffendre. Si ce n'estoient leurs seigneuries, ou ne nous sçaveroit, que faire, et sommes toujours ainsy maingies, taillés et gabellez par eulx et pour leurs seigneuries. Nous ne le debvons souffrir ny endureir.

(Must we be taxed to make them rich and keep their lands for them? These four lords and their men would not have taken the city; we were there to defend it. If they hadn't been lords, they wouldn't have thought of dealing with us in this way, and yet here we are, consumed, tithed, and taxed to the hilt by them and for their lordly estates. We must not suffer or endure it

---

[31] Ibid., 245–47.

[32] Ibid., p. 221.

[33] Nicholas, *The Later Medieval City*, pp. 138–39.

[34] F.-Y. le Moigne, p. 156.

any longer.')[35]

The remaining townspeople were reduced to seasonal invective and, instead of civic elections, rebel leaders from the gilds asserted themselves.[36] One minor representative of the *seigneurial* class, *chevalier* Nicolle Grognier, was caught and hung.

Civic organization did not always develop in an orderly method which one might call mutually-agreed progress. In Louvain and Metz it often swung between opposing groups, each seeing their own practices as the original and true system, and Bishop Robert claimed ancient tradition prior to 1205 for his 1553 changes. The multiple readings possible for events on St John's Day contributed to the confusion, and another of Bishop Robert's reasons for intervention in 1553 was his accusation of festive disorder in the citizens' own elections. He claimed they were childish parodies of serious business, perpetrated by those flawed creatures, 'young men':

> '[L]e plus souvent y avoit des jeunes gens comme enfans séans en siège de justice pour observer leurd. ordonnance, et jamais n'estoit le nombre desdits treizes accomply, et y avoit le plus souvent jeunes gens qui n'avoyent jamais allés ne venus, ne fréquenté pays ne veu comment on doit régir pollice et gouverner une telle honnorable cité et un tel peuple et une telle république.

> (Most often you find young men like children, lodged in the seats of justice following their own orders... most often young men who don't attend, nor visit the region nor have any idea how to police and govern such an honourable city and republic.)[37]

This is a curious point to raise if David Nicholas is right and the ruling bourgeoisie had turned themselves into a new patrician class governing Metz in a feudal manner.[38] As already said, the list of 1555 reveals a mixed class selection and, in 1556, these retiring magistrates instructed every parish to elect: 'un homme de bien, de bonne fame, bonne renom-

---

[35] Huguenin, ed., *Les chroniques de la ville de Metz*, p. 131.

[36] '[L]a plus grant partie du peuple ensemble se mutinant contre lesdits seigneurs, gouverneurs de la cité, et entreprendre le gouvernement de la cité et firent juges et officiers d'eulx meysmes'. Ibid. Cf. the sixteenth-century ballad, 'Revolte des Bourgeois de Metz contre leurs Seigneurs', Anon., *Les Chroniques de Metz* (Metz, 1525, printed 1855), p. 93.

[37] La Hière, ed. Zeller, p. 225.

[38] Some relaxation in eligibility for *juré* service could have been caused by the decimation of the patrician families due to plague and war. See F.-Y. le Moigne, p. 156.

mée, idione et suffisant et de bonne reputation pour porter l'office de
treize pour la justice temporelle'.[39] Therefore, it would appear that in
Messine eyes, men of means and of reputation could be found among the
ordinary middle classes.

It was very likely that in some places seasonal wild behaviour on 24
June continued in parallel with more serious business. In Tournai in 1422,
the town gates were closed from 23 June to 14 July, with only the pedes-
trian gates open and each patrolled by 'cinq hommes de garde'.[40] Similarly, during the serious disturbances in the same town in 1566, when the
people left Tournai *en masse* on 30 June to hear the Protestant preacher,
the gates were locked in case they rioted on their return, but the crowds
deliberately returned peacefully.[41] The border between what was serious
business, and what disordered festivity, or between what was legal and
what was rebellion, was confused. Franchises which the lower classes
considered long-standing rights were permanently open to the challenge
by the upper classes that they were insurrection, while the events in Metz
in 1405, though trying to re-establish old citizen rights, resulted in
rebellion against a newer status quo.

And the free speech at the Nativity of St John, 1405, which began the
violence, brings to mind the possibility that some other recorded slanders
could also have been the airing of grievances over issues of civic injustices—for example, the priest in Metz, in 1512, calling Lord Nicole
Remiat a liar. In 1504 one Nicol Remiat was involved in a promise of
electoral autonomy for Viéville-en-Haie (a nearby village)[42] and the
possibility arises that the priest used the seasonal liberty to challenge the
non-appearance of the more substantial liberties. Another neighbouring
town of Trondes made a declaration in 1505, apparently to protect its
freedoms: 'La Mairie de Trondes est par élection de la Communauté en
fault au jour de la nativité St Jean Baptiste par chacun an'.[43]

Where a town's independence did thrive its success revealed one
power waning and another growing. And because the *jurés* were elected
for one year only, the principle of the calendar cycle provided a reminder

[39] La Hière, ed. Zeller, p. 245.

[40] *Extraits analytiques des anciens registres des consaux de la ville de Tournai 1422–1430,* ed. by H. Vandenbroeck (Tournai, 1863), I, p. 255.

[41] Pinchart, pp. 59–60.

[42] H. Lepage, *Les communes de la Meurthe,* II (Nancy, 1853), p. 679.

[43] Archives de Meurthe-et-Moselle, Nancy MS G. 1389, p. 447.

that their power, too, was limited, though both points could only be symbolically apparent if the election of civic lords was held on 24 June.[44] In some places, it would seem the date was not inflammatory. For example, in the sixteenth century, in the small town of Arlon close to Luxembourg, loyalty was acknowledged to the Holy Roman Emperor, yet the declaration continues with the town's own elections: 'le jour de la nativité de Saint-Jean'.[45]

At the other extreme, the situation in Louvain reveals the difficulties the date could create if confrontational attitudes were set up in council chambers. While, in Metz, at the time *Galeran* was written, the town had eliminated seigneurial opposition from its council meetings and appears to have been running well under consensual government.[46] Jean Renaut's work was not the only major tale featuring this city in the early thirteenth century; there is, too, the anonymous *chanson de geste, Hervis de Mes*. This does not mention St John's Day, but the author pays tribute to 'la commune de Mes la forte cité, 'Mes... la mirable cité,' and its 'frans borjois',[47] whom Hervis is encouraged to copy, rather than follow chivalric example. As in *Galeran* and in some other literature of the thirteenth century, the bourgeoisie as protagonists might be treated as innovators of a fresh and therefore uncorrupted system.

Pope Urban IV spent much of his papacy battling against the trend towards secularization and the growing power of city communes.[48] Coincidentally, he was also the founder of the Feast of Corpus Christi, which was first introduced in Turotte in 1246 and was observed throughout Europe by 1317. It was the last Feast day to be added to the Church's Calendar, and was part of the movement in the Church to reach out to the

---

[44] Because of this, Florence is not an example, despite its long-standing 24 June celebrations with the Baptist its patron saint. The method of election or appointment of the town's lords was subject to several changes, but the date was never 24 June. See R. Davidsohn, *Storia di Firenze*, IV, Pt 1 (Florence: Sansoni, 1962), pp. 99–120; IV, Pt 3 (1965), pp. 562–70.

[45] *Coutumes des Pays, Duché de Luxembourg et Comté de Chiney*, ed. by M. N. J. Leclercq, 4 vols (Brussels, 1867), I, pp. 179–80.

[46] In 1256, the decision to institute the new mayoral system was decided by '*li Maistres Eschevins, & li treze Jurié, & li Comuneteiz de Metz*'. François, *Metz*, III, Part ii, *Preuves*, p. 198.

[47] *Hervis de Mes; chanson de geste anonyme (début du XIIIème siècle)*, ed. by J.-C. Herbin (Geneva: Droz, 1992), ll. 2391, 5347, and 7422.

[48] *The Lives of the Popes in the Early Middle Ages*, ed. Mann, XV, pp. 148–73.

people. The earliest date on which the Feast could fall was 21 May and the latest, 24 June.[49] Therefore, either by accident or by design, from 1317 on, the worldly focus which had developed around St John the Baptist's Day was shadowed by a new Church festival reminding the people of the 'basic claim on which Christianity had come to rest' (Rubin, p. 179), as though the original Christianization of the Solstice had been seen to have failed. There is no stated evidence that the Church's purpose was to challenge secular midsummer customs and the absence of Church comment on all but wheel-rolling shows the contempt with which they were held. It was the rise of strong Italian city states, such as Florence and Venice, which was of more concern. However, the content of the liturgy for Corpus Christi day is not totally unrelated to features associated with midsummer. In the service, as written by Thomas Aquinas, the body of Christ is expressed through 'a corporeal under-standing of a sacramental substance' (Rubin, p. 188). This suggests that Christ was established, on a metaphysical level, as the real lord of the *été* season. Also, Thomas's hymn in the liturgy, 'Pange lingua', 'thrives on oppositions, in a manner most suited for the exploration of the paradoxes in the eucharist' (p. 193), while his sequence, 'Lauda syon', is an appeal 'to faith at the moment of doubt' (pp. 192–93). Paradox, doubt, and a distancing from Christian doctrine are all features of Chrétien's mid-summer adventures, of the *Yvain* in particular.

Chrétien was not, of course, at odds with the Church, but the genre of anti-clerical satire developed soon after and Jacquemart Giélée included a midsummer context for his attack on corruption in state and church power. And, in Renaut's *Galeran,* it is the failings of a religious woman which are attacked in midsummer free speech. Just as the people of Metz found their freedoms encroached on by empire-building Bishops, so too Fresne's future is put in jeopardy by the abbess Ermine, and repeated references to St John's Nativity remind the reader of injustices being perpetrated outside the splendour of the celebrations held on that day.

---

[49] M. Rubin, *Corpus Christi: The Eucharist in Late Medieval Culture* (Cambridge: Cambridge University Press, 1991), pp. 164–74.

CHAPTER 6

Jean Renaut's *Galeran de Bretagne*

… Tout droit a Mez en Loerraine,
Le jour de feste saint Jehan.

S cholarly knowledge of this highly readable work only dates from
1877 when the sole manuscript copy was discovered in Paris and
its qualities immediately prompted A. Boucherie to prepare an
edition.[1] Until recently, however, the identity of Renaut has often been
confused with that of Jean Renart, author of *l'Escoufle*. In the 1996
introduction to his modern French translation Jean Dufournet summarizes
the debate, giving the present-day consensus that Renaut was in fact a
different author who wrote *Galeran* between 1205–08 or 1216–20.[2]
Dufournet also shows how far from Arthurian literature *Galeran* is in
many ways. Some critics have considered it an early masterpiece of
'realism'[3] and, although Dufournet does not himself go quite so far,
Renaut's experiment with contemporary settings is handled as expertly as

---

[1] *Le Roman de Galerant, comte de Bretagne, par le trouvère Renaut, publié pour la première fois d'après le manuscrit unique de la Bibliothèque nationale*, ed. by A. Boucherie (Montpellier: Société pour l'Etude des langues romanes/Paris: Maisonneuve et Leclerc, 1888). The one other edition is *Jean Renart: Galeran de Bretagne: Roman du XIIIe siècle*, ed. by L. Foulet (Paris: Champion, 1926, repr. 1975). The *Galeran* manuscript no. is BnF MS fr. 24042.

[2] *Renaut: Galeran de Bretagne*, ed. and trans. Dufournet, pp. 8–9.

[3] R. Lejeune, *Grundriss der Romanischen Literaturen des Mittelalters*, IV. *Le Roman jusqu'à la fin du XIIIe siècle* (Heidelberg: Carl Winter, 1978), Pt 2. 'Jehan Renart et le Roman réaliste', pp. 400–453. Dufournet, pp. 9–10.

Guillaume le Clerq's later adoption of burlesque, while the subjects Renaut explores are rather more substantial.

Women's education is briefly, but thoughtfully, included; so too Galeran's psychological state of mind, and particularly brilliant are the cameos of the bourgeois world seen through the lives of Madame Blanche and her daughter, Rose, in the city of Rouen.[4] These provide moments of proto-realism in which women, too, have an active part to play, contributing to a narrative rich with paradox, dualities, conflicts and oppositions.[5] For Renaut did have one source in common with writers of Arthurian romances; he developed the possibilities of a midsummer context as fully as did Chrétien or the author of the *Perlesvaus*. Renaut may have rejected Arthurian myth (Arthur is briefly mentioned as the king 'que le chat occist')[6] but his 'penchant' for St John's day is impossible to overlook:[7] significant events in the plot happen three times at the festival of the Baptist's Nativity. And, despite the danger that repeated use of the date and its implications will produce a hackneyed series of predictable tricks, Renaut created another original and multifaceted narrative. One of his innovations is the use of 'lordship' in the city of Metz and, at the appropriate point, I will consider some possibilities for it.

Like the *Yvain,* errors associated with midsummer—arrogance, poisoned speech and the pursuit of self-exaltation—appear at a Christian festival. In *Galeran* this is Ascension and the failings are displayed by Madame Gente, a beautiful aristocrat married to the good old man Brundoré. Despite her name, she is 'plaine d'orguei' (l. 82) and another married lady in their court, Marsile, draws Gente's envy because she has the virtues Madame Gente lacks and, when the gathering compliment Marsile on her new-born twins, Madame Gente, like the bad fairy at the christening, cannot resist adding that the priest says twins can only come from two men ('ja nous die clerc ne prestre,/... deux enfans, s'avant pechié/ N'a a deux hommes et allé', ll. 158–61). However, God forgets no outrage and soon Madame Gente herself gives birth to twins, two girls

---

[4]   Faith Lyons, *Les Éléments descriptifs dans le Roman d'aventure au XIIIe siècle,* Publications Romanes et Françaises 84 (Geneva: Droz, 1965), p. 57.

[5]   Dufournet, pp. 22–26.

[6]   *Jean Renart: Galeran de Bretagne*, p. 154, l. 5071. Foulet misattributes the work to Renart, instead of to Renaut, but his line numeration is more reliable than that of other editions of the original text.

[7]   Lyons, p. 84.

born during the absence of her husband. Shamed by her own words, she has an officer, Galet, take one baby away. The other, called Flourie, is nourished with great riches, while the abandoned child descends ('Une heure fait l'enfant descendre', l. 637), unbaptized, and almost loses her life ('l'enfant.../ de fain crie', ll. 746–47). However, Galet arrives at the Abbey of Beauséjour, and leaves her under an ash tree, and the aristocratic Abbess, Ermine, adopts the child—calling her Fresne after the tree—reassured by the money in the cradle that her efforts will be rewarded.

Ermine is also fostering her nephew, Galeran, infant son of the Count of Brittany. He and Fresne share an idyllic childhood, which results in their mutual devotion; but, at the point when Galeran asks Fresne to marry him—an offer she rejects as an impossible mockery—, messengers arrive to announce the death of both of Galeran's parents. Fresne's view is proved the more accurate as, instantly, he is obliged to take up his high station in life. After many adventures, honours and, eventually believing Fresne to be lost, Galeran meets Flourie and prepares to marry her because she looks like Fresne. Hearing of the wedding, Fresne arrives at the Church wearing the shawl she was found in and singing a *lai* Galeran had composed for her. In one moment she is recognized as his true love and twin sister of the intended bride, who, fortunately, had never taken her role in the marriage too seriously.

Renaut begins their adult adventures with an explicit connection between Fortune's wheel and midsummer, incorporated in both of the ways discussed in Appendix A. For an abrupt change in status comes into conflict with the other way of interpreting her power, that is, as the wheel governing the seasons of life. This clash of opposites—natural progression against disruption—is led up to through an account of the couple's blossoming love in the early summertime of their lives. One moment the story is a romantic idyll, set 'un pou après le jour de may' (l. 1983), and the perfectly matched pair are discussing marriage, when, abruptly, a messenger arrives just after breakfast on a day of the Saint John: 'Tout qu'un jour de la saint Jehan,/... advint/ Un des haulx hommes de la terre' (ll. 2342–43). He is a high-ranking ambassador, followed by a great company of men. They prevent Galeran's move to the midsummer kingship of marriage by announcing the other change in his fortune. The world of nightingales and streams is abandoned as everyone in the Abbey defers to the influx of courtliness and the demands which the messenger brings, producing a scene full of midsummer behaviour, and dense with repetition of *hault* and *hautein*, curiously at odds with the sad message. The noble messenger, anonymous at this point, salutes the Abbess Ermine, and she wishes him the joy of the high feast day due to a powerful and honourable man ('fait joye et haulte feste/ Com a puissant hom et honeste', ll. 2363–64). The news he brings is, as he says, not good; her sister (Galeran's mother) and Count Alibran have both died suddenly, but: 'n'ayez de trop douloir cure,/ Se fortune vous est trop dure,/ Car sa rouele souvent tourne/ En tel lieu dont elle est retourne' ('do not be too sad if Fortune is harsh towards you, for the wheel often returns to the place it began and in its turn joy will replace sorrow', ll. 2376–78).

The reasoning behind his metaphor is based on the classical under-standing of Fortune's power, therefore an appropriate thought for the day, but a curious one in view of the fact that the messenger addresses a woman of the Church. However, instead of rebuking him, the Abbess responds with great cries, she faints, and on coming round, laments that she wished she were dead. Again, this is a natural response, but one more appropriate to the season, and to a secular character, like le Clerc's Galiene, than to a woman of God. The reader is also aware that behind these public histrionics lie two secret and more devastating changes of fortune, in which Renaut again uses a clash of opposites, for a rise and a fall occur at the same time. Because Galeran will rise, Fresne will fall, as happened before at her birth. She had grown secure in his company, and at this moment has to rethink her life as an abandoned child. But, instead of railing on Fortune, Fresne's distress is later expressed in appeals to God (ll. 2633–40).

From here on Galeran is constantly reminded of his need to prove himself, when all he wants, or says he wants, is to return to Fresne. The responsibility which falls on him is not, as one would expect, to rule Brittany—in fact Galeran instructs a relative, the messenger Brun de Clarent, to take charge. The demand on Galeran is first to renew his father's vassalage to the King of England, and then to prove himself worthy of support. The need for prowess is insisted on by the Abbess, who says she never thought her sister would bear a child not to be proud of. How shaming it will be if he takes the opposite path to that of valour and is, instead, seduced by a beggar girl ('Si Galeran bien ne se prueve/... Ainz est d'une garce suozprins', ll. 2979–81). The abbess has worldly values and the story which follows is based on the conflict between such goals and Galeran's love. The word *duel* is used throughout, ambigu-ously, to mean either sorrowing or a duel within himself. And much of the midsummer combat between opposites in the tale is this interior struggle. Galeran's public quest for self-exaltation and lordship is set against the integrity of his deepest thoughts, with the result that his, and Fresne's, lives are nearly destroyed. As in *Yvain*, love and worldly exaltation are at odds, though most of the pressure on Galeran to distinguish himself comes from his relations.

One has to say 'most' since a clear exception is found near the beginning. With the messenger's arrival at Beauséjour Galeran had learnt that he was '[u]n des haulx hommes de la terre' ('one of the world's great men', l. 2345); nevertheless he had promised Friar Lohier, their confidant, that 'if his reception in Brittany was good' he would come back and marry Fresne (ll. 2506–12). He is in fact received rapturously, 'com l'en doit faire a seigneur' (l. 2690), but instead of going back he becomes carried away by the glamour. Renaut writes that in the excitement of the planned visit to England, Galeran did not then think of her ('Galeren ne pensa puis d'el', l. 2698) and instead resolves to become a knight. Jean Dufournet's modern French translation interprets this line as, 'he thought of nothing else but becoming a knight'.[8] The result is the same in terms of his actions, but Renaut's original text establishes the broken promise. In England Galeran is again given a lavish welcome and the English king offers him a knighthood in his own service. But now love draws the knight home to Brittany, though he cannot make this his reason. Instead, the king of England supports a chivalric quest, with gifts of money, horses and men. Galeran returns as, 'sire de sept citez.... Sires est Galeran sans faille' (ll. 2744–49), but instead of a triumph comes an internal battle with love which crushes and torments him ('Mais or li sourt une bataille/ D'Amours qui le presse et tourmente', ll. 2750–51). The first return to Brittany when he could, perhaps, have combined position in the world with marriage to Fresne, is passed, and now set on a separate road, schizophrenia begins. At the point when he should be jousting with his fellow knights decline sets in, his health and looks deteriorate and he realizes, '[s]i je n'y voys prochainement,/ Recevoir m'en couvient la mort' ('if I don't see her soon I shall die', ll. 2784–85). He returns to Beauséjour and becomes engaged to Fresne before the priest, saying: 'Je suis cuens, vous serez contesse,/... Ainz que passé soient cinq moy,/ Vouldray pour vous chevalier estre' ('I am count, you will be countess,/

---

8 '... puis de retourner en Bretagne pour se préparer à être fait chevalier. Galeran ne se préoccupa de rien d'autre.' *Renaut: Galeran de Bretagne*, p. 71, l. 2698.

never doubt it./ But for five months I wish to be a knight for you', ll. 2868–71).

At this point both the Abbess and Brun de Clarent interpose, emphasizing that Fresne does not count in the world. Brun tells him he will ruin Brittany if he does not marry more wisely; Galeran cannot raise Fresne to his station, since he is a count and lord of land. ('Qu'il est cuens et sire de terre…/ Ne de delez Fresne lever', ll. 2929–31). And Ermine berates Galeran, on the personal level, for coming to see a foolish waif, and so turning himself into a schoolboy again—the opposite to the great man he should be. ('Qui amez une garce folle;/ S'estes revenuz a l'escolle,/ Qui a hault homme est a contraire', ll. 3011–13.) Despite these onslaughts, Galeran has to keep hold of both aims. He has no heart for his knightly quest until he obtains her picture embroidered on a sleeve. In this way his love is united with the world's chivalric demands and, comforted by her picture 'next to his heart' (l. 3276), the five month promise slips by more substantially than it did for Yvain, and Galeran follows the knightly path for seven years ('La la garda plus de sept ans', l. 3277).

Exactly one year into this quest Galeran enters Metz for his first engagement on the day of St John ('Tout droit a Mez en Loerraine,/ Le jour de feste saint Jehan', l. 3315). The repetition is half-way through the story and marks his continued ascent up the path of public good fortune. Faith Lyons points to the details with which the activities in the city are described: Galeran rides through a lively street market, where all kinds of game, fish, meat, and spices are sold, and which also includes the money-changers of Metz (ll. 3360–95). Among the city's activities are those of the knights who have arrived for the festival: ten thousand of them, coming and going in the streets on their fresh horses, looking for rooms in houses and hotels. Some take presents to the women and girls in the town, others play chess, or games of chance, in the streets (ll. 3340–50). The observer, Galeran, is also observed and admired. The citizens of Metz are said to recognize his nobility because he is so handsome and sits (or is enthroned) so well on his horse ('Qui siet sur le cheval si droiz,/ Est roys ou ducs ou quens sans doubte', ll. 3406–07). This throws up an interesting point, since in contrast to his relatives' arguments on birth and breeding, Galeran had observed that, in a strange country, it is money and rich trappings which are needed for people to treat you as a lord ('Monnoie, esterlins et besans/ a fait le jour peser et querre:/ Aller veulst en estrange terre,/… li richez est a houneur,/ Si le tiennent touz a seigneur', ll. 3278–86). The reaction in Metz bears this out and the superficial judgement, combined with the season, show Galeran as a midsummer king, whose prime of life is accentuated by his finery. The only midsummer aspect missing from him, apparently, is arrogance. He gives money to the poor knights less well accommodated in the city ('or et argent abandonne/ Aux povres chevaliers honteux/ Qui sont sejournans es hostielx', ll. 3584–86), and his aim is to be of service to the great lord, Duke Helymans, who governs both the city and this festival. The Duke also judges by appearances, observing that Galeran looks like a man of breeding ('Haulx homs me semblez au visage/ Et a l'abit et au coursage', ll. 3515–16), while Galeran retains his modesty, recalling the previous year's midsummer paradox. His parents' deaths have, he says, brought him honour ('Leur mort m'en a mis en l'onneur', l. 3526).

The next midsummer setting comes towards the end of the story. Galeran is still in Duke Helymans's service, he has been knighted, and is treated as a son by him and the Duchess. Their daughter, Esmée, is fruitlessly in love with him, but Galeran has incurred the wrath of another knight, Guyant, because unintentionally, he robbed him of her affections. The two knights find themselves in combat with each other in a tournament and in a game of chess; Guyant is humiliated each time, and his fury results in the agreement that they will hold another great combat outside Reims, '[a]ux octieves de saint Jehan' (l. 5136), to decide finally whose power is on the wane.

Following the mention of this season Esmée has '[u]n songe hideux qui l'afolle' ('a hideous dream which drives her mad', l. 5143) for through it she realizes that she has no power over Galeran. The nightmare combines St John's eve traditions with the torture of Sisyphus, as her task in it is to roll a great stone up a mountain. Once at the top it rolls down to the bottom. She tries again, and again it falls to the bottom ('elle portoit une grant mole/ Amont une montaigne sus,/ Puis la relessoit rouler jus,/ Et puis querre le revenoit/ Reporter sus li convenoit', ll. 5144–48). The dream is prophetic for, after his departure from Metz, Galeran meets Fresne's twin sister, and all dallying with Esmée ends.

The meeting with Flourie, Fresne's double, brings in further paradoxes and oppositions. Galeran's first impulse on seeing her is to kiss her twenty times, earning the rebuke from her: 'vourrez jouer come espoux' (l. 5248). On the one hand he wants to believe that Nature has recreated Fresne for him, since he can only marry her; on the other he knows that Flourie was right and 'que ses cuers faulcement veult' (l. 5513). He falls into a half-hearted wooing, deceived in his senses but clear in his mind, and the division results in increased torment, since he realizes again how much he misses Fresne. During this midsummer 'romance' he is conscious of paradoxes; he does not want 'to change the sun for the moon', but his feelings are drawn to Flourie. It is, he says, 'un merveilleux contraire' (l. 5526) and the internal duel affects him in the ensuing 2 July battle with Guyant. The sleeve with Fresne's picture in it, and tied to his lance, is now also a memento of Flourie and Galeran fixes his eyes on it rather than on his adversary but, unlike the story of Lancelot, the results are not comic. Galeran fights suicidally, expressing his despair in a challenge to Guyant put in terms of Fortune's opposites: 'Vieigne a moi jouster pour la vive,/ Et je jousteray pour la morte', (ll. 5934–35). Needless to say, Galeran wins, although wounded both emotionally and physically, for the folly of Guyant's arrogance and cowardice proves the greater handicap.

The accusation of 'playing' with Flourie could also apply to the tournament. Although put forward as a real battle in which knights are killed, it is also described as play. The two sides meet on a field 'souz un tertre' ('under a small hill', l. 5589) and the names given to Galeran's men and horses are largely allegorical, as in Huon de Mery's battle between the sins and the virtues. In Renaut's poem the names are either fantastic—the nearest to mythological unreality that the author comes to—or they are based on a horse's unbridled wildness. The list ends with Hardibras (strong arms) who never goes either to battle or a combat without two lances, and who rides a horse called Arrogance (see Appendix C).[9] Yet this is Galeran's, not Guyant's, army; therefore, one wonders whether we should hold him more responsible for events than the author superficially says. Although there is no Chateau Orgueilleux, Galeran's quest is the worst of the three listed in Chrétien's *Perceval* (see Chapter 8), and there are suggestions in Renaut's text that Guyant is not so much Galeran's opposite as his alter ego, for, despite their quarrels, they remain friends. Galeran's personality was initially split between the desires for fame and for Fresne, and the first appears to be personified in Guyant as a way of giving Galeran's selfish side a more flamboyant and outwardly vainglorious display than we actually see in the character. And his inner emotional duel is thus given an outward form through the combat between the men.

---

[9]   In Huon de Mery's *Li Tournoimenz d'Anticrit,* a similar personification, Bras-de-Fer, is a vainglorious figure who serves Antichrist.

Once Guyant is publicly put down, Galeran forces his tormented mind to marry Flourie, but Fresne's appearance at the end resolves the decline in both their personal fortunes. If there is blame on Galeran, it is limited, for the midsummer dates and his youth recall the mixture of childishness and adulthood, in which offences are pardoned. Philippe de Navarre had not yet written his *Quatre ages de l'homme*, but Abbess Ermine and Brun make similar points in their chiding of Galeran. His return to his old home to see his childhood sweetheart is, she says, the behaviour of a schoolboy finding it difficult to grow into a man ('s'estes revenu a l'escolle,/ Qui a hault homme est a contraire', ll. 3012–13), with *haut homme* providing a useful ambiguity between his new position in society and his natural adulthood.[10] There is the further irony, however, that it is Ermine who is preventing him from growing up by hindering the marriage. Galeran's initial lapse is reinforced by such influences and his behaviour acquires the changeability and untrustworthiness associated with the season in which the tale is set.

Reminders of summer are dropped into the narration throughout. The jewels in baby Fresne's basket are said to be 'belles com beau jour d'esté' (l. 446) and, on his quest, Galeran expresses his belief of returning to her 'com un cler jour d'esté' (l. 2946). When Esmée tries to amuse Galeran, she honours him with the floral chaplet from off her head: 'li fait grant feste:/ Un chapel qu'ell' a en sa teste/ Li met sur le sien et assiet' (ll. 4553–55). Flourie is christened at St Eloy's Church (l. 686)—St Eloy's day was 25 June—and, although the final wedding is only said to be on a Sunday, the bread baked for it is 'plus blans que n'est lis en esté' (l. 6790). There is too, an insistence on the title 'lord', which has been described as courtly politeness between characters,[11] but this extends to the way Fresne addresses the priest, Lohier. Her calling him 'Sire', l. 1383, and 'Biau sire', l. 1484, is as inappropriate to his vocation as it was, in the *Yvain*, attached to the name of St John the Baptist. Its inclusion in *Galeran* similarly maintains lordliness as the central midsummer issue. Further, the plot of *Galeran* develops through Fortune's reversals and antitheses, with pairs of characters repeatedly propelled in opposite directions. Sometimes Renaut creates a balance, writing of Galeran's combat with Guyant: '[s]'un y gaaigne, [sic] l'autre y pert', ('if one wins

---

[10] Similarly, Brun tries to teach Galeran that his attachment to Fresne is like that of an *enfantis*. He will not become a *hault hom* until he breaks the ties and leaves home (ll. 3050–58).

[11] Lyons, p. 61.

the other loses', l. 5870). However, the way the scales are loaded in favour of some and against others can be rather less acceptable. Fresne descends three times against the rise of someone close to her: the first at birth, again when Galeran leaves Beauséjour, and she descends for a third time as he rises higher in Metz.

For, after Galeran becomes part of Duke Helymans's court, the narrative returns to Fresne, who is waiting for him to keep his promise. For her there is no great celebratory season: 'chascun moys y va et vient' (l. 3616) and fortune continues to be jealous of her ('Or li est fortune envieuse', l. 3729), for not only does her protector, Lohier, die but Galeran's letters, which are her only contact with him, are discovered by Ermine, and Fresne's continued descent is precipitated by an explosive exchange between them.

Here the arrogance of those set above others is starkly presented. Seated on a horse, the Abbess throws contempt on Fresne for her presumption: 'Fresne, il estuet son cuer refraindre/ De chose ou l'en ne puet attaindre;/ Vous estes jaunes comme cire' ('... you must control your heart over something you cannot have. You are impressionable like wax', ll. 3775–77). Fresne meets the challenge head on and asks whether the Abbess isn't presuming on her relationship with God. Humility, Fresne retorts, is the way to the 'high house' ('Par veillier et par jeüner,/ Par aulmosne, et par oroison,/ D'aller en la haulte maison', ll. 3809–10). Ermine then attacks what she sees as Fresne's ambition to be a queen, a search which will turn her instead into a harlot. Fresne maintains her self-belief, and challenges the restrictions which deny an improvement in status to those of low birth. She will, she says, leave Beauséjour: she has not been given a humble heart ('Je ne suis mie de cuer basse', l. 3874), she has been brought up as a lady and now, '[u]n conte dont je fusse amee,/ Encor puisse je estre clamee/ Contesse et dame de grant terre!' ('if I must love a count, still it can be that I shall be called countess and lady of great lands', ll. 3887–93). This is revolutionary talk in terms of medieval society and the flyting escalates until Ermine calls Fresne a slut, prophesying that her pride and lechery will result in her being hanged from the same ash tree she was named after (ll. 3919–33). In a realistic picture of arrogance, '[l]'abbaesse, qui tant est fiere' (l. 3773), is presented in a fit of midsummer rage on a prancing horse (see Appendix C).

Scandalous language in aristocratic women of the Church might sometimes have been the reality, but I would argue that it was the midsummer examples of flytings which made this portrayal acceptable. Festive traditions allowed realities to be exposed through an artistic inversion of the norm, and examples of the lower classes challenging the authority of those above them at this season could have provided the model for Fresne's equally bold and unmaidenly response. When alone, she continues her scandalously honest thoughts, in prayer to the Virgin Mary: 'Doulce marraine, Ce siecle est plein de toute peine;/ De traÿson, d'orgueil, d'envie/... Gens y ont une fole tesche: Qui plus y est et plus y peche; le plus grant y est plain d'ordure. / Ce que chascuns petit y dure', ('... this world is so full of pain: of treason, of arrogance, of jealousy. People can be taught the fool's dictum: the greatest are full of the greatest sins. The greatest are full of filth. The lowly endure it', ll. 4015–22). Although the actual season here is not St John's Day, its laws govern the story, providing a context for railing against the high and mighty by a destitute woman. Her comments can also, indirectly, include Galeran, since, at this point, he is so content carrying her sleeve, that he is oblivious of the realities of her life.

Galeran's combats are fantastic, the verbal combat Fresne finds herself in is down to earth, and the same difference can be found in their respective departures from Beauséjour. Galeran had had a noble escort, while she leaves alone on a mule, and with no belongings except her harp with which she plans to earn her living. And, instead of meeting honour and splendour, Fresne's adventures are problematic. Through them Renaut continues to depict the nobility from the perspective of those below them, rejecting both concepts of high and low, and seeking a middle way from the bourgeoisie.

Fresne arrives in Rouen and mistakes the house of a wealthy widow for a hotel. This woman, Dame Blanche, is 'debonaire et... courtoise' (l. 4170): she has all the qualities of concerned respect lacking in the courtly women. When Fresne greets her and her daughter, Dame Blanche welcomes her warmly to the town. She asks Fresne who she is, and Fresne's reply rejects the system which dominates so much of the story. She replies, as Renaut writes, 'senée' ('wisely', l. 4184) that she has no relatives at all; she was born in neither high nor low station: 'Dame, moy ne les miens ne vant,/ Ne nes abés, ne ne les hauls' (ll. 4186–87). Despite this, she does hit the lowest point, and her courage cracks, when told the house is not a hotel and all the hotels in Rouen are full. Were it not for the bourgeois courtesy continued in Rose, who offers to share her own room with her, Fresne would be lost at the bottom of Fortune's wheel.

Her life with them has a kind of sanity lacking in Galeran's unhappy
glory. She earns her living from needlework, goes to church, takes pity on
the poor, enjoys sensible games like chess at feast days, and, for obvious
reasons, rejects suitors (ll. 4294–319). She continues the middle way:
'Trop ne se vante ne humilie' (l. 4310). Despite, or because of, this the
impression she gives is that she is an aristocrat: 'Qu'a conte soit fille ou a
roy' (l. 4323). Only when she hears of Galeran's impending marriage
does a *duel* begin in her as she laments her loss, loneliness, and low birth.
But finally reason returns: 'Je fusse sage' (l. 6494) and she puts into
action the plan of singing in the church the *lai* that only she and Galeran
know. However, even after her reconciliation with the courtly world, the
argument for moderation remains through the criticism the reader has
already read of aristocrats whose claim to superiority results in arrogance.
Dame Blanche had directed the reader's attention to this when she said
that the hotels in Rouen were full, adding that tricksters and deceivers
often snatch these services from the needy: 'Bien fait qui pour Dieu
l'ostel preste / A ceulx qui en sont besoigneux./ A maint bon toulst li
engigneux/ Et li guillierres le bienfait: Le bon souvent mescroire fait/ Li
maulvés homs que l'en houneure'.[12] This inevitably makes one reconsider
Duke Helymans's festival in Metz, with his ten thousand knights filling
its hotels.

Initially, one might ask, why did Renaut choose Metz for the centre of
courtliness in a poem written after 1205 when, from then on, Metz was
famous for its bourgeois independence? Why was Madame Blanche, with
her admirable principles, not set here instead of in Rouen? In keeping
with St John's Day principles, there does appear to be a deliberate use of
irony and inversion here, and these are more strongly inflected in the
description of Duke Helymans's control over Metz. Renault says that he
ruled the city and the surrounding region, and the feast of St John was
enjoyed by all people without grief or villainy, because he had sent in a
thousand conscripted knights to patrol the streets. Helymans was wise,
powerful and gentle, loved by high and low. He, and his ten thousand
knights in all, would be staying in the town the full eight days of the
octave, and every year they held this great court:

Le jour de feste saint Jehan./ N'a le jour en la ville enhan,/ ne villennie, ne

---

[12] 'People should, in the name of God, give hospitality to the needy. Tricksters and
deceivers have often snatched the benefits from the upright and often the good are not
believed because of the malice of those above them' (ll. 4228–33).

doulour, Car un sires de grant valleur/ Y a mil chevaliers oar ban,/ Qui tient Loerraine et Breban/ Et Bourgoigne jusqu'a Losenne;/... Honnourez et cheriz de tous,/ Et de haulx et de bas amez,/ Li dux helymans est clamez... . /Et il les huit jours a sejour/ Et chascun an y tient court grant. ll. 3316–3337.

Even without knowledge of the real situation in Metz, it is hard to believe that this sort of domination would be welcome in any city[13] and the facts regarding Metz were that secular lords as well as Church dignitaries were discouraged from living there from the beginning of the thirteenth century.[14]

However, at the end of the account of Helymans's midsummer control, Renaut adds: 'Telle feste court, ce me semble,/ Mais or est morte en nostre aage,/ Pas ne regnent li seigneurage' ('Such festive courts, it seems to me, are dead in our age: Lordship does not rule', ll. 3396–98). He presents Metz, therefore, as in a bygone age which contrasts dramatically with the present in which he is writing since, from 1205, the 24 June had been appropriated by the burghers as a symbol of their own independent lordship. The setting in Metz would appear to be an in-joke, providing two divergent readings. Renaut's courtly readers might lament over the line, 'Lordship reigns no more in our age', while wealthy burghers could see the change as an improvement. Renaut's use of St John's Day in Metz supports the argument that the burghers who had chosen that day to celebrate their civic power were conscious that they were enacting a symbolic reversal of power structure. In the same way that midsummer traditions themselves straddled festivity and politics, there is a political element to this romance, and the fact that such a well-written piece appears not to have been widely disseminated could indicate that it brought trouble to its author.

Renaut is also surprisingly open in his use of secular belief in Fortune and her cycle, with references to her kept separate from shameful falls into a valley. Fresne's place of birth was on a hilltop, called Roche Guyon, but Galet's departure from there is given no geographical placing yet, when Madame Gente insults Marsile, Brundoré's honour is said to be 'avallé... à terre de honte' (ll. 162–63), and when Galeran fights Guyant, that dubious character is discovered downhill. Galeran's courtesy prevents him from taking unfair advantage: 'Je suis amont et vous aval;/

---

[13] See this treated ironically in Huon de Mery, below, p. 168.

[14] See Nicholas, *The Later Medieval City*, p. 104.

n'aiez paour qu'ainsi vous fiére' (ll. 5990–91).

However, these terms are not applied to the lovers' opposite sets of adventures. In contrast to the structure of the *Yvain*, where the high road to power and glory in the first half leads to Yvain retracing his steps in shame and humility in the second, in Renaut's tale there is no simple contrast between self-glorification and self-abasement. Galeran finds himself uncomfortable on the high road and Fresne rejects the concept of hers as low. And, although there can be no happy resolution for Fresne without the discovery of her family, yet she consistently puts forward revolutionary, classless ideas. Before the interruption of her Maytime idyll with Galeran, she had prayed to God that a way might be found for a sensible woman of low birth to marry above her. The only shame in such marriages, she argues, is if the woman is foolish: 'Honte prent qui prent femme folle,/ Si se desconfist et afolle;/ Mais femme sage, c'est li voirs,/ Vault mieulx que parage n'avoirs'.[15] And at the end of the tale, Fresne achieves this for Rose, finding her a husband from the nobility (ll. 7790–93). The continual questioning of divisions in society in this romance would seem only possible in a context of midsummer inversion where traditions of free speech allowed the expression of the unthinkable. Yet, the section where the middle class provides the example of aristocratic virtue is in a setting suggestive of realism rather than of inversion. As with the subject of lordship in Metz, it is possible that readers from different classes perceived different meanings or, as already suggested, possibly Renaut's work was found a touch too challenging.

St John's day principles were as central to Romance literature as they were to be three-and-a-half centuries later, in England, in Renaissance Drama. Despite its semi-pagan cosmology ruled by Fortune, there appears to have been an open-minded approach to traditional customs in the twelfth and thirteenth centuries, one which mirrors the open-minded observations of Churchmen such as John Beleth and William Durand.[16] The result was highly creative works of literature which could be entertaining as well as moral, and *Galeran* stands out, along with *Yvain*, and *Erec and Enide,* as a romance which is no less interesting for its lack

---

[15] 'Shame is brought by choosing a foolish woman: that is the way to unhappiness and ruin. But the truth is that a wise woman is of more value than high birth and riches' (ll. 1911–14).

[16] Mimesis, too, was sanctioned by the Church in the twelfth century, before being attacked again in the fourteenth. *Tretise of Miraclis Pleyinge,* ed. by C. Davidson (Kalamazoo: Western Michigan University, Medieval Institute Publications, 1988), p. 11.

of frivolity. Instead of the wit of Chrétien, Renaut provides psychological complexities and in some ways his touches of realism provide a closer point of contact for the present-day reader when, for example, the liberties of seasonal licence are used to show a convincing quarrel, rather than the more absurd insults of Kay.

CHAPTER 7

Bourgeois Satire

Adam de la Halle's Jeu de la Feuillée *4 June, 1276.*

'... c'est une veritable *sotie'*

Gaston Paris

Gustav Cohen, however, considered *Le Jeu de la Feuillée* a play appropriate to St John's eve because it is the fairies in it who provide the focal point. The first of May and Pentecost were also possibilities, yet Cohen thought St John's Nativity, a time 'dedicated to Nature cults', was the more likely.[1] Despite this, there is nothing unworldly in Adam's writing: mortals do not experience the transcendental; rather it is the fairies who are metamorphosed, taking on human characteristics and even failings.[2] Their urbanization produces behaviour opposite to that expected of fairies, but it is in keeping with the tone of Adam's city farce, as commented on by Jean-Claude Aubailly[3] and by Richard Axton, who wrote that the night-time setting, during which the townspeople of Arras wait for the fairies to appear, is a kind of Watch ✓

---

[1]   G. Cohen, *Le théâtre en France au Moyen Âge* (Paris: Rieder, 1931), vol. 2, p. 19, and J. Rony, *Le 'Jeu de la Feuillée': texte et traduction* (Paris: Bordas, 1969), pp. 6–7.

[2]   H. Braet, 'Désenchantement et Ironie Dramatique chez Adam de la Halle', in *Between Folk and Liturgy,* ed. by A. J. Fletcher and W. Hüsken (Amsterdam: Rodopi, 1997), pp. 89–95.

[3]   J.-C. Aubailly, *Le théâtre médiéval profane et comique* (Paris: Larousse, 1975), p. 29.

and 'the Midsummer show in medieval Chester was known as 'the Watch'.[4]

There are, among these comments, promising signs of a midsummer date for the play's original presentation but, in fact, these are not realized. The performance has now been established as 4 June 1276, when it was put on overnight by the Puy of Arras during a '*grand siège* of jongleurs and bourgeoisie'.[5] Yet, Cohen and Axton do identify midsummer features in it, and a closer look at the organization of Arras's summer entertainments provides a useful background. The Puy, of which Adam was a member, was the élite, but not the sole, literary society: the second was the Confrérie of minstrels and bourgeoisie. The Puy elected its leader, or Prince, on 1 May and the Confrérie held its annual celebration on 14 August, the eve of the Assumption of the Virgin Mary.[6] The Puy was a secular society but, since the Confrérie was a Marian foundation, it is not surprising to find that her Assumption into heaven provided their annual focal point. Therefore, while the secular celebration of the Puy was held on the day which traditionally began the secular summer season, the religious celebration of the Confrérie fell two weeks before the time when such summer festivities usually ended. The meetings of the two societies appear to have given Arras the *termini a quo* and *ad quem* for its summer liberties and *Le Jeu de la Feuillée* was performed almost half-way between. It could well have been written as a composite summer play, combining all possibilities appropriate to the period, with the May theme of love mingled with St John's day eccentricities, not unlike the mixture in Chrétien's *Erec and Enide*.

The acting area for the play is one '"open" in every sense; characters appear to "enter" from the street and to "exit" to real places nearby',[7] and

---

[4]   R. Axton, *European Drama of the Early Middle Ages* (London: Hutchinson, 1972), p. 147.

[5]   R. Berger, 'Le *Jeu de la Feuillée*. Quelques notes', in *Arras au Moyen-Age: histoire et littérature,* ed. by M.-M. Catellani and J.-P. Martin (Arras: Artois Presses Universitaires, 1994), pp. 221–22.

[6]   See J. Dufournet, *Adam de la Halle: à la recherche de lui-même, ou le jeu dramatique de la feuillée* (Paris: SEDES, 1974), p. 224, and R. Axton, p. 145.

[7]   R. Axton and J. Stevens, *Medieval French Plays* (Oxford: Blackwell, 1971), p. 210. The stage used was probably the public square known as *la place de la fuellie* (Mad Square) because it was the setting for events which ranged from the most sacred to the most damning: the display of sacred relics and public executions. The word *feuillée* in the title could be folly, or refer to the canopy of leaves placed over the shrine of Notre Dame, when it was set in the square between Pentecost and the Assumption.

the content of the play is a mixture of fantasy and fact. Fictional
characters, such as the fairies and the mad fool, were probably played by
members of the town's literary societies, but named figures from Arras's
society seem to have been performed by those people themselves, who
entered the acting area to be ridiculed by their neighbours before making
way for the next 'victim'. For the dominating feature of Adam's play,
other than the visit from the fairies, is free speech by the townspeople
about each other. Petit de Julleville described the text as 'a mordant satire
in which all the people of Arras feature, each to be ridiculed in his turn...
an Aristophanaic comedy in its bitterness and licence: and similar, too, in
its sparkling fantasy and a capricious unruliness in the incoherent
design.'[8] The word 'incoherent' is one way to account for the play's lack
of plot development, but Axton and Stevens see in this a revue style
intended to present 'a fantastic hotchpotch of characters and themes' in a
series 'of formal set pieces or "turns", commenting on topical issues'.[9]
The personalized line of attack is acceptable entertainment because the
author makes himself the opening target: this may be Adam's play but, in
it, his ambitions are seen as pride and pretension, and they are treated as
the central subject for ridicule.

His first assertion is that he will leave his newly-married wife and
return to Paris to continue a literary career so as to prove that his
ambitious talk was not empty boasting: 'Or ne porront pas dire aucun que
j'ai antés/ Que d'aler a Paris soie pour nient vantés'.[10] Adam, therefore,
shows the same self-centred concern for fame as that shown by Yvain,
and he is even more explicit than Gawain in describing the encumbrance
that a wife can be to a husband's pursuit of honour. Further, he puts this
in terms of a progression through the seasons, from the first delight in
love in early summer to midsummer disillusionment, and including the
heat recently identified by Philippe de Navarre as part of a young man's
own disposition. Adam declares:

> Car pris fu ou premier boullon,
> Tout droit en le varde saison
> Et en l'aspreche de jouvent,

---

[8]   L. Petit de Julleville, *Les comediens en France au Moyen Age* (Paris: Cerf, 1885), p.
48.

[9]   Axton and Stevens, *Medieval French Plays*, p. 211.

[10]   *Adam de la Halle: Œuvres complètes,* ed. P.-Y. Badel (Paris: Librairie Génerale
Française, 1995), p. 286, ll. 5–6.

> Ou li cose a plus grant saveur,
> Car nus n'i cache sen meilleur
> Fors chou qui li vient a talent.
> Esté faisoit bel et seri,
> Douc et vert et cler et joli,
> Delitavle en chans d'oiseillons,
> En haut bos pres de fontenele
> Courans seur maillie gravele.
> Adont me vint avisions
> De cheli que j'ai a feme ore,
> Qui or me sanle pale et sore.
> Adont estoit blanke et vermeille,
> Rians, amoureuse et deugie.
> Or le voi crasse, mautaillie,
> Triste et tenchans. (ll. 57–74)

(I was taken at the moment I boiled,/ Right in the middle of the green season/ And in the rebelliousness of youth/ When 'that thing'[11] tastes most strongly,/ And when what's good for you is obscured/ By what you fancy./ The summer was beautiful and serene/ 'Soft and green, cloudless, lovely,/ Ringing with the song of birds.'/ In the hilltop forest close to a spring/ Which rippled over the pebbles/ There, I had a vision/ Of the girl who is now my wife/ 'And seems so pasty and dull./ Then she was all white and rosy'/ Laughing, loving and refined./ Now I find her crass, ill-dressed,/ And a bad-tempered scold.)

This progress from early delight to contempt is completed with a metaphor of kingship, expressing the magical, yet delusory, power of love, able to turn a ragamuffin into a queen ('une truande... une roïne', ll. 85–86). Adam's complete reversal in his feelings for the woman, once his wife, is very like the post-Pentecost metamorphosis in Erec. As Shakespeare's Rosalind was to say, 'Maids are May when they are maids, but the sky changes when they are wives' (*As You Like It*, IV. 1. 140–41). Folie, too, in *La Folie des Gorriers* claims: 'I make lovers dance and revile each other, all in a summer'.[12]

The only support for Adam comes from his father. His companions reward him with jeers and the insult of 'lout' ('caitis', l. 12), commenting

---

[11] Translations in quotation marks are by Axton and Stevens.

[12] *'Je fais dancer les amoureux/ Et despandre dans un esté.'* La Folie des Gorriers, ll. 152–53. *Recueil général des sotties,* ed. by E. Picot, SATF (Paris: Didot, 1902), I, p. 151. See heading to chapter 3.

that he suffers great delusions ('grans abusions', l. 15). Adam complains of being mocked, yet the fairy, Maglore, takes up the same derisive role and wishes that Adam,

> ... qui se va vantant
> D'aler a l'escole a Paris,
> Voeil qu'i soit si atruandis [the same insult as that Adam used about his wife]
> En le compaignie d'Arras
> Et qu'il s'ouvlit entre les bras
> Se feme, qui est mole et tenre,
> Si qu'il perge et hache l'aprenre
> Et meche se voie en respit. (ll. 684–91)

(... who boasts/ that he's going to go and study in Paris/... becomes utterly infamous through his Arras associates, and that he so forgets himself in the arms of his soft and tender wife that he neglects and ruins his studies, and abandons his planned road.)

There could hardly be a less fortunate intervention for his youthful, midsummer ambitions. The man with the leading role, as author and character, is subjected to the greatest contempt, which is further endorsed by the otherworld intervention. And Maglore's intensification of the bickering in the town, through her fortune-telling, also includes an attack on the town's privileged élite.

For, in contrast with the freedoms gained in Louvain and Metz, the *échevins* remained in control of thirteenth-century Arras, and had adopted the exploitative traits of feudal society towards the bourgeoisie,[13] 'governing the town solely in their own interests'[14] and taxing its citizens to line their own pockets. Dissatisfaction culminated in a rebellion in 1285, which took place in the same 'mad' square where Adam's play had been performed. The riot took place at Pentecost and was as violent and ineffective as the later Pentecost rebellion in Lyon.[15]

---

[13] See J. Dufournet, *Adam de la Halle: à la recherche de lui-même*, pp. 225–31, and M. Ungureanu, *La Bourgeoisie naissante: société et littérature bourgeoises d'Arras aux XIIᵉ et XIIIᵉ siècles* (Arras: Centre National de la Recherche Scientifique, 1955), pp. 37–40.

[14] '[...] dans le seul intérêt de leur caste'. Ungureanu, p. 39. R. Berger disagrees with this assessment, but he does not attempt to explain the unrest in Arras. See *Littérature et société Arrageoises au XIIIe siècle.* (Arras: Commission Départmentale, Pas-de-Calais, 1981), p. 95.

[15] See Ungureanu, pp. 69 and 53 and Chapter 1, above.

Adam's play of 1276 has been seen as part of the growing unrest and, though it clearly did not intend to ferment insurrection, it did identify and hold up to ridicule the most disliked patrician families, by displaying them as figures on the wheel of Fortune brought in by the fairies. When the identity of these figures is asked the good fairy dare not answer, but Maglore claims that her declared wish to speak ill provides a permit. It is as though licensed-fool indemnity is announced before she names two of the town's *échevins*, Sir Ermenfroi Crespin and Jacques Louchard, who have been set up in honour on this wheel. Each man is a king in his own domain: 'Mis les a Fortune en honnour./ Chascuns d'aus est en sen lieu rois' (ll. 792–93). A third, more sympathetic figure, Thomas de Bourriane, is falling from top to bottom, pushed off by the two 'escars' ('misers', l. 796). Another unhappy prognosis follows, this time for the town of Arras for, Maglore continues, 'Au mains regnent il maintenant/ Et leur enfant sont bien venant/ Qui raigner vauront aprés euls' ('the two men reign at the moment and their children are coming along well. They intend to reign after them', ll. 797–99).

Other figures mocked by both citizens and visitors range from the pantomime figure of loose-living Dame Douce, to those Popes responsible for Adam's uncomfortable financial predicament as a married cleric, taxed as other citizens, even though lacking the necessary income. Adam's father points out the imperfections of the system, and Gillos brings the subject to a conclusion, playing with the concepts of fortune, death, and a fall: 'Li papes qui en chou eut coupes/ Est eüreus quant il est mors./ Ja ne fust si poissans ne fors/ C'ore ne l'eüst desposé!' ('The Pope who was to blame is fortunate to be dead, for no matter how powerful and strong he had been, he would have been deposed!' ll. 462–65) One of the three Popes who have been identified as possibilities was Alexander IV, who died on 25 June 1261.[16]

Another figure given the 24 June treatment is Robert Sommeillon, the newly-elected Prince of the Puy in Arras, and for whom the fairy, Morgue, languishes in admiration. Robert, she claims, is an example of the best in chivalry. He jousts everywhere ('amont et aval', l. 722) in her name at meetings of the round table knights.[17] Fairy Crokesos deflates this ideal with appropriate midsummer accusations, saying that Robert boasted of his affair with Morgue, so putting her fairy-husband, Hellekin,

---

[16] Ungureanu, pp. 99–100.

[17] The Puy of Arras held round-table tournaments. See Axton, *European Drama*, p. 144.

in a jealous rage and, as an invisible supernatural agent, he then caused Robert's horse to stumble so that Robert fell off, dishonoured, in the lists (ll. 732–41). This fate is, however, the familiar reward for pride and lechery (see Figs 11–13). And despite the charges Morgue continues to defend Robert against those whom she calls mockers (ll. 732–42).

There is a possibility that the poetry competition discussed in the play is to take place on 24 June. The fool says this is yet to be held by the Puy, which would mean after 4 June, and the claim is made that one Master Walter will be acclaimed king at it:

> A sen Pui canchon faire doit,
> Par droit, maistre Wautiers As Paus…
> L'autr'ier vanter les en oï.
> Maistre Wautiers ja s'entremet
> De chanter parmi le cornet
> Et dist qu'il sera courounés. (ll. 408–09, 412–15)

> ('In his Puy they've got to put on/ The songs of Master Walter-aux-Paus… I heard them boasting the other day:/ Master Walter was practising/ To play a tune on his instrument;/ He reckons to get the winner's crown!' Axton and Stevens, p. 227.)

The fourteenth of August can be ruled out, since this was when the Confrérie met. But, as Master Walter boasted about his future kingship, one is reminded of other literary examples in which boasting is connected with a midsummer-day elevation, and the possibility arises that the Arras Puy elected the king of their poetry competition on the day of St John the Baptist's Nativity.

The saint of the play's proceedings, however, is the mythical St Acaire, patron saint of fools[18] and, through this stalking horse, men of the Church receive equal derision. St Acaire's relics are filched from the profiteering monk and the fool is summoned by his father to adore his patron saint. But the fool's filial reply is splenetic insult: 'Fiex a putain! Leres! Erites!/ Creés vous la ches ypocrites?/ Laissée[s] m'aler, car je suis roi!' ('Heretic, robber, son of a bitch! Do you believe those hypocrites? Let me alone for I am a king', ll. 393–95). Later, after the monk has regained the relics on payment for the night's drinking, St Acaire is further mocked in parodic reverence for his intervention in assuaging the watchers' thirst (ll. 1008–24). Yet the drinking scene, itself, had provided another quarrelsome episode, with Guillos rebuked for slandering the wine

---

[18] Ungureanu, p. 93.

(l. 944) and Adam criticized for no longer eating with them. Because he has set his sights on being a student he acts as though he is now 'above' everyone else (l. 948).

As this brief account shows, every episode in this play contains quarrelsome accusations of pride and corruption at every level of society, as found in epitaphs and slanders, and they become comic through their profusion and variety. Adam is the central protagonist, both as a mocker of marriage and of the town, and also in being central to the mockery. He has the midsummer qualities of youth: 'Biaus fiex, fors... et legiers' (l. 196). These produce disloyalty and selfish ambition, but, like Renaissance satirists, Adam's own failings give him a clear perception of the failings of others,[19] including those in political power above him. As in many works which reflect midsummer traditions, liberty is taken to oppose perceived injustices, and those of the *échevins* are embedded— possibly for safety's sake—in satire on every aspect of Arras's life.

Midsummer features in Sotties *and* Farces.

As critics since Gaston Paris have noted, there is much in common between Adam's play and the fifteenth- and sixteenth-century Shrovetide theatre. Adam's 'emphasis on folly, [the play's] bizarre stock characters and its shrewd satire of the ecclesiastical and civic establishments... anticipates by two centuries the Parisian law clerks' theatre of the *basoche.*'[20] *Sotties* and *farces* were also written in an episodic, revue style, and they contained mocking comments on individuals as well as on society in general. For example, in *Farce joyeuse des Galans et du Monde*, the third Gallant says: 'Plus nyais que jeunes moysons/ Nous sommes tous troys' ('All three of us are more naive than young moysons').[21] Picot suggests that *moysons* could have been used instead of *moines* because it was the name of someone from Rouen society whom the author wished to mock.[22] However, the example is interesting for its inclusiveness: the gallants do not attack the inflated pretensions of the

---

[19] See A. Kernan, *The Cankered Muse* (New Haven: Yale University Press, 1959), pp. 155–57.

[20] Axton, *European Drama,* p. 144.

[21] *Farce joyeuse des Galans et du Monde*, ll. 37–38. Picot, *Recueil,* I, pp. 11–46.

[22] Ibid., p. 17, n. 2.

character discussed, but instead diminish their own stature by comparing themselves to him. In the *mundus inversus* of carnival festivities folly is shared, and the point of *sotties* is to present the audience with this universality, as a mirror in which to recognize themselves.

Yet, in *Les Menus Propos*, 'St John, who liked the solitary life' ('sainct Jehan, qui la veult sengler'),[23] is included along with reference to 'karesme prennant' ('Shrovetide', l. 41), and a study of other *sotties* leads to the conclusion that there was no watertight division of subject matter: midsummer characters and themes might be inserted along with those of carnival. I have already pointed to the comment in *La Folie des Gorriers* on the changeable nature of lovers during their summer season, and one recurring character in *sotties*, whom I would suggest was based on midsummer literary precedent, is Mundus—appearing as the character, Le Monde. Mundus symbolized the peak of all possible material well-being and was characterized as a rotund figure flourishing in an abundance of riches. In *Mundi inversi,* however, he is appropriately powerless against the follies of a society which abuses his wealth. In the *Farce Joyeuse*, above, his cumbersome girth puts him at a disadvantage as the three gallants mock and flatter him for his riches, his high growth, calling him a master in his doublet whose good days are not yet over.[24] The ineptitude of these parasites is foretold in the fact that they travel to see Le Monde on mules, rather than horses ('Nos chevaulx?/ Ilz sont trop dyvers;/ Nous avrons chascun une mule', ll. 66–68). Le Monde sees through them and they quarrel, but it is Order who sends the gallants away to the Abbey of Frevaulx—'Cold Valleys' (l. 397). A similar moral lies behind *Farce nouvelle moralisée: des Gens Nouveaulx qui mengent le monde et le logent de mal en pire*[25] though with a more damning conclusion. *Gens nouveaulx*, new men in power, use the cyclic argument to justify their unprincipled rise, claiming that the previous reign is over, and each man must reign in his time:

> Le Premier: Gouverner, tenir termes haulx,/ Regenter a nostre appetit/
>   Par quelques moyens bons ou faulx:/ Nous avons du temps ung petit.
> Le Second: Les vieulx ont regné, il souffit;/ Chascun doit rener [sic] a

---

[23] Ibid., p. 66, l. 17.

[24] *Farce Joyeuse à cinq personnages: troys galans, le Monde qu'on faict paistre et Ordre.* Rouen *c.* 1445, Picot, I, pp. 37–38, ll. 299–314.

[25] *Circa* 1461. Picot, I, pp. 119–36. André Tissier includes it under the genre mentioned in its title in his *Recueil de Farces (1450–1550)*, IV (Geneva: Droz, 1989), pp. 299–342.

son tour.' (ll. 25–30.)

Monde has no champion, and cannot prevent their taking him *aval* (l. 245), first to the city of Bad and then to the city of Worse.

However, the fullest summer theme associated with Monde is found in the Toulouse play, the *Sotise à huit personnaiges*, by André de la Vigne, which Picot concluded must have been performed during the 1507 carnival.[26] Yet, near the opening, Sot Abus scorns Le Monde with the comment that: 'you've been somewhere this summer where they've turned your head' ('croys moi que tu as esté/ En quelque lieu a cest esté/ Ou l'en ta tourné ton serveau', ll. 97–99); and this suggests that the summer rather than the winter season was the time of performance. The play also contains several features of the feast of St John's Nativity, with references to a saint of that name and, unlike the earlier political satire, *Sottie de l'Astrologue,* played in the autumn of 1498,[27] *Sotise à huit personnaiges* names public figures in its accusations.

It is Le Monde, rather than the *sots,* who provides narrative comment, and he begins by describing a summer context. God, he says, has rewarded him with a lustrous sun and all the riches of the earth. The world could be God's original Paradise, for the young live in it vigorously without effort: 'D'ung beau soleilh luysant me guerdonna;/ Tel guerdon ne a le Monde en ses desportz;/.... Fruitz, grands apportz, chevaulx, beufs, asnes, porcz;/ Et sans effortz demeurent toutz es fortz/ Et jeunes...'.[28] However, the world is the opposite to Paradise since a fouler form of man, 'l'humain qu'est tout immonde' (l. 15), flies to be outdoors, joining in various games of chance. The fields are his garden, where he cultivates dirty vices. With his companions they put themselves beyond control. ...if mankind is blind to remorse... he will say as he contemplates death: "What a sorry figure is poor World"' ('il s'en fuyt d'este hors,/ Donnant a sortz par bien divers assortz,/ Ses champs, ses ortz a nourrir vices ortz,/ En ses consors se mectant hors de bonde.... a tout les vivens grandz remortz/ Quant j'aré mortz leur corps tant furibonde/ Alors diront, roghant leurs ruddes mortz....' ll. 21–27). This appears to be an onslaught against summer customs, similar to those Claude de Rubys said took place in Lyon, and which Jacques Bruneau implied happened in the fields outside Angers. The field in which de la Vigne sets the play itself

[26] Picot, II (Paris: Didot, 1904), p. 12.

[27] Ibid. I, pp. 198–99.

[28] Ibid., II, p. 22, ll. 10–15.

provides the argument, for the audience sees a potential paradise turned into an extension of hell. Despite Le Monde's apparent authority in the opening speech, he is powerless against Sot Abus and his companions, who act out the pastoral iniquities Le Monde had described. Abus boasts to Le Monde that his own work has rejuvenated and made green le Monde's trees—'Hé! n'ay je pas par ma labour/ Amprès de tes branches ensiennes,/ Affin que plus longuement tiennes,/ Faict venir tous ces arbres vers?' (ll. 41–44)—but when Abus goes to gather the fruit, shaking the six trees, a Vice drops down from each. The tree of Dissolution produces Sot Dissolu, dressed as a churchman; Sot Glorieux, a man of war, emerges from the hot tree; Corruption lets fall Sot Corrompu, a lawyer; Deceit produces Sot Trompeur, a merchant; Ignorance, Sot Ignorance, a natural fool; and finally, the Tree of Folly produces a female *sotte* of that name and the angriest of them all. They wake the World to mock at him and display his gross rotundity, commenting that King Pepin did not have so sudden a rise and fall as he,[29] and that they should do away with him so that the next king can rise: 'Le roy Pepin/ Ne fut honc si subite escheue./ Or.../ Necteyons pour l'autre avancer' (ll. 489–92). Sot Dissolu claims that they will be 'deaf to the world's comments, proud, ignorant, and extortionate, to empty the world of everything, following Abus's orders' ('Ainz estourdiz, fiers, ruddes, estordis,/ Tous desgordiz d'accomplir tes [Abuz'] preceptes', ll. 508–09). Monde laments that fools, folly, and rebellion put the world to derision (ll. 420–21) before he is taken to Derision's house, beaten, and dragged to Confusion where he is lost until the Sots' own decline at the end of the play. This opening satire is inclusive, exposing folly in all professions; later the targets become specific.

Once the old World is removed the *sots* set about devising a new one, with each Vice putting forward his own method of folly as the founding principle: the lawyer argues for paper, the merchant for scales and the man of war for lances, but all agree that the name of the New World will be Confusion. They themselves form its pillars, climbing up onto six raised areas. At one point Sotte Folie slips and the comment is: 'Elle tumbe... Par sainct Jehan, elle ne vit plus!' (ll. 637–38). This is one of three references to a Saint John, all in the same section of the play, and,

---

[29] Picot translates 'escheue' as 'succession', derived from 'eschoite' or 'escheute'. However, the *Dictionnaire de l'ancienne langue française, et de tous ses dialectes du IXe au XVe siècle* (Paris; Vieweg, 1884) translates 'escheue' as 'esseve', or flowing away. It is possible that the skilful rhetorician, de la Vigne, intended both meanings in the one word.

since their discussion here is gossip about individual churchmen and statesmen (some of whom are named), the mention of St John appears to invoke the appropriate seasonal licence for free speech. Eventually, Sotte Folie provokes the men into a leaping competition, to prove who serves her best. The competition degenerates into fisticuffs and the New World, which they were supporting, falls and is broken. The *Sots* are driven to finding somewhere other than the world in which to live—hell is suggested—while Le Monde has the final word in a repeated moral refrain against depending on the temporary pleasures of this world: 'Ce n'est pas jeu que se fier au Monde:/ Bien est deceu qui se fie en ce Monde' ('Worldly pride is not a game; Who trusts in the World is deceived', ll. 1539–40, 1552–53, 1565–66, and 1572–73).

World, here, is the Order figure, expelled for the duration of his *inversus*. It is he who provides the detached comment while the *sots* are completely absorbed in the blind arrogance of the young and strong. Seasonal, youthful aberration is here used in an open, condemnatory way to symbolize Vice. And, instead of the free movement and speech between 'actors' and 'townspeople' as in *Jeu de la Feuillée,* a more formal concept of the Speculum is maintained: on their entry each *sot* mingles with the audience to comments from Abus that he'll find his like among them. The inverted world provides a mirror image of the real world, symbolic of it but theatrically separate from it.

Both seasons could be used to expose failings[30] and Ian Donaldson's understanding of the Carnival method of writing could also describe Adam de la Halle's play for, there too, society is shown 'collapsing under the strain of scandalous and widespread folly and ineptitude, centred in those traditionally thought to be society's pillars'.[31] However, not even in the *Sotise à Huit Personnaiges* is there quite the same face-to-face, comic bickering of Adam's play. Much of the *Jeu de la Feuillée* is dramatized slander, a fact which characters under attack repeatedly protest against. The play is a unique scripted survivor from medieval summer games before they were assimilated into other forms, and an example of pure midsummer truth-telling. It could also be called the cultural opposite to the twelfth century Arras play, the *Jeu de St. Nicholas,* which 'reconciles'

---

[30] Pierre Gringore's *Sottie contre le Pape Jules II* is one of the most outspoken and was performed on Shrove Tuesday 1512. Yet, even with the protection of Louis XII, Mère Sotte plays Mère saincte Église only, not the Pope by name.

[31] I. Donaldson, *The World Upside-Down: Comedy from Jonson to Fielding* (Oxford: Clarendon Press, 1970), p. 8.

classes, 'celebrates' 'the pursuit of profit', and depicts 'social relations...
as harmonious and mutually dependent'.[32] In contrast, Adam exposes rifts
within the élite bourgeoisie as well as between it and the rest of the town;
rifts are also shown between competing members of the Confrérie and
Puy, and between the author and the rest of the town. Adam's meaning
and method are not unlike those of Woody Allen in *Deconstructing
Harry*.

---

[32] C. Sponsler, 'Festive Profit and Ideological Production', in *Festive Drama*, ed. by M.
Twycross (Cambridge: D. S. Brewer, 1996), pp. 66–79 (pp. 73–75).

SECTION IV:

The Moral Perspective

CHAPTER 8

Midsummer Satires of Pride

En tous tamps y faisoit esté./ Jamais n'avroie devisé/ La richece Orguel le meschin.

La Vie d'Enfer...

Pride is the feature common to midsummer lords and ladies in the works considered so far, yet, up to and including *Le Jeu de la Feuillée*, the result has been secular entertainment not moral lesson. Enjoyment of this vice, of course, comes from the well-known belief that it precedes a fall. A character's arrogance is combined with error of judgement which ensures his or her downfall in degrees ranging from comic humiliation to total destruction. In the most symbolic examples the character is a clown, heedless of an obvious reality with which (s)he then collides: a formula found even in the work considered the basis for medieval moral allegory, Prudentius's fourth-century *Psychomachia*. In this, Pride loses her battle when her wild charge ends in a pit dug by her own forces:

> ... shouting, she now spurs her swift war horse,
> And dashes madly forward with loose reins...
> But quick she falls into a hidden pit,
> Deceit had slyly dug across the field.[1]

It is a curious paradox that during the Middle Ages pride was viewed as the chief sin and therefore the most dangerous[2] yet, in allegory, it is

---

[1] Prudentius, *Psychomachia*, ll. 253–58, trans. by Sister M. Clement Eagen, *The Poems of Prudentius*, II (Washington: Catholic University of America Press, 1965), p. 89.

[2] M. W. Bloomfield, *The Seven Deadly Sins* (East Lansing, MI: Michigan State College

usually portrayed as carrying these seeds of self-destruction which undermine the threat. Prudentius's personification lacks even the threatening
appearance found in later portrayals of Antichrist, since she comes to the
battle decorated with useless ornaments.[3] It is possible that continued
confidence in pride's inherent weakness allowed for its playful treatment
in the later romances, for the combination of flamboyance and error in
Méléagant and Kay is not unlike that in Prudentius's Superbia.[4] Chrétien
also includes abstract personifications called Pride, minor characters who
often point to the same flaw in major ones, for example, Orguillious de la
Lande in *Erec and Enide*, a post-Pentecost symbol of arrogance who is
defeated by the up-and-coming contender for the title.

However, the most interesting use of such personifications is in
Chrétien's last romance, *Perceval*, written about 1182.[5] In this there are
two figures with the name—one male, one female—and one might expect
some serious moral comment since they are integrated into the story's
thematic development, but instead Pride, particularly Orguelleus de la
Lande, is a cipher incorporated into a seasonal context in such a way that
it is the seasonal attributes which dominate over the moral and this may
explain why the author of the moral *Vie des Pères* disliked the work. But,
because of its playfulness, *Perceval* provides a clear example of a work
which uses pride as a central theme, in a non-judgemental way.

The incomplete tale begins in spring: 'at that season when trees burst
into leaf and grass, woodland and meadows grow green; when in the
morning the birds sing sweetly in their own tongue and every living thing
is fired with joy' (Owen, p. 375). Perceval himself is newly fledged from
his mother's care. He is a rustic fool on pilgrimage to courtliness, but his
rough ignorance encounters aspects of courtly arrogance and pride along
the way, from the good-humoured contempt of the first knights (ll. 231–
50) to Kay's more pointed abuse, and finally to the defeat of pride's
personification, Orguelleus de la Lande. The season mentioned before
this combat is Pentecost, which is held in proper solemnity at Arthur's
court and, up until this, Perceval had had meteoric success. But when the

---

Press, 1952), pp. 145 and 183.

[3]   See B. McGinn, 'Portraying Antichrist in the Middle Ages'.

[4]   Bloomfield does not include Arthurian literature. See *The Seven Deadly Sins,* pp. 108
and 120.

[5]   *Perceval ou le conte du graal*, ed. by Jean Dufournet (Paris: Flammarion, 1997),
introduction, p. 11.

action continues his fortune swiftly changes from good to bad. He is shunned and locked out of the castle where the previous evening he had been welcome, and in the forest the subject of death is introduced when he finds a girl lamenting the slaying of her young man (l. 3640). She tells Perceval that his Mother, whose health he had prayed for at Pentecost, has also died, of grief, because he did not return to see her. At this point, Perceval's own grief is limited. After hoping his Mother's soul is with God, he shows a carelessness, or arrogance, towards matters of life and death: 'since she is put in the earth, why should I search further?' ('Et puis que ele est mise an terre,/ Que iroie je avant querre?' ll. 3621–22). The girl, too, is changeable in her advice on whether or not he should pursue the murderer of her lover, who turns out to be Orguelleus. This section of post-Pentecost change sits between two references to fortune: the girl calls Perceval 'mesavantureus' in line 3584, while, after the combat with Orguelleus, Perceval wishes his now humble opponent 'bone avanture' (l. 3992). Therefore, the nadir to Perceval's and the maiden's adventures is when each has a high-summer encounter with Orguelleus, who 'nule chose ne demande/ Se bataille non et meslee' ('likes nothing better than war and combat', ll. 3818–19). Orguelleus, like Méléagant, is a caricature of danger and Perceval's defeat of this symbol of pride then puts an end to the sequence of ill-fortune in the story, turning the cruel personification into a penitent man. The fact that the troublesome figure occupies the story between two references to 'mis' and to 'good' fortune suggests that his role is simply to exemplify the worst that Fortune can do during the season of change.

The characteristic of pride is later reintroduced with the description of the castle, to which some knights are drawn.[6] Chastel Orguelleus at the top of Mont Douloureux (ll. 4685–720) is the first of three different types of quest. The second, which Gawain pursues, is the rescue of a damsel besieged in her hilltop castle, and the third (Perceval's) is the quest for the grail (ll. 4685–740). The first quest is for vainglory, though this is not stated in the text. The second involves selfless service, and therefore bestows true worldly honour; and the third, the spiritual quest, has no

---

[6] From Chrétien's brief allusion to the Castle of Pride, the concept quickly became a moral commonplace. For example, Rutebeuf's 'La Voie de paradis', ll. 149–201, *Œuvres complètes de Rutebeuf*, I, pp. 336–70 (346–48); *Gliglois: A French Arthurian Romance of the Thirteenth Century*, l. 786ss, ed. by C. H. Livingston (Cambridge, MA: Harvard University Press, 1932), pp. 86–88; and *Les Livres du roy Modus et de la royne Ratio*, ed. by G. Tilander, SATF (Paris: SATF, 1932), passim.

worldly aspects at all. Vainglory offers most variation in terms of midsummer analogies, and all of Chrétien's protagonists are infected with it to some degree. The second is the path Yvain follows to purge his pride, and the third is the most elusive to capture in romance form. Yet it can be given a midsummer perspective through John the Baptist's asceticism, as in *Perlesvaus*. By contrast, in Chrétien's *Perceval*, nothing decisive comes of Perceval's decision and the moral distinctions between quests are not explicit. Instead, the three types are presented in a morally neutral context as though they had equal value and it is left to the reader to perceive that the quest chosen reflects on the quality of the knight who chooses, as do the caskets in Shakespeare's *Merchant of Venice*.

The more didactic satire of the thirteenth century not only approached the problem of pride in an openly derisive way, writers also used Arthurian characters as one measurement of it, sometimes humorously, as in the boast by Jacquemart Giélée, in *Renart le Nouvel*, that the cock, Chanticler, has done more valiant deeds in one day than either Perceval, Lancelot, Gawain, or Tristan, or, in *Le Roman de Fauvel*, where it is said that Lancelot was not better nor more beautifully armed than was the horse, Fauvel.[7] Yet there are also damnable implications. In *Renart le Nouvel* Orgueil is knighted with the arms of vainglory, discord, treason, and covetousness, which had not been seen since the time of Arthur: 'Cote a armer de vaine gloire,/... Tes ne fu puis le tans Artu;/De descorde et de traïson/ Ot en my un rampant lion,/ Et s'ot hiaume de couvoitise' (ll. 261–67), and it is said that 'amour fine' unites Orgueil and Renart (l. 1196). And, in De la Mote's *Voie d'Enfer et de Paradis*, a tapestry depicting the love of Lancelot and Guinevere hangs in Pride's castle at the entrance to Hell.[8]

Similarly, the perception of midsummer underwent a change. In *Erec and Enide, Yvain*, and Renaut's *Galeran* it had provided the context for temporary, seasonal pride in young men. Hot-headedness and the pursuit of self-glorification were part of an unavoidable cycle; therefore, any anti-Christian behaviour came from redeemable characters, and the inevitability of the cycle provided a forgiving matrix: even the abstract

---

[7] *Renart le Nouvel par Jacquemart Giélée*, ll. 5057–61, ed. by H. Roussel, SATF (Paris: Picard, 1961), p. 210; and *Le Roman de Fauvel par Gervais du Bus*, MS E, l. 1102, ed. by A. Langfors, SATF (Paris: Picard, 1914–19), p. 176.

[8] Jehan de la Mote, *La voie d'Enfer et de Paradis: an unpublished poem of the fourteenth century*, ll. 213–14; ed. by M. A. Pety, Studies in Romance Languages and Literatures 20 (Washington: Catholic University of America Press, 1940), p. 29.

personification of Pride in *Perceval,* is shown to be capable of redemption. The temporary nature of any season was the key to this lenient view. In moral satires, however, the summer season itself became identified with Pride as an abstract, unchangeable, and anti-Christian force. Texts which reveal this shift are Huon de Mery's *Le Tournoi de l'Antéchrist,* (*c.* 1234), Jean de Meung's continuation of *Le Roman de la Rose* (1270–80), Jacquemart Giélée's *Renart le Nouvel* (*c.* 1288), and Jehan de la Mote's *Voie d'Enfer et de Paradis,* (1340). Huon's work straddles the romance-morality divide; therefore, its subtleties show more clearly after a study of Jehan de la Mote's poem, since this reflects settled changes in the tradition probably effected about 1288 by Giélée. But in all these later works, the worldly implications of St John's Day are clearly associated with Lucifer's influence—as already seen in the sixteenth-century *Sotise à huit personnaiges.*

Voie d'Enfer et de Paradis

Jehan de la Mote's poem of 1340 is the most explicit. As the title states, the first part explores the road to Hell and the second, the way to salvation. This is not presented as a battle between the forces of good and evil; there is, instead, a choice. The Narrator expresses his wish to see Hell, and midsummer is associated explicitly with his arrival there. Heaven is not given any season but Jehan ends the poem by saying that the work was completed a few days before Christmas, 1340. In this way he marries a fictional use of season in the first part with the progress through the actual time taken for the poem's composition in the second and the writing ends in the season of the birth of faith, so reflecting the narrator's final allegorical experience.

The poem was written for Simon of Lille who had moved from Flanders to become a leading goldsmith and 'bourgoys de Paris'.[9] Therefore, it is not surprising to find that the exploration of Hell is not only a midsummer adventure, but that Hell also turns out to be the home of the aristocracy, while the Virtues whom the Narrator later comes to know are personifications of bourgeois values such as Work, Self-Sufficiency, and Diligence.

---

[9] Pety, ed., *La voie d'Enfer et de Paradis,* p. 8. The sole manuscript (BnF fr. 12594) came to France from Flanders about 1695. Sister Pety's published dissertation on and of it remains the only edition.

The story begins with the Narrator in his bed, in melancholy mood, and overcome by an urge to know the dangerous region. Immediately, Despair enters to show him the way and tells him he will spend seven nights in Hell, one night at the house of each of the Seven Deadly Sins. The entrance is through the Castle of the country's crowned prince (ll. 242 and 251), Pride. This Castle of Pride is large, strong, seated on a rock, and cleverly engineered with moats, gates, and towers, including bell towers which are there to ring out in Pride's exaltation. Inside, the Narrator finds a garden with many flowering bushes, bright birds, and fountains (ll. 148–52). After exploring further, he and Despair return to the garden, to its many flowering trees (ll. 232–34) and where, we learn: 'En tous tamps y faisoit esté' ('every season, there, was summer', l. 235). There is a similar association here to that in Rutebeuf's 'Voie de Paradis', where the natural beauties of summer are also indicative of vice: 'in summer... the earth makes itself proud with flowers'.[10] In de la Mote's castle, there is the further custom of 'Ainsi alames devisant / Jusques pres complie sonnant, / C'on sonne en esté de hault jour' ('sounding the alarms at compline on the high day of summer', l. 517–19). This sounds like those recorded incidents when, on 24 June, kings displayed their power, or success in battle, with a cacophony.

The interior of the castle contains the ultimate in princely grandeur. It is magnificently sculpted, decorated with gold and silver, and luxurious tapestries cover the walls. One tells the story of Lancelot, another that of Alexander. This castle is a trap for the unwary for it gives the appearance that, indoors, hell's residents live in permanent man-made comfort while, outside, they enjoy the permanent pleasures of summer. The attractions of summer flowers and good weather are hellish because they illustrate the mistake of anticipating the afterlife as a place where the body's needs, not those of the soul, will be catered for; and the Narrator says 'Mes corps el castel s'en entra' (l. 156), whereas, later, he finds it is his soul which is threatened: '[e]n l'eawe qui si froide estoit... ot grant plenté/ D'ames' (ll. 2281–84), for, after his senses are seduced by the splendour of Hell's entrance, what the narrator then experiences proves to be opposite to the promise.

Once accepted as a son of Pride (l. 264), and given a suitably fashion-able dress, the Narrator explores the feudal state of Hell. Envy's castle

---

[10] 'Mi marz tout droit, en cel termine/ Que de souz terre ist la vermine/ Ou ele a tout l'yver esté/ Si s'esjoïst contre l'esté,/ Cil arbre se cuevrent de fueille/ Et de flor la terre s'orgueille[...]', 'La Voie de paradis', ll. 1–6, *Œuvres complètes de Rutebeuf*, I, p. 341.

sits on the hill just below that of Pride, to which she looks up with the same ill-grace as she looks down on dwellings in the valley below her. After visiting her and the other deadly sins, the Narrator discovers how complete an illusion Pride's castle had been when he falls into the power of Anger, a wild outdoor man inhabiting a cold and barren region (ll. 787–828). Anger's glacial lake is full of the souls mentioned above, and tormented by the cold, '[e]n tous temps, yver et esté' (l. 2289). Permanent warm weather, enticing entrants, turns to permafrost once the souls are trapped and the Narrator is only saved from this fate by a habit of repeating his Ave Maria.

The way to Heaven, then shown him by Confession, is not some alternative to a path through the world, such as the ladder shown in the *Hortus Deliciarum* (Fig. 10, p. 219) and mentioned about 1288 by Jacquemart Giélée. The narrator's route through this fourteenth-century poem retreads a geography similar to that of Hell, with the difference that the landscape is governed by opposite values. Hell had its mountain of Pride and desert of Anger; the way towards Heaven is through the mountain of contemplation and valleys of good renown... resting at night in discreet castles: ('Par mons de contemplacîon,/ Par vauls de boine renommee... /Par castiaus de june discree', l. 2833–39). During his journey, the Narrator discovers that toadying to the great is not the only way to live. Independent work is the more holy way. It is shameful not to work, since through it, God is honoured at all seasons ('Ne t'en caut se t'es riches homs,/... Tant dois tu Dieu mieus honnerer;/ De labour est toudis saisons', ll. 2905–08). Festivity is still allowed, at Generosity's house, where Charity wears the crown, and Generosity's discreet castle lacks the pretentious high towers of Pride ('Comment qu'il n'i ait haute tour/ Ne castel, ne fossees entour', ll. 3184–85). Throughout the second half, the argument is for a middle way of living, and the character who personifies this is Measure, who, interestingly, has a daughter called June (ll. 3193–203). Though Jehan does not explain his use of the English word, it could be his way of finding a meaning for the mid-month of the year, opposite from the traditional one of excess. Divested of traditional expectations since it is borrowed from a foreign language, June can be viewed as the offspring of measure, since it is a month equidistant from either end of the year. In the house of Measure, and with the help of the other Virtues, Reason, Moderation, Sufficiency, Obedience, Gentleness, Humility, and Diligence, the Narrator learns modest behaviour and catches a glimpse of the true glories of Heaven.

Although the writing is a little prolix, the allegory is better constructed than is often allowed.[11] The antitheses develop consistently, and of greatest interest is the contrast made between the values of feudal Europe and those of Jehan's 'modern' society, in which seasonal analogies are condemned along with the old system.

Huon de Mery's Le Tournoi de l'Antéchrist

This earlier poem is divided similarly into experiences of Hell and Heaven, but here there is no choice for the Narrator: the despair is involuntary and, once in this state, he is only saved by psychomachia when God's forces defeat those of Antichrist, into whose power the Narrator has fallen. It is possible that the allegory was based on Huon's own state of mind after taking part as a knight in Louis IX's traumatic campaign of 1234.[12] *Le Tournoi* is hard to categorize, but it could be called a hybrid romance-morality. Huon admired Chrétien; he acknowledges him four times and borrows the forest of Broceliande from *Yvain*. It is possible that, under the same influence, the opening hellish experience is treated as romance, using summer themes for the rule of Antichrist, who, Stephanie Orgueur tells us, was considered 'the king of all the sons of Pride'.[13] It is notable that, although M. W. Bloomfield calls the Antichrist of this poem 'the devil',[14] Huon does not depict him as a serious threat. Instead, the opening appears to satirize the Narrator, and the world from which he had fled.

The otherworld adventure begins with the Narrator arriving 'par aventure' (l. 74) at Chrétien's Perillous Fountain, on 'la quinte nuit de

---

[11] See M. A. Pety, ed., p. 22.

[12] Little is known of the author, other than the probability that he was in the service of Louis IX. However, the poem exists in twelve manuscripts, which indicates its contemporary popularity. There have been four editions: *Le Tornoiement de l'Antechrist par Huon de Mery*, ed. by Prosper Tarbé (Reims, 1851); *Le Tornoiemenz Antecrit*, ed. by Georg Wimmer (Marburg: Elwert, 1888); *Le Torneiment Anticrist by Huon de Méri*, ed. by M. O. Bender, Romance Monographs 17 (Mississippi: The University of Mississippi Press, 1976); and *Huon de Méry: le Tournoi de l'Antéchrist*, ed. and trans. by S. Orgeur (Orléans: Paradigme, 1994), following Wimmer's text, but adding an extensive introduction and a modern French translation.

[13] Orgeur, introduction, *Huon de Méry: le Tournoi de l'Antéchrist*, p. 15.

[14] Bloomfield, p. 134.

moi' ('the fifth night of May', l. 94), after 'four full days of riding' ('Chevauchai IIII. jours entiers', l. 69). Simple arithmetic thus reveals that he fled the battle on 1 May, the start of the summer season. A clash between the worldly and the spiritual is introduced by the date of 5 May, since this was the eve of the feast of St John the Evangelist, the author of *The Revelation*, and the Evangelist is present at the end of the tale, at the feast held after the tournament in the city of Hope. This clash of meaning in the dates would seem to prefigure the psychomachia to come.

The one other stated date is for the final feast which was held 'La veille d'une ascensïon,/ En esté, a I. mercredi' ('on the eve of a day in Ascension, one Wednesday in summer', ll. 3165–66). Since the possible dates for Ascension begin before 5 May and end on 3 June, a maximum of a month is left for the journey to the tournament. However, in this work, linear time is not as important as are shifts between spiritual attitudes, and the dates carry more meaning as indicators of the narrator's state of mind than as a register of calendar events; the inclusion of the word, *esté*, in line 3166, provides a final reminder of the worldliness, symbolized by the summer season, which has been overcome through God's intervention. Huon de Mery begins the work with two apparently unconnected observations: 'N'est pas ioseus, ainz fet bone oevre/ li troveres qui sa bouche euvre/.../ Mes qui bien trueve pleins est d'ire,/ Quant il n'a de matire point': ('writing a story demands the opposite to sloth' and 'if an author cannot find a subject, he feels anger' (ll. 1–4). However, after the narrator is transported to the other world, the sun rises on the imposing horseback figure of Bras-de-Fer and, in his challenge, Bras-de-Fer displays both these summertime attributes, energetic action, and hot temper: 'monte sanz arest!... Te dirai sans contremander', ll. 275–79). They are placed in comic contrast with the Narrator's cowardice as he falls head first from his saddle in fear: 'car j'avoie trop grant hidour,/... la teste avant trebuchier/ Li convint du destrier a terre' (ll. 237–47).

Bearing in mind that Huon sketches in his seasons very lightly, other moments in Hell bring to mind summertime activities. Firstly, after the feast in the City of Despair, it is said that Antichrist 'issi de la vile;/ Bacheliers menoit X mille' ('came out of the town, leading ten thousand unmarried young men', ll. 533–34) and even the lowliest of them carried a banner. The author boasts on their behalf: 'Onques compagnie plus fiere/ ne mena Erodes n'Eracles' ('Not even Herod or Heracles had a prouder company', ll. 536–37). These recruits later become different Vices, mostly sons of Pride (ll. 602–65). Yet Huon de Mery's choice of description for them is 'bachelors' and it is a curious coincidence that it was the unmarried men who made up the youth groups in small towns[15]— the author also uses the word *ville* not *cité* at this point. Therefore these troops resemble a mass of uncontrollable youths on their way to their games in the fields outside the town. The association reduces the threat from hell's forces, while satirizing the destructive capability of young men indulging their seasonal liberties. In Louvain, in 1267, one of the restrictions on craftsmen at midsummer was that they had to have permission from the town council before parading in public with banners and pennants.[16] Therefore, the pride characteristic in Huon's troops, which we are introduced to afterwards, would appear to relate equally to the condition of youth as well as to the sin which leads to hell, and there is a point of comparison here with the seasonal context of Chrétien's *Orguelleus*. However, Huon's rag-tag body of men further parodies fourteenth-century warfare for, earlier, Bras-de-Fer had anticipated a drunken *fête* in the City of Despair among five thousand hellish knights: 'Bien a C. mil covers de fer/ Des meillors chevaliers d'enfer... N'i aura serjant ne garçon/ Qui ne soit ivres enque nuit/... Tote nuit feste grant et liée' (ll. 297–311). The satire on chivalric realities had continued with the scene of two thousand squires fighting in the streets over accommodation: 'Escuiers i vi bien II. mile/... Des escuiers as ostiex prendre/ Que meint en i vi entreprendre/ Pour biaus ostiex avoir a force' (ll. 359–65). The effects of thousands of knights massing in one town are presented here rather more realistically than in *Galeran,* though Renaut might have intended his description to be an *écart* obvious to the reader. And, as the action of Huon de Mery's work develops, the separate otherworld established at the opening gives way to a sense that hell is, in the Miltonic sense, present in this one. When Antichrist leaves the city of Despair with his Vices, or revellers, or knights, the city shakes with the noise of their parting cacophonous music, called a 'noisy demonstration of pride' and further suggestive of midsummer *alarmes*: 'De la vile issent a grant frainte:/ La avoit meinte lance peinte... / Et meinte trompe et meinte areine./ De la fierté, c'Antecriz meine,/ De toz sens la terre trembloit' (ll. 897–903).

---

[15] N. Z. Davis, *Society and Culture*, pp. 104–05.

[16] 'Après avoir promis de renouveler les échevins chaque année à la Saint-Jean, le duc décrète que les métiers ne pourront sonner la cloche ni paraître en public avec leurs bannières et penons qu'après en avoir obtenu l'autorisation du Conseil.' J. Cuvelier, 'Les Institutions de la ville de Louvain', p. 122.

The fall of these forces at the Tournament is told through the diurnal, rather than annual, progress of the sun, with midday forming a microcosmic solstice: 'Li soleuz, qui d'eure ne ment/... Monte de degré en degré/... Et devers medi se torna' ('The sun, which never lies, climbs degree by degree in the firmament... and about midday it turns', ll. 2231–35). At this moment the Virtues begin their attack and by 3 p.m. the Vices lose control, Antichrist himself is obliged to take part, and, soon after, 'li rois du firmament' (l. 2968) takes him prisoner. By evening when 'li soleus... par le pui avala/ De vespres el val d'occident' ('the sun fell into the pit of evening and the valley of the west', ll. 2992–95), Antichrist's forces had lost. This battle is a foregone conclusion: not only do the Vices bear the seeds of their own defeat, but also the poem 'contains the unusual feature of giving the initiative to the forces of good'.[17] As in Prudentius, it is Christ's troops who instigate the battle.

Further, the character of the Vices' leader relates more to medieval and classical literature than to the dangers of hell, for in the early Middle Ages Antichrist was seen as a supernatural grotesque.[18] In the *Tournoi de l'Antéchrist* there is no physical description, but he behaves, and others respond to him, as a normal human being. His physiognomy could not be too repulsive since we are told that on leaving Hell, Pluto's wife, Proserpine, gave him a diamond helmet as a love token, so making Pluto jealous. 'Prosperpine... estoit si desdigneuse / Tant estoit d'Antecrit esprise' ('Proserpine was disdainful, so taken was she by Antichrist', ll. 553–61). Not only is this a borrowing from classical legend rather than from *The Revelation*, but Proserpine also behaves as a Guinevere. However, Antichrist's reception in the Town of Despair is like that for a real medieval king, since he was met by at least two thousand rich bourgeoisie, the richest of whom helped him dismount from his horse before he presided over the great feast. Huon's Antichrist contains nothing of the supernatural, nor anything overtly vicious. Sometimes he is reminiscent of Chrétien's Arthur in *Yvain*, who is also an Antichrist in the first half of Chrétien's tale, and sometimes the narrative reads more like an imitation of medieval life. As the editor says, 'the frame of the tale is the medieval courtly world' (p. 18), and the courtly aspect could provide an allegory for the forces which had brought about the Narrator's original

---

[17] Bloomfield, p. 134.

[18] McGinn, pp. 3 and 12.

despair. In Huon de Mery's work the conflict is not between a hellish Antichrist and God, but between a worldly Antichrist and God.

In all, Antichrist reflects medieval leaders as found in seasonal game, in literature, and in society, and Huon de Mery's eclecticism shows further in the placing of the romance characters themselves, Arthur, Gawain, Yvain, Lancelot, Perceval, and Kay, in the ranks of the Virtues along with Generosity, Nobility, and Watchfulness (ll. 1975–80). Despite this apparent sanctification, Huon in fact continues the satirical perspective through Kay, who is anything but virtuous. On his shield he carries: 'les armes detraccîon/ Endentées de felonie/ A ramposnes de vilenie/ A III. touteaus fez et farsiz/ De ramposnes et de mesdiz...' ('the arms of detraction, edged with disloyalty, with villainy rampant, and three fools, and filled in with arrogant raillery and slander', ll. 2008–15).

It is Antichrist's envoy, Bras-de-Fer, however, who is the most absurd, and the hollowness of his bravado is revealed at the Tournament when he is defeated before battle by a ray from the eye of Mary in Heaven. Struck down, he retreats in despair to the appropriate city. As forerunner to the Antichrist, Bras-de-Fer appears to be an Anti-John the Baptist, so explaining why he does not take part in the Christian battle. The reason he gives at the opening for his impatience is that his 'master will soon be here'. The Narrator asks, 'But who is the lord coming after you, and what is his name?' ('ci vieigne/ Misires. Monte inellement!/... Mes qui est li sires qui vient/ Apres toi et et comment a non?' ll. 264–73).

Huon de Mery's figure of bravado is in complete contrast to Jean de Meung's better-known Anti-John the Baptist, False Seeming, in the *Roman de la Rose*. Yet Jean de Meung, too, appears to have been aware of 24 June traditions, for False Seeming's cunning is not in evidence at the point when we meet him; instead he displays the paradox of open pride in his deviousness. He admits 'si n'ai mes cure d'ermitages/ J'ai lessié desers et bacoges/ Et quit a saint Jehan Baptiste' ('little love for hermitages, woods,/ And deserts. Wilderness and hut and lodge/ I leave to John the Baptist', ll. 11701–03).[19] On the surface there is the irony that a man from a religious order following the Baptist's principles mocks those principles. Looked at more closely, further ironies emerge, for all that False Seeming says inverts the Baptist's principles and, in so doing,

---

[19] *The Romance of the Rose*, trans. by H. W. Robbins (New York: Dutton, 1962), p. 241. Cf. *Guillaume de Loris et Jean de Meun: Le Roman de la Rose*, ed. by D. Poirion (Paris: Garnicr-Flammarion, 1974).

recalls secular midsummer traditions. A man, for whom religion is his calling, should be humble, yet, the editor notes, 'he boasts of his own faults'.[20] False Seeming is also ambitious for wealth, cultivating the rich and robbing the poor. John the Baptist's name was invoked to remind people of the instability of material success; False Seeming reminds us of its desirability. He has even built himself a palace (ll. 11576 and 11677), and has earned himself the title of 'King of Ribalds' ('rois de mes ribaus', l. 10938, 'rois des ribaus i seras', l. 11984). His behaviour is the opposite to that of his religious calling and to the religious meaning of the Baptist's Nativity. However, his free speech and mockery fit the secular traditions of the day. As he admits, he is the opposite to this forerunner of Christ and a more serious threat than Bras-de-Fer, or even Antichrist himself, in the *Tournoi de l'Antéchrist*.

By comparison, the humour in Huon de Mery's poem can make it appear slight, but his writing appealed to a secular readership and recent revaluation awards him a seminal role in thirteenth-century literature.[21] Huon, himself, claimed originality: 'Car tel matire ai porpensée/ C'onques mes n'ot en sa pensée/ ne sarrasins ne chrestïens' (ll. 19–21). His fresh thinking appears in the free construction, through which Huon combined several different sources, and it also appears in his original combination of reality with fiction. The opening battle, which causes the Narrator such trauma, is identified as that between Louis IX and Mauclerc, the Count of Dreux: a man with kingly qualities, and the unrealistic belief in his ability to preserve Brittany from the might of the king. From the actual situation, therefore, Huon constructs an opposition between a proud mock king and a *real* real one: an appropriate plot for summer, since the tale is based on actual political events. It has also been suggested that the trauma for Huon resulted from his sympathy with Mauclerc and, if Mauclerc had been Mery's model for Antichrist, it could account for the fact that Antichrist's error is wrong-headedness rather than evil. Also, if the poem did provide an outlet to express Huon's political unease, this too would have been appropriate to a midsummer context.

Seriousness in Huon de Mery's work is reserved for the Narrator's conversion at the end. Before then, summer and midsummer elements provide a satiric way of diminishing the threat from the Antichristian

---

[20] *The Romance of the Rose*, ed. by C. W. Dunn (New York: Dutton, 1962), p. xxiv.

[21] Orgeur, introduction, p. 7.

forces. As a festive leader, he cannot be a strong antithesis to God. It is Antichrist's power which is ridiculed while, unlike False Seeming, he has no ability to belittle the power of God. The seasonal aspects contribute to the optimistic resolution by being connected with a satanic world power to be overthrown and this results in an anti-festive perspective on the games themselves. As in most works up to the early thirteenth century, midsummer traditions are viewed negatively, but not too seriously.

Jacquemart Giélée's Renart le Nouvel[22]

The plot of this beast fable reveals the completion of an irretrievably damnable association between Pride and midsummer. Both are shown as features of a satanic worldly power which increases its hold instead of declining, and the Festival of St John becomes a time which marks this progress of devilish pride on fortune's wheel of hell. The totality of the change in midsummer tradition is achieved through Giélée's use of Renart who is summed up as treachery in the hearts of men. Giélée writes: 'Li cuer sont mais plain de renart' ('the heart is full of renart', l. 36) and Pride, a young man, son of King Noble, uses this support to overcome his own in-built, seasonal weaknesses. Giélée also attacks corruption in Church affairs: 'Couvoitise a fait sont pont/ En che monde, seur coi monter/ Fait les prelas et desmonter:/ De Dieu en montant se desmontent/ Quant plus as temporeus biens montent....' ('Covetousness has made a bridge to the world, and prelates have stepped down from the ascent to God and climb towards worldly goods', ll. 13–18). (Fig. 10, p. 219.) The danger no longer comes from a self-declared leader of opposition to Christ, an open enemy who can be identified and dealt with; the danger is the enemy concealed in the hearts of so-called Christian leaders.

The poem is in two parts which, in works such as *Yvain* and the *Voie d'Enfer*, create a cyclical process, in which danger is unleashed in the first part, but from which characters progress to redemption and hope. In

22 The provenance is Flemish and the four extant manuscript copies are held at the BnF in Paris. Three contain illustrations of Fortune's Wheel. There have been two editions: one by J. Houdoy, *Renart-le-nouvel, roman satirique composé au XIIIe siècle par Jacquemars Giélée de Lille* (Paris: Aubry, 1874) and the one currently available, *Renart le Nouvel par Jacquemart Giélée. Publié d'après le manuscrit La Vallière (B.N. fr. 25566)*, ed. by Henri Roussel, SATF (Paris: Picard, 1961).

Renart, the two-part structure serves to emphasize negative control, for Giélée takes the plot in a direction opposite to the one anticipated. As Henri Roussel says, the poem is far better written than is often claimed[23] and Giélée, in fact, constructed one of the best pieces of satire of the fourteenth century.

Part I begins with Lord Noble, the lion, trying to maintain chivalric order but weakened by the subversion from his son, Pride (which suggests that Noble cannot escape being the Antichrist). Noble holds a solemn court, with jousting, on his birthday, which was also Rogation Day, i.e. Monday, Tuesday, or Wednesday before Ascension. ('Mesires Nobles li lions/ Tint court de grant sollempnité/ Au jour de se nativité;/ Che fu au jour de Rouvisons', ll. 46–49). The overt aim of the Tournament is the exaltation of pride, and when its personification is dubbed knight he is given his Arthurian arms of vainglory, discord, treason, and covetousness. And the first midsummer reference occurs at these festivities. All the knights who take part: 'Se fiert ou tournoi et sen pan/ I soustint bien par saint Jehan' ('They pride themselves on the Tournament; they are there to uphold their reputations in it, by St John', ll. 635–36).

Instead of gaining glory, Orgueil is humiliated by Ysengrin which, in Chrétien's *Perceval* was the correct result: the personification of arrogance received his fall and was reformed. In *Renart*, however, there is no acceptance of moral justice. The fable is an allegory for the real world, where pride and humiliation are irreconcilable opposites, and Orgueil's defeat demands the revenge which is then taken by his Renart deliberately killing Ysengrin's son, Primaut, in the tournament. Treachery in the hearts of men is exposed at the heart of the idealized chivalric jousts. Renart is imprisoned, but escapes; and the plot of the two parts of the satire follows the same cycle: each time Renart is cornered, he survives to come back and flourish in a more firmly entrenched position than before. And although at the opening Orgueil is the leading Vice, Renart, his more cunning alter-ego, gradually takes control. Orgueil is the old-fashioned, youthful figure, and less dangerous, perhaps, because familiar. Renart is portrayed in a novel way, more threatening because more intelligent.

After the death of Primaut and Renart's subsequent escape, the fox is besieged in his castle, Maupertuis; he is rescued by Orgueil and, in return,

---

[23] See H. Roussel, 'À propos de l'épilogue de "Renart le Nouvel": quelques reflexions sur l'allégorie de Fortune', in *Alain de Lille, Gautier de Châtillon, Jakemart Giélée et leur temps*, ed. by H. Roussel and F. Suard (Lille: Lille University Press, 1980), pp. 307–31 (p. 330).

Renart crowns him in Orgueil's own castle with the traditional, satanic (or Alexandrian) words: 'roi de tout le monde' (l. 1237). But, in Part II, after a sea battle between Noble and Renart, which the fox wins on about 'li sains Jehans' (l. 5164), it is Renart who is then said to be 'lord of the land./ It causes much grief and pity, that Renart is raised so high' ('Renars est sires du païs,/ Dont c'est et doleurs et pités/ Que Renars est si amontés', ll. 5198–200). It is a peculiarly depressing moment, for comedy in satire is only sustained if hope is held out that there will come an end to the rise of oppression. But the cycle confirmed by the midsummer battle is that worldly arrogance and its corrupt power revive at the point when we expect their fall. The message is not unlike that of Maglore's regarding the Arras *échevins* in *Le Jeu de la Feuillée*, written not long before.

Renart's rise and rise in fortune is marked by varying uses of the valley and mountain analogies as, for example, *si amontés* in line 5199, quoted above. And, when Noble besieges Renart's castle of Maupertuis, set high on a rock (l. 838) the king's forces try to scale the walls. They fail and descend *aval* (l. 995) both literally and figuratively. The metaphor is repeated in Part II when a posse of furriers similarly attempts to infiltrate Renart's new stronghold of Passe-Orgueil. They, too, have to admit defeat and '[d]eschendent de la roche aval' (l. 5751). Renart's speech to Orgueil at Pride's coronation had contained the lines, 'Nous en savons peu par le mont/ Qui se desmonte et qui s'esmont' ('We know a few men in the world (or on the mountain) who are descending and some who are climbing', ll. 1259–60). The complete cycle, however, does not apply to Renart himself, as we begin to learn in Part II. For, at the end of Part I, Renart had recovered Noble's favour with the help of the Church; he had returned to his ancestral home, Maupertuis, and celebrated with a festival, singing contemporary popular love songs[24] with his wife. These are songs of triumph, appropriate to the end of the first part, and they should mark Renart's temporary eminence. The reinstatement, with its triumphal feast, looked like the highest point the Vice would attain, and the expectation was for a change in Part II. Instead, at the beginning of Part II, 'Li rois... voit par mi le fons d'un val/ Renart' ('King Noble sees Renart at the bottom of a valley', ll. 2654–57). It turns out that, in comparison with the rise yet to come, Renart's previous success had been nothing. King Noble

---

[24] N. Van den Boogaard, 'Jacquemart Giélée et la Lyrique de son Temps', in *Alain de Lille*, ed. H. Roussel, pp. 333–53.

dismounts, Renart falls to his knees in a feigned act of humility, and King Noble continues the raising of Renart *amont* (l. 2666).

However, Giélée uses the mountain metaphor against Orgueil. Before his coronation, set high in his castle on the rock, Orgueil's vassals send him a golden sceptre to make him 'king and emperor of the world' ('Pour che que roi et emperées/ Soit au mont', ll. 1201–02). *Mont,* here, appears to mean mountain rather than world for, a few lines later, Giélée uses the *monde* spelling at the coronation, when Renart gives Orgueil the satanic accolade: 'Sire, t'ies roi de tout le monde' (l. 1237). There are, in this speech, a sequence of puns on 'world' and 'mountain' (see Appendix C) which make the spelling in line 1202 deliberate double meaning rather than scribal accident. Therefore, Orgueil receives his sceptre from his subjects as 'King and Emperor of the mountain': a reductive image which mocks his pretensions to global power. This figure is no more worthy to be a king of the world than a rustic in his prime playing the role, and further vocabulary continues the subversion. Renart uses the *tu* form of address in line 1237 above, although in the following line he uses *vous:* 'Car ou monde n'en a si monde/ Qui de vous ou de moi n'ait taque'. Therefore, at the moment of the coronation there is mockery of Orgueil's royalty by the vassal crowning him, revealing the real relationship between them. In festive game, the courtier's acclamation similarly contained derision and, in this moral piece, we see Orgueil only made king for a limited season. When his time is over he becomes secondary and his place is taken by the more dedicated reprobate who is unaffected by seasonal insecurity. The arrogance of youth is superseded by endemic arrogance.

On his way to permanent eminence Renart passes through several mock king stages. One is at the end of Part I as the lord of Maupertuis, and the next is at the beginning of Part II when Renart acts as go-between to win the adulterous love of Lady Harangue for Noble. As a result, Renart is made the king's bailiff and, when Noble sets up his court at Pentecost, it is the fox who carries the royal standard in procession before him. As bailiff, Renart gains actual power over Noble's people, which brings them 'grans doleurs' (l. 2969). The reward is given to 'Renart le rous' (l. 2960), red Renart or Renart the wheel, Fortune's favourite. The pun reminds the reader of Renart's upward revolve, and also recalls the fact that, to other animals, Renart *is* Fortune's wheel, in control of their lives by giving judgement over the cases brought to Noble's Pentecost court. Soon after, Renart has to flee again, this time because of the complexities of the love affair; and, in two exchanges of letters with the king, we meet Renart in his third mock king role—this time as outlaw. The defiant opening of each letter is in the royal style, as some English outlaws wrote in the fourteenth century,[25] and beginning with the plural pronoun: 'Nous, Renars, sire de Maupertuis et du païs entour' (ll. 3637 and 4337).

By now, Renart has fled overseas to his new stronghold of Passe-Orgueil and the decisive sea-battle between him and Noble takes place off the coast, on about the 'sains Jehans' (l. 5164), when the real king loses and the mock king is confirmed in power. After this, Renart makes peace with the world on his terms, happy to release his prisoners because, when king Noble returns to land, he is obliged to accept Renart's control: 'Et li roys Nobles Renart fist/ Segneur de ses consaus et dist/ K'il gouvrenast son regne et lui' ('And King Noble made Renart lord of his counsels and said that he would rule him and his reign', ll. 7057–59).

The suggestion throughout the narration, and supported by Giélée's use of the midsummer date, is that Renart is in control of Fortune's wheel and that her traditional rules, whether applied through seasonal or wheel analogy, do not apply to him. Confirmation comes at the end, when Fortune says: 'Renart, je te voel courouner/ Sour ma roe et en haut lever' ('Renart, I wish to crown you and raise you high on my wheel', ll. 7679–80). Renart refuses because of its downward turn (l. 7687), but Fortune replies:

> Jamais au tans ki ore va
> N'ert tournee un seul tour par moi.
> Tu en as abatue Foi,
> Loiauté ai desous mes piés, …
> Sire Renars, par vo vretu [sic],
> Orgiux a mis Humilité
> Bas a mes piés.... (ll. 7692–700)

(Never again, I will not turn it any more because you have beaten faith; Loyalty I have beneath my feet.... Lord Renart, by your virtue, Pride has placed Humility low at my feet.)

This is a reverse ending to all other battles between good and ill from the time of Prudentius to that of Huon de Mery's *Tournoiemenz* and, though never declared as such, Renart is a highly effective Antichrist.

---

[25] Billington, *Mock Kings*, pp. 11–12.

Three times in the poem (ll. 2337, 3554, and 3919) we are told that the contestants for power did not hear God's thunder, but the line is satiric rhetoric, for God is, in fact, absent. Instead, through the fox, a satanic Fortune, who addresses Renart as her Lord, has the forces for good where she wants them, therefore she will make the wheel stand still, so ensuring corruption will dominate for all time. The top of the wheel is, therefore, safe for Renart: 'Montés, Renars, car a vo destre/ Arés Orguel, et a senestre/ Ert dame Guile... / Fai jou en me roe...' ('Climb, Renart, with Pride at your right and Dame Guile on your left/ Climb, and play on my wheel', ll. 7703–09). 'A icest mot Renars monta/ Sour le roe tous coorounés/... Vestus de l'ordre des Templiers/ Mi partis as Hospitaliers./ A ses piés fist ses fix seoir/ Sour le roe... Ains est courounés conme [sic] uns roys,/ Fausser fait jugemens et lois,/ Fortune a se roe escotee/ Si que mais n'ert par li tornee'. ('At this Renart climbed onto the wheel and was crowned,... dressed as a Templar and Hospitaler, and his feet were fixed on the wheel. Thus is he crowned like a king, to make false judgements and laws. And Fortune jams the wheel so that she can't turn it', ll. 7716–30).

Giélée even completes the analogy between the wheel and the mountain by describing the stationary wheel as a raised piece of solid landscape: 'li roe ne puist tourner/ Quant on i ert assis en roce' ('the wheel could not turn, as though Renart sat on a rock', ll. 7786–87). This removes the wheel's association with seasonal progress through time which would bring changes (see Appendix A). It is no longer a device which brings good and bad in equal measure; instead, its mountain-like solidity returns the reader to the opening affirmation that men in power have come off the ladder to God, and now make an ascent to satanic materialism up the mountain of worldly ambition. Giélée anticipates this conclusion in his use of 'li sains Jehans' (l. 5164), making it, too, stable in the satanic cause. If inversion of the norm is a festive expectation, then Giélée uses inversion to defeat the festive expectation. And pride, which traditionally brought about its own fall, either by the revolving seasons or through its own error, is here bolstered by renart in the hearts of men which sits with Orgueil on the mountain of pride.

John Flinn concluded that Giélée added little that was new to satirical tradition because the moral, that evil is endemic, is similar to that in *Le Roman de Fauvel*.[26] It can be seen, however, that Giélée in fact

---

[26] J. Flinn, *Le Roman de Renart* (Paris: Presses Universitaires de France, 1963), p. 277.

revolutionized the concepts he used. Prior to him, Pride had straddled two
traditions: the seasonal, youthful and forgivable, and the irredeemable
and satanic, with the first undermining the threat of the second. In *Le
Tournoi* even Antichrist obeys the rules of the Tournament. He cannot
resist God's summons and is defeated in honest combat. Despite their
bravado the Vices are the passive combatants, and their flaws weaknesses
rather than strengths. The result is a foregone conclusion and the seasonal
parallel further reduces their stature.

In Giélée season and pride have irredeemably damnable associations.
So too does Fortune, for the first time in any of the works so far considered. Prior to this, her connection with the mid-point of the year provided
a licence which had made her incorporation morally neutral. Giélée, in
his reversal, does not avoid seasonal licence, but makes all associations
with it irredeemable. The only hope lies in acknowledging the decay of
past principles and in finding a new way forward, a form of reasoning
which is not unlike that of Renaut, who has Fresne reject Fortune's
concepts of 'high' and 'low'. Giélée, though, concludes with some
ambivalence: 'Fuions Renart, que c'est nos mors,/ Car il aslonge de Dieu
l'ame/ Et le met en le puant flame/ D'infer, dont Dame Dex nous gart'
('Let us flee Renart, for he is our death,/ for he alienates the soul from
God, and places it in the stinking flame/ Of hell, from which may lady
Dice [Chance] guard us', ll. 7026–29).

Pride was a versatile basis for characterization since an author might
apply it in differing degrees: if a seasonal aberration, then festive
indulgence and comedy predominate, though moral danger can be
included. *Fergus* and *Yvain* are both festive romances but Chrétien's is
obviously the more serious. At the other end of the spectrum *Renart le
Nouvel* is a highly serious satire on the machinations behind a damnable
thirst for power. Giélée used the seasonal structure to increase the sense
of danger by repeatedly raising expectations of a midsummer change,
only to frustrate them. And it would appear that it was this modification
which influenced later writers such as Jehan de la Mote and the author of
the *Sotise à huit personnaiges*.

There was no imperative to include midsummer, Fortune, and pride in
order to develop complex literature. Christine de Pisan has no seasonal
analogies, but her wide-ranging classical and literary knowledge in *La
Mutacion de Fortune*, creates a unique moral allegory. But where the
seasonal link was retained, the result was direct comment on social and
political issues. Jehan de la Mote, Huon de Mery, Jean de Meung, and

Jacquemart Giélée all had specific targets in their sights, thus retaining the fundamental midsummer liberty of free speech on current issues.

CHAPTER 9

Religious Theatre

[L]e théâtre est né du culte. Loin de proscrire le drame, la religion l'avait
d'abord adopté...

Petit de Julleville

Having begun by looking at midsummer play and its Christianization, there is a satisfying circularity in finishing with religious
drama. Just as *Perlesvaus* reveals that the ambiguities of the
solstice can lend themselves to religious themes in novels, so too there
were solsticial possibilities for writers of Christian theatre; the wildness
of secular *jeu* was not the only option. For the fact that man is subject to
fortune's cycle of mutability at all was attributed to Adam's failure in
Paradise, a point which was staged in the twelfth-century play, the
Mystère d'Adam. This Anglo-Norman work was written during those
years at the end of the twelfth century when Church authorities developed
a creative attitude towards mimesis and towards popular customs.[1] This
possibly explains why Adam, in the *Mystère,* is a young man (l. 98)
whom God makes lord of all the world (l. 61). The youthful sovereign is
placed in an elevated paradise[2] where seasonal change is unknown (l. 54);
his youth, too, will be endless (ll. 58 and 98). Therefore, Adam casts
away an already perfect existence for the apple, a reversal in his destiny
which is expressed in the lines: 'senz nul rescus sui jo mort,/ Tant est

---

[1] Davidson, ed., *Tretise of Miraclis Pleyinge*, p. 11, and *Mystère d'Adam: texte du
manuscrit de Tours,* ed. by Henri Chamard (Paris: Colin, 1925), pp. vii–xi.

[2] Stage directions are for a high place in the Church, below heaven. *Mystère d'Adam,*
trans. by H. Chamard, pp. 3–4.

chaite mal ma sorte!/ Mal m'est changé' ma aventure' ('My lot has fallen
so badly that unless I am rescued I must die. My fortune has changed to
ill', ll. 317–19). At the end of the scene Adam repeats, 'there is nothing
for me now but death' (l. 386).[3] Before this, fortune, chance, and death
did not exist for him; they only become features of Adam's fallen state
and in later religious plays, particularly in Michel's *Passion*, men and
women are shown trying to regain the original paradisal eminence
through satanic means, only to discover the temporary and illusory nature
of any success since now they have no choice but to inhabit the mutable
world.

Lucifer's own fall is the archetype. In all the Mystery Cycles it is his
pride which leads him to compete for God's kingship, resulting in the
most extreme fall from heaven to hell. This is now so familiar that one
thinks of it as a Bible story. Yet, it does not appear in the Creation story
of the Old Testament. It was only by 1200, a time which saw growing
interest in the subject of arrogance, that 'it was generally agreed that
Lucifer fell because of pride, i.e. insubordination and unwillingness to
accept his proper place in the divine order.'[4] As said in Chapter 1, the
name meant light-bearing and was, originally, an accolade—there was
even a fourth-century Christian zealot known as Lucifer![5] During the
Middle Ages the meaning was modified, until the name acquired an
association with damnation in parallel with the reinterpretation of midsummer and, in the *Mystère du Veil Testament,* played in Paris in 1500,
the light-bearing devil receives a midsummer punishment for his pride.
Lucifer appears among the angels as the only one to have a sun shining
behind him,[6] and the basis of his pride is the exceptional beauty and

[3] *Mystère d'Adam*, ll. 317–20. Adam is without pride at the opening and mockery of the
youthful lord, by Satan and other devils, fails to provoke him.

[4] Bloomfield, *The Seven Deadly Sins*, p. 382, n. 16. The date is interesting, in view of the
increasing examples, then, of successful insubordination in Europe against the feudal
system.

[5] *The Ecclesiastic Cyclopaedia,* ed. by J. Eadie (London, 1862). 'The Isaiah story [of
Lucifer's fall from heaven] is simply an ancient astral myth, based on the disappearance of
Venus at the break of day [and] the Old Testament Satan was no more than a kind of
celestial prosecutor, whose function it was to test Man's virtue and accuse him when it
was found wanting...' J. M. Evans, Paradise Lost *and the Genesis Tradition* (Oxford:
Clarendon Press, 1968), p. 34.

[6] *Le Mistere du Viel Testament,* ll. 60–61, ed. by Baron de Rothschild, SATF (Paris:
Didot, 1878), p. 3.

brightness that it gives him (ll. 238–44). But when he and his angels climb, they discover they are on a wheel which God rotates, saying: 'Non ascendes sed descendes' (l. 407). Like the sun at midsummer Lucifer cannot escape the complete orbit, which, for him, results in hell without the possibility of future rising.[7] God, here, is staged as in control of the wheel. The image affirms hierarchical order in the heavens and also in the world since Lucifer is depicted as the archetypal midsummer rebel whose adventure ends in self-destruction. As in literary works depicting pride, Lucifer's revolt, in medieval dramas, is often portrayed as a combination of vice and failure of judgement which turns him into a comic figure of weakness rather than a serious threat.

But it is Lucifer's continued rivalry with God that instigates the action of the Passion plays. When Satan succeeded with Adam, Lucifer's authority supplanted that of God in the world, thus necessitating God's intervention through his son. Solsticial principles are not always used overtly, but they are there in the sub-text: one can see that the mutability, caused by Adam's error, itself undermines the threat to God from Satan's worldly powers. Satanic materialism is transient, therefore ultimately powerless against God's eternal authority; and, frequently, festive motifs are used to illustrate the futility of Lucifer's apparent success. For example Arnoul Gréban, in his *Mystère de la Passion* (first played in 1452), stages Lucifer's court as a twisted imitation of heaven: 'Roy Lucifer'[8] is the 'Domine' (Prologue, l. 1494) who makes Satan lord over the world. The two devils, like Antichrists, assume the roles of God and Christ and, when Satan succeeds in Paradise, Lucifer awards him with a precious diadem and the title of 'roy de tous noz heraulz' (Prologue, l. 713). Subsequently, on leading in the souls of Adam and Eve, Satan is further honoured as 'roy de la feve' (Prologue, l. 1483). The titles are intended as honours, but the transience of the elevation, particularly for the well-known one-day, winter king, provides a derisory contrast with the eternal rule in God's kingdom.[9]

---

[7]   In 1162 John Beleth added a fall into Hell to the solar analogy for the Baptist, making John's visit a precursor to Christ's Harrowing. *Rationale Diuinorum*, p. 303.

[8]   Omer Jodogne, ed. (Brussels: Publication of the Royal Belgian Academy, 1965), Prologue, l. 992. Ten manuscript copies are extant, some incomplete. The one used by Jodogne is BnF, MS fonds français 815. A later production of Gréban's play appears to have been staged in Poitiers in 1486. See Jean Bouchet, *Les Annales d'Aquitaine* (Poitiers, 1644), p. 296.

[9]   Billington, 'King and Queen Games in English Mystery and French Passion Plays', in

Yet, in Gréban's play, Satan does govern the world until Christ breaks
Hell open, and mock king titles are further used for Christ by the devil's
allies, Herod, and the torturers. These are obvious mockery, not intended
as worldly honour, and the name-calling culminates in midsummer insults. Initially, when Herod fails to make Christ speak, he orders him to
be dressed as 'un de mez folz le plus cornu' (l. 22358). Christ is dressed
in a white robe and horns are put on his head. For the audience, the image
anticipates Christ as sacrificial lamb, but a different interpretation comes
from the torturers for whom the horns make Christ the 'roy des cornars'
or king of cuckolds (ll. 22849–53). It is likely that this title was taken
from domestic *charivari*,[10] which could occur at any festive season. However, they also replace the white gown with an 'abit de roy... le plus
villement qu'on pourra... ung vieulx pourpre tout troué/ plus dessiré
qu'ung vieulx haillon' ('the vilest king's costume that can be found... an
old purple gown full of holes, more tattered than an old rag', ll. 22859–
60). The mockery in this game has more to do with ridiculing kingship
than cuckoldry, and issues of kingship, central to the fears that the
worldly authorities have of Christ, are also central to midsummer games.
The tattered king's dress is augmented with a sceptre and the crown of
thorns which is called 'couronne de noblesse/ pour ung grant prince
seculier' (ll. 22925–26), and Christ is mocked as the most pathetic-
looking king: 'Dieu! quel roy' (l. 22871). Alexander Carpenter referred to
a 'summer game of torturers' in his *Destructiorum Viciorum*, and another
'Somer Game' analogy for Christ's Passion in drama appears in a contemporary sermon.[11] Therefore, it is hard not to conclude that, in
Gréban's scene of torturers described above, he borrowed from
midsummer tradition, to contrast the eternal prince, in kingly rags, with
the winter grandeur assumed by Satan, as a crowned and courtly 'king of
the bean'.

In the later *Mistere de la Passion JesusCrist*—derived from Gréban—
Jean Michel added titles which make midsummer associations more

Custom, Culture and Community in the Later Middle Ages, ed. by Thomas Pettitt and Leif
Søndergaard (Odense: Odense University Press, 1994), pp. 96–97.

[10] See N. Z. Davis, *Society and Culture*, pp. 97–99 and C. Mazouer, 'Spectacle et théâtre
dans la chevauchée des Conards de Rouen au XVIᵉ siècle', *Fifteenth-Century Studies*, 13
(1987), 387–400 (pp. 391 and 394).

[11] See N. Davis, 'The *Tretise of Myraclis Pleyinge:* on Milieu and Authorship', *Medieval
English Theatre*, 12 (1990), 124–51 (p. 131), and Davidson, ed., *Tretise of Miraclis
Pleyinge*, p. 18, respectively.

explicit. The torturers call Christ king of the suffering ('roy des souffreteux'),[12] king of cowards ('roy des couars', l. 24937) and, crucially, 'king of unfortunates' ('roy des malheureux', l. 25033). The implications of the soldiers treating Christ in this way are complex. On the one hand, low-class men speak what they think is the truth about the pretensions of a jumped-up leader, whose change in worldly fortune is satirized in play. On the other hand, as further analysis shows, in Michel's text, Christ proves the futility of Fortune and of all solsticial beliefs associated with her. And the date of the original performance appears to have contributed to this argument.

Jean Michel's four-part play was performed in Angers on six days between Sunday, 20 and Friday, 26 August 1486, ending shortly before the *decollatio* of John the Baptist.[13] The events which had led up to the Baptist's *decollatio* provide the main action of Day 1, beginning with a sermon from John, followed by his baptism of Christ, and ending with John's execution and burial. In Days 2 to 4, Christ's greater ministry is shown, followed by his Passion, and ending with his execution and burial. In this play, the Baptist prefigures Christ in both his message and in his personal history, and Christ's death was performed at the end of Day 4, close to the commemoration of the Baptist's *decollatio.*

This is one of several major differences between the Michel text and that of Arnoul Gréban, the most significant aspect of it being that Michel did not show Christ's Resurrection. Rosemary Woolf was so sure the scene would be there, that she included it in her summary.[14] A second, yet related, difference is that Lucifer and his cohorts are connected to their supporters on earth by belief in Fortune: therefore the world where Christ's ministry and death take place is one which is ruled by this pre-Christian belief. And, as was customary in the writing of religious drama,

---

[12] Jean Michel, *Le Mystère de la Passion (Angers, 1486)*, l. 25032, ed. by O. Jodogne (Gembloux: Duculot, 1959), p. 365. Jean Michel was a medical, not a theological, doctor and fifteen manuscript copies of his play survive, although it was probably not performed a second time. O. Jodogne's editions of this and of Gréban's text are the only ones available.

[13] No explanation is given for six rather than four days for the performance of a four-part play. See 'Extrait d'un manuscrit de Messire Guillaume Oudin,' *Revue de l'Anjou et de Maine-et-Loire*, 1 (1857), p. 141, in Billington, 'Social Disorder', p. 217.

[14] R. Woolf, *The English Mystery Plays* (London: Routledge and Kegan Paul, 1972), p. 66. In 1491 Michel wrote a separate *Mystère de la Resurrection de Nostre Seigneur.* See Petit de Julleville, ed., *Histoire du théâtre en France: les mystères*, II, p. 446.

Michel added many anachronisms, some of which were original. One group of soldiers call themselves *gueux,* which had been the name of the outlaws who had terrorized Anjou during the Hundred Years War, ended only a few years prior to the play's performance.[15] A soldier from a more respectable cohort jokes with the *gueux* about the fate of hanging waiting for both them and for Jesus. He is reminded by a cleric: 'Now, now, it has to be a cross' ('Or, sus, sus, il fault une croix', l. 26084). And, as noted above, Satan and Christ are both given names from medieval festive game. Anachronisms were part of medieval theatre's emphasis on a living Christ in contemporary society.[16] Since Chronicles show that open expression of Fortune belief was widespread in the fifteenth century, Michel's use of her relates to his own society, as well as to the time before Christ, thus reminding the audience of the need for Christ's redemption in their own fallen, fifteenth-century world. Michel even gives a line to Peter, before his conversion, in which he says that fishing in the right place will bring them 'good fortune' ('je croy, par ma carte marine, que nous aurons bonne fortune', l. 3946–47). Judas, of course, is steeped in belief in her (l. 3865) and the word is in frequent use by Pilate (l. 2384), Satan (l. 2239), and Lucifer who, at one point, parodying God, pardons the devils' 'fortune' (ll. 2295 and 2301). However, the fullest development of fortune belief is in Michel's use of the cyclic passage from birth to death for all the unredeemed, for whom the emphasis is on reigning in the midsummer of life.

The models are Lazarus and Mary Magdalene who, before their conversions, appear as an Orgueilleus and Orgueilleuse exulting over their position as prince and princess. In Day 1 Lazarus enters, richly dressed as a knight, with a hawk on his arm and followed by his dogs. His servant calls Lazarus a prince (l. 5856) and Lazarus sings of the delights of youth and worldly riches. The refrain is: 'car il n'est plaisir que en jeunesse/ ne heur que de jeune adventureux' ('For there is no pleasure but in youth nor time like that of youthful adventures', ll. 5804–05, 5822–23, etc.) He rejoices in the seasonal cycle, for 'Fortune souldaine/ qui tout bien amaine,/ m'est doulce et humaine/ et au plus hault de son demaine/ me mect en sa roue. Jamais je n'eus peine... fier comme ung vaillant cappitaine' ('changeable Fortune, who leads to all good things, is gentle

---

[15]   See Billington, 'Social Disorder', pp. 218–19.

[16]   V. A. Kolve, *The Play called Corpus Christi* (Stanford: Stanford University Press, 1966), pp. 121–23.

and humane to me and has placed me at the highest point of her kingdom, on her wheel. I never feel pain... I am proud like a bold captain', ll. 5844–52). Lazarus is also explicit about the fitness of this cyclical system for those living in the mutable world: 'Le monde est par le temps conduyt/ et Fortune en est la maistresse,/ car, comme le temps se poursuyt,/ ainsi Fortune ses fais dresse. Les mondains sont pour leur pocesse, de mondanités curîeux' ('The world is driven by time, and Fortune is its mistress, for as time follows itself round, it is she who governs events. Those who are part of the world want possessions; they are interested in worldly things', ll. 5836–43). Lazarus is both a lord in the social hierarchy and, more significantly, a lord in the temporary midsummer of his youth, who exits in pursuit of new pleasurable *passe-temps*. But Michel's message is completed by the following scene, of the death of Jayrus's daughter, and Christ's resurrection of her—a reminder to the audience of the frequent untimely interruptions to a young person's pleasure which Lazarus himself is soon to meet. Lazarus will depend on Christ even for his physical well-being. Since Michel's play was performed in different 'mansions' on a single stage, the action was continuous, and moral meanings could be displayed by such contrasts without their being written didactically into the text.

Mary Magdalene appears in Day 2 and her refrain, too, is praise of the worldly life: Fortune has given her riches and Nature, beauty. She is caught up in all worldly joy and pleasure, living in a castle as a princess: 'Ou Fortune donne richesse/ et nature belle jeunesse/ avecques courage de sorte,/ plaisire mondain veult que on s'asorte/ en toute joyeuse lÿesse... je tiens estat de princesse... jay mon chateau de Magdalon' (ll. 8469-504). There is greater condemnation of Mary than of Lazarus, for she openly delights in gratifying the senses, even indulging the seven deadly sins, and primarily pride: 'Je suis en orgueil si hautaine...' (ll. 8590ff.). As though taking Philippe de Navarre's warning as licence, Mary says that brazen sinning at the top of the wheel is excused by her youth: 'Si donc en jeunesse quiers joye,/ Nature en moy ne se forvoye./ Je ne fasse que droit jeu, droit compte,/ Pour ce, personne ne s'esmoye/ si delict mondain me convoye,/ car Fortune au plus hault me monte' ('Therefore, if youth seeks joy, Nature is fulfilled in me; I am only playing the appropriate game. No-one can be angered if worldly pleasure guides me, for Fortune has placed me at the highest point', ll. 8620–25). Interestingly, it is she, rather than Lazarus, who uses the word 'heat': she is 'chault' (l. 8634) for worldly things. One can read the depiction of

Mary in two ways; it either reflects antipathy to women or it provides greater hope for the women in the audience for, unlike Lazarus, Mary becomes one of the blessed followers.[17]

Her wheeltop exultation is also contradicted by the following scene, where Tubal, the paralysed man, laments at the bottom of the wheel: 'je viz de vie fortunee/ en rigueur de Fortune nee... Fortune a sa roe tournee/ de tous poins a ma doleance' ('I see my life ruled by chance./ Born in the rigour of Fortune's laws... She turns her wheel at all points, to my sorrow', ll. 8648–54). And again Jesus reverses the wheel's progress for Tubal, restoring him to 'permanently vigorous health' (l. 8733). Tubal is saved by Christ, both from Fortune's power over him and from belief in her.[18]

The most daring combination of reigning with youthful elevation is in Michel's version of Satan's mountain temptation of Christ. In dialogue not in Gréban, Satan says he will, if Jesus wants, make him master of all he can see because Christ is 'elegant,/ sage, rassis, beau, jeune et grand,/ vertueux, digne de regner' (ll. 3004–06). 'Handsome, young, and tall' are irrelevant qualities, except in terms of summer kingship of youth at the top of Fortune's wheel.[19] In the Temptation scene, the height of the wheel

---

[17] E. A. Witt, in *Contrary Marys in Medieval English and French Drama* (New York: Peter Lang, 1995), sees both Gréban and Michel as writers promulgating anti-woman views. But Witt fails to take into account the dramatic context and the social conditions of the time. See Billington, 'Review', *The Early Drama, Art, and Music Review*, 19 (1996), pp. 54–56.

[18] At this point in the play Lazarus, Jayrus's daughter, Mary Magdalene, and Tubal are figurae of the *regno* and *sum sine regno* positions on the wheel. All four positions are explicitly explained and acted out in the French *moralité*, *Bien Advisé Mal Advisé*, while Fortune's comment after Regnavi's declaration of undiminished loyalty is the appropriate one of: 'Par saint iehan ce me plaist sire'. *Moralités françaises, Réimpression fac-simile de 22 pièces allégoriques imprimées aux XVᵉ et XVIᶠ siècles*, ed. by W. Helmich (Geneva: Slatkine, 1980), I, p. 80. There is also a woodcut of the wheel on fol. giii, Helmich, I, p. 79. Also, in *Moralité de l'Homme juste et de l'Homme mondain*, each vice makes obeisance to Homme Mondain as he sits on the *'Roue'*. (Helmich, I, p. 544). Cf. Yves Le Hir, 'Indications scéniques dans la moralité: *Bien Advisé et Mal Advisé'*, *Bibliothèque d'Humanisme et Renaissance*, 46 (1984), 399–405, and A. Hindley, 'Les VII Pechie Morteil: Dramatizing Sin in the Old French *Moralité'*, *Romance Studies*, 32 (Autumn 1998), 21–32.

[19] In the *Passion de Palatinus* (*c.* 1390) Cayfas sees Christ, in the distance, being brought before him and asks: Who is this man, whom I see 'si forment armez?/ Et qui est cil qui est entr'aus/ Qui de grandeur est li plus haut/ Et li plus jeune,' *La Passion de Palatinus: mystère du XIVe siècle*, ll. 289–93, ed. by G. Frank, CFMA (Paris: Champion, 1922), pp.

as a metaphor for this midsummer peak is supplied by the mountain on which Christ stands, with Satan there dressed as a devil-king. The stage directions read: *'Sathan en habit de roy'* (ll. 2959–60). A regal robe over his devil costume reveals him as the source of worldly power, the satanic controller behind Fortune's gifts of material success. And, as in Giélée's interpretation, this mountain setting is more damning than the wheel. Mary's and Lazarus's exultation in their kingship is part of a cycle they have not sought. The seasonal wheel they describe sweeps up all men and women whether they will or no, therefore the good fortune might as well be enjoyed before the bad follows. The mountain, however, is emblematic of ambition to greater fortune, and greater power, than come naturally in the cycle (see Appendix A). And, again, Christ demonstrates that man can release himself from Fortune's laws, and the threat of subsequent damnation, by his simple rejection of Satan's material promises.

In this pervasive Fortune environment where all that matters is to reign, it is not surprising to find Christ's deeds misunderstood by his enemies as competition for worldly power, and they accuse him, among themselves, of robbing them of their lordship: 'nostre honneur perdu... nostre revenue/ en diminue est nostre avoir/ car, jadis, soulîons avoir/ entre nous... l'honneur et la crainte des gens... appellés estions seigneurs .../ mais, maintenant... chascun le suyt, chascun l'honnoure' ('our honour is lost to

---

12–13. J. Ribard makes the point that in the Middle Ages it mattered that Jesus should have these qualities, since outward appearance reflected inner qualities. However, the words young and high (tall), have opposite connotations, put explicitly by Michault Taillevent in his 'Passe Temps', where to be 'young, handsome, and tall' is part of youthful worldly folly: 'S'on est beau, jeune, grant et fort,/ Let et malostru on devient/ Et de ce monde a grant effort/ On s'en reva ainsi qu'on vient. Riens n'y vault, enviellir convient,/ Et puis Mort vient qui tout acourse', *Un poète bourguignon du XVe siècle*, ed. Deschaux, p. 157. And, in Michel's play, St Peter uses the phrase in the speech before his betrayal (see below). However, it appears that the author of the *Passion of Palatinus* laid the groundwork carefully so as to give a Christian reinterpretation of the phrase. Immediately prior to Cayphas's observation came the incident in the Garden of Gethsemene where Mark tried to cut off the ear of a soldier. On restraining him, Christ said 'I do not wish to defend myself/ I hang on the cross of my own free will... I will suffer death without pride' (ll. 263–68). This reminder allows the use by Cayphas of those physical attributes which usually result in pride, without any negative reflection on Christ, since he does not hear them. The negative reflection is on Cayphas, who is himself limited to perceiving only physical qualities. See J. Ribard, 'Théâtre et Symbolisme au XIIIᵉ Siècle', in *The Theatre in the Middle Ages*, ed. by H. Braet et al., Mediaevalia Lovaniensia, Series I/ Studia XIII (Leuven: Leuven Univ. Press, 1985), pp. 103–18 (p. 115).

him... our income and wealth... Before, we had the honour and fear of
men... we were called lords... but now everyone follows and honours
him', ll. 1156–82).[20] To begin with, enemies and false followers persist in
seeing a worldly rise in Christ's fortune. On one level, therefore, this
four-part play can be seen as Christ's own wheel of fortune, which
reaches its apex at the end of Day 2 and beginning of Day 3, with the
finding of the ass and the entry into the high, or hilltop, city of Jerusalem
('la haulte Jerusalan', l. 15320). Christ's reception there is his worldly
zenith, where Christ could, if he wished, realize Satan's promises.
Temptation, in this play, is not limited to the earlier brief scene, but the
Christian perspective, free of pride, is established in the choice of the
ass's foal. As Simon, says: 'pas n'appete mondain honneur/ quant il
monte sur une anesse' (ll. 15299–300). Yet, this does not affect the way
others see him and Christ's reception in Jerusalem is that for a worldly
king. Without understanding what they say, the Jews call him 'le hautain
roy/ et le redempteur glorïeux' (ll. 15578–79), 'le roy benin sans rigueur/
qui doibt regner' (ll. 15542–43). Ironically prefiguring the Crucifixion,
they repeatedly and triumphantly call him 'roy des juifs' (ll. 15624–35).
As in the Gréban, Christ does not exult; instead he bewails the future fate
of the city: 'Jerusalan, pleure, pleure, ton roy!' (l. 15839). Having
rejected the people's offer, the worldly renown bestowed on him against
his will declines towards his death in Day 4. There is also a parallel with
the four-part sequence in the twelfth-century story of Alexander. Day 1 of
Michel's play shows Christ's initiation into his mission, Day 2 his
youthful exploits leading to great fame. Day 3 sees his decline and Day 4,
his death.[21]

   As his worldly influence ebbs, Christ's kingship is mocked, as de

---

[20] They do not use the word 'fortune' in relation to themselves—only to the state of Israel
(l. 11542).

[21] The *Passion d'Arras,* written in the early fifteenth century, is also in four parts and, in
the introductory address to the audience, the preacher calls it an experiment through game
'Car vous en verre plainement/ Par nostre jeu l'experiment' (ll. 40–41). Day 1 is of the
Nativity and ends with Jesus's boyhood. Day 2 opens with John the Baptist's ministry and
death and ends with the arrest of Christ. Day 3 follows the Passion and burial of Christ,
and Day 4, his Resurrection and Ascension. There is the suggestion of an inverse wheel
movement, falling before rising. The theme of the play, the preacher says, is to follow the
course of the sovereign of all the heavens who came down 'A summa celo egressio
eius:/du souverain de tous les cieulx' (ll. 49–50). He experiences the worst the world can
do and returns after redeeming it. See *Le Mystère de la Passion d'Arras,* ed. by J. M.
Richard (Geneva: Slatkine, 1976).

Julleville noted, with remorseless vigour;[22] he is insulted with the midsummer-king names and ragged costume and is beaten. The plot of the second half of the play moves relentlessly towards his death and burial.

Because the Harrowing of Hell and the Resurrection are omitted, it is not surprising that the play has been seen as a failure in terms of religious theatre, despite the brilliance of the writing. Yet, in view of the excellence of the writing, it seems we need to examine the text in greater detail and recall the numerous scenes throughout the four days, where, as already said, Christ overcomes Fortune's circular movement on behalf of others, curing madness, illness, and, most importantly, death. There are more scenes in the Michel than in the Gréban of Christ's power over mortality. The crucial one is again that of Lazarus, towards the end of Day 2, and this is preceded by Christ's reassurance: 'Je suis surrection et vie:/ celui qui bien en moy croyra,/ c'il est mort, encor vivra' (ll. 13675–80). This belief, further confirmed by the devils, comes immediately before Christ's mistaken summit in worldly Fortune, but it is Lazarus' resurrection which is the apex of Christ's true message. Similarly, before the Crucifixion, God the Father gives his reassurance to the saints in limbo that their freedom is imminent (ll. 25390–424), and at Christ's death on the cross, the devils anticipate his arrival in hell to carry this out.[23] Therefore, the more important sub-text is that Christ's burial is not the end of the Christian play, although it is of the pagan play; and, ironically, after the crucifixion, St Michael reminds Jerusalem of her prophesied decline in summer king terms: "Quant ton roy te laisse/ en fleur de jeunesse,/ ta couronne cesse,/ ton bien se depart, /tu pers ta noblesse.../tu pers ta richesse' ('When your king leaves you in the flower of youth, your crown fades, your comfort leaves, you lose your nobility and riches', ll. 28542–49). In this play, only those who live on Fortune's terms are faced with her reversals.

The drama is maintained through the constant struggle between pagan and Christian alternatives, for example, as noted above, in the disciple, Peter. His pre-conversion belief in fortune anticipates his later failing and, in Day 4, at the moment before his betrayal of Christ, he returns to these beliefs, aware that his youthful strength and vigour is a 'fortune'

---

[22] *Les Mystères,* I, pp. 224–25.

[23] Petit de Julleville was incorrect in saying that we see Christ undertake the Harrowing. Ibid., II, p. 445. As with the omission of the Resurrection, no moment of Christian triumph is shown at all.

which could change instantly to death, if he is found supporting Christ:

> Tu es robuste, fort et grand
> et n'as ozé porter garand
> a ton maistre tant doulx et saige!...
> Mais si Fortune va tourner
> et de son malheur m'atourner,
> je suis mort sans remission. (11. 21233–54)

> (You are well built, strong, and tall
> and haven't dared support
> your master, so gentle and wise...
> But if Fortune decides to turn
> and takes me along into misfortune
> I shall be well and truly dead.)

And 'sans remission' also carries the meaning of 'without forgiveness for sins', ironically suggesting the eternal death Peter is risking by following the Fortune argument. Peter's return to the pagan way of thinking makes him, momentarily, a better contender for the summer title, 'roy des couars'.

The mountain of Pride, where the Temptation took place, is also territory to be redeemed, and John the Baptist's opening sermon, in which he prophesies its humiliation (1. 1577), is shown not to be the only answer. John had been explicit that the mountain symbolized Lucifer's vice which infects men: 'les haultains les presumptueux' (1. 1586), such as we see in the elders, Judas, the *tyrans*, Barabbas—all of Christ's enemies.[24] In the Temptation scene the mountain as metaphor for worldly, satanic pride had been played out literally; while a low-life parody of such hilltop arrogance also appears in an exchange between soldiers (*tyrans*) and the jailer, Brayhault. He greets them aggressively and the rejoinder is: 'A, dea, tu es sur ton fumier,/ tu parles hault!' ('By god, you're standing on your muck-heap/ you're speaking haughty!' ll. 24620–21). It suggests that, despite Anjou's level countryside, mounds could be used to illustrate man's attempts at self-elevation.

The mountain in Michel's play, however, was placed on the stage immediately below heaven. It was the closest physical point to God, and Christ's defeat of Satan on it marks its Christian recuperation. Satan's boast that he is 'seigneur de tout le monde' (1. 3035) deflates with

---

[24] This theme is taken from the Gréban text. See Billington 'King and Queen Games', p. 97.

Christ's simple rejection. With a clown-like explosion of rage and despair he runs back to hell, to leap into its hottest part,[25] while Christ is sustained with food, and is glorified by God and the angels. Again, it is the visual presentation, here, rather than the text which shows where power really lies and, subsequently, the mountain is not levelled, but becomes Christian territory.

A further midsummer tradition used by Michel is free speech, firstly through the historical voice of John the Baptist when he walks into Herod's palace in his rags, and tells the king he must stop his adultery. Herod is not the obvious tyrant of English *Mystery* plays. He responds to John, as he does later to Christ, trying to win his trust and compliance. Interestingly, Herod considers both John and Christ as types of fool, the first, one who talks too much, and the second too little, and with the same result, for each is executed. Herod is the prime example in the play of corrupt, but subtle, worldly authority, holding the power of death over men. This is contrasted with the actions of Christ, whose spiritual power repeatedly gives men and women life.

The midsummer liberty of free speech is taken further by the author when he addresses social failings of the time, particularly of the Church's organization in the fifteenth century. One insidious effect of prolonged war was the wrong sort of men taking orders. In 1431 at the Church Council of Nantes it was observed that:

> [M]agnus error hodie reperitur in Dei Ecclesia, dum innumerose persone et abjecta vita, scientia et moribus insufficientes, ad sacerdotium et quod longe damnabilius est ad curam et regimen preferuntur animarum....'
>
> (Today great error is found in the Church of God, where many men leading contemptible and worthless lives, lacking in learning or morals, arrive in the priesthood and what is even more damnable are preferred to the care and ordering of souls....')[26]

Articles of reform issued in 1493 reveal just how far religious communities had diverged from their calling,[27] and Michel throws down his own gauntlets to the churchmen in his audience. One challenge comes

---

[25] The potential in the devils for comedy could well have been drawn on in some *sotties*. The sixteenth-century *Sottie nouvelle à six personnaiges* (Picot, ed., III, l. 209) opens with a boast by the Roy des Sotz: 'Je suis des sotz seigneur et roy'.

[26] *Les conciles de la province de Tours: XIIIe–XVe siècles,* ed. by J. Avril (Paris: Centre National de la Recherche Scientifique, 1987), p. 426.

[27] See Billington, 'Social Disorder', pp. 219–21.

in the scene of Peter's betrayal of Christ for, unlike Gréban, Michel includes the third denial, the cock crow, followed by Peter's remorse when he recollects Christ's words that his name would be the stone of the new Church:

> Pierre qui ay le cueur pierreux
> d'avoir la pierre habandonnee
> sur quoy Sainct Eglise est fondee.... (ll. 22157–59)

> (Peter, with a heart of stone,
> has abandoned the stone
> on which the Holy Church is founded....)

He pleads for forgiveness:

> O doulx Jesus, qui es souverain bien,
> regard moy, s'il te plaist, en pitié.
> Las, j'ay peché, mais a toy je revien.... (ll. 22187–89)

> (Oh, sweet Jesus, who is the sovereign good,
> look at me, please, with pity.
> Alas I have sinned, but I return to you....)

This pleading continues for over forty lines, begging that his moment of worldliness should not lose him his eternal life: 'My fearful heart and my worldly senses/ have revealed their stupidity.../ Alas, the good I have merited/ on your account, Jesus, I have suddenly lost;/ for this I sigh and weep many tears.../ crying: alas, don't close the heavens to me', ll. 22197–205). Peter here is a very flawed first Pope and, in the context of fifteenth-century churchmen abandoning their religious principles, the long lament provides a public challenge to the many churchmen in the audience over their own possible betrayal. It is interesting to note that Judas was played by a priest, canon Thibault Binel.[28] Other priests played God and the Virgin Mary and, although these might be sanctified roles, priests were not supposed to act at all.

Finally, it would appear that Michel incorporated romance tradition in his depiction of pre-conversion, or antichristian failings. Lazarus and Mary Magdalene, are clearly based on concepts of chivalry, Lazarus in his hawking and hunting, while Mary is more explicitly connected to Arthurian mythology in her claim to be acquainted with the round table ('Je puis bien tenir table ronde', l. 8522): Angers, as well as Arras, had its

---

[28] Ibid., p. 222.

Puy. Yet, in the religious context, Arthur's court had become the form in which to express frivolity and self-gratification to the point of damnation.

An even more bizarre adaptation of this can, I think, be suggested for Judas, who becomes Pilate's wildly erring steward and who, despite his attempts towards redemption, only succeeds in damning himself. In Michel's extended story, in Day 1, he is presented as a Perceval who is as aggressive as Kay; and his parents, Ruben and Cyboree, enter—rich but unhappy—lamenting the disappearance of their son, who has gone to seek his Fortune' (l. 3592) following the same road as Pilate (l. 3563). Judas then enters their garden looking, significantly, for apples required by his master. Ruben does not recognize him and challenges him; Judas kills Ruben and then marries his mother, Cyboree.[29]

In support of the marriage, Pilate argues that Judas is a man 'pour estre... grand seigneur' (l. 3815), and should make amends to the widow of the man he has killed, by marrying her. This romance treatment of the Oedipus myth is utterly fanciful, but Judas becomes an example of the inversion of Christian purity, and a mock lord during the time when Christian order does not prevail: an appropriately disordered *maistre d'hotel'* (l. 3764) for Pilate, whose judgement is equally flawed. Further, during the marriage debate Cyboree undergoes a Laudine-like reversal,[30] first lamenting the ill fortune of Ruben's death and accusing Pilate's steward. The next moment she agrees to the remarriage, and her protests become humble. Judas and she, Cyboree says, are opposites in fortune: 'vous estes homme de grant fait,/... jeune, fort, plaisant et affect/ d'honneur, entre gens avenant' (ll. 3856–59). Crucially, Judas is young and strong. By contrast she is 'aage, simple et ignorante,/ veufve, adeullee piteusement,/ sans port d'amys et pou sçavante' (ll. 3860–63): this, despite the fact that Pilate had described her as full of honour (l. 3813). In reply, Judas says he has never been more enamoured; blond or brunette has never fired him more: 'jamais... ne me chault clere ou brune' (ll. 3869–70). The scene makes most sense as a damning parody of summer romance tradition, and is helped by its late-summer performance, while,

---

[29] For studies on the Oedipus myth in the portrayal of Judas see M. Accarie, *Le Théâtre de la fin du Moyen Age: étude sur le sens moral de la Passion de Jean Michel* (Geneva: Droz, 1979), pp. 251–63 and R. Axton, 'Interpretations of Judas in Middle English Literature', in *Religion in the Poetry and Drama of the Late Middle Ages,* ed. by P. Boitani and A. Torti (Cambridge: D. S. Brewer, 1990), pp. 179–98.

[30] First noted by E. DuBruck, in 'The Perception of Evil in Jean Michel's *Mystère de la Passion* (1486)', *Michigan Academician,* 15 (1982–83), 253–63 (p. 256).

in another scenic contrast, Michel follows Judas and Cyboree with a perfect mother/son exchange between Mary and Christ.

Through staging and textual subtleties, Michel created a composite kaleidoscope of many aspects of social and literary licence associated with summer behaviour, all used to build around Christ a highly corrupt society in need of redemption. This is largely the reason why, at the Renaissance, the play was condemned for not being sufficiently respectful to him. Critics have objected to the fact that the torturers enjoy their task, and that scenes of Mary Magdalene's frivolity interrupt the sanctity of Christ's transfiguration on the mountain.[31] In the second case, time was needed for the actor playing Christ to change into the trans-figuration costume and to be lifted to the top of the mountain. Michel uses it to show that, despite the cosmic revelation, worldly values do in fact still dominate in the world. Similarly, Mary Magdalene's initial interest in Christ is a physical one. She would like to add him to her admirers, but is herself conquered on a spiritual level. In all these points, Michel confronted worldly realities head-on. The Hundred Years War had left a legacy of anarchy, and he appears to have been too aware of the harsh conditions people were emerging from to condemn ordinary people for the superstitions and practices they had turned to—he even portrays some of the ignorant villains as victims.[32] Therefore, Lazarus and Mary Magdalene are not to be condemned for their sinfulness, but to be rescued from it. Nor does Michel reject all festivity: the Apostle John says Christ deserves a welcome in Jerusalem, as a 'roy plein de simplesse' (l. 15200) and *feste* forms a large part of Christ's ministry. Many scenes include hospitable eating and drinking, from the dinner with the debt-collector, to the wedding at Cana and the miracle of the loaves and fishes. In the marriage at Cana there is a also a midsummer moment. Marriages might be seen, as said, as a form of kingship, the topmost point of fortune for young people on the seasonal cycle (Fig. 4). When the wine runs out Mary appeals to Christ that 'la feste fort s'empire/ Et tourne a honte et a escande/ sur l'espoux' ('the festival is going very wrong, and is turning to shame and scandal on the couple', ll. 5204–06). Since Christ's intervention prevents this, once more he stops the wheel from its downward turn and allows the festivity to continue.

This moment is the nearest Michel goes to endorsing midsummer

---

[31] Petit de Julleville, *Les Mystères*, I, pp. 224–25.

[32] Billington, 'Social Disorder', p. 233.

traditions; the association with pride at midsummer makes a positive Christian incorporation of the season difficult. This, and its association with Fortune, not only fits it for the pre-Christian world, it also provides symbols of un-Christian behaviour. However, it is possible that the author of *The Passion of Palatinus* did attempt to recuperate midsummer associations by making their symbolic context Easter.[33] And there is a further adaptation in the fifteenth-century Brussels manuscript transcription of Augustine's *City of God.* This is not theatre except in the fact that the illumination presents a scene, to be interpreted (cover illustration). Augustine sits, reading, on a hilltop; the sun is high overhead, and King Clovis stands as secular supporter of God's word on the right-hand side of the picture. In the explanatory Introduction the scribe wrote that St Augustine must be called the king of the early Church: 'MonS. saint Augustine entre les docteurs de leglise primitive Il peut & doibt estre compare [à laigle] Et clame Roy. Aussy come laigle est repute Roy et souverain des oiziaux.'[34] Therefore, in this dubious setting, Augustine is also claimed as a lord and king. However, careful alteration has been made to avoid the sin of pride. The sun may be high overhead, in the June position, but it is obscured by a cloud, and the figures below focus on the book. As the scribe explains, the sun, here, is the wisdom of God which cannot be seen directly. Only through the book can such wisdom be glimpsed by mortal men. Judging by the scribe's own comments, as well as other evidence considered here, it would seem that the significance of the illustration lies in a reinterpretation of festive traditions. Just as the devil should not have all the best tunes, the illuminator, here, shows that Christianity can be celebratory in its appreciation of the good things of the natural world, without damnation.

---

[33] The Passion took place at Passover, called, in line 2, '*La sainte Pasque*'. The singular form, *pasque* means Passover, yet the inclusion of, 'holy', and the capital 'P', bring Easter to mind. See n. 18.

[34] Bibliothèque Royale, Brussels, MS 9015, fol. 1ᵛ.

Conclusion

Just as there were diverse systems of calculating Ages in the individual's lifespan, so too there were various ways to assess the passing of time. Peter Travis has considered five: the philosophical method of relating it to eternity, 'the science [*computus*] by which medieval scholars sought to forecast the precise date of Christ's resurrection and thus the precise dates of all the other movable feasts in the liturgical year',[1] time measured according to the fixed co-ordinates of the astrolabe, and the two methods which most affected people's lives, the clock and the seasonal calendar.

One view which has developed through a too definitive reading of Jacques le Goff's *Time, Work and Culture in the Middle Ages* is that dependence on the clock neatly superseded the influence of seasonal computation during the course of the Middle Ages due to the growing dominance of bourgeois trade over the regulations of the Church. However, as Gerhard Dohrn-van Rossum demonstrates, although more exact timekeeping provided by clocks was essential to maintain businesses, different social groups did not restrict themselves to any one system but, instead, adopted the method appropriate to the task in hand.[2] Church

---

[1] Peter W. Travis, 'Chaucer's Chronographiae, the Confounded Reader, and Fourteenth-Century Measurements of Time', *Disputatio*, 2 (1997), pp. 1–34 (p. 3).

[2] G. Dohrn-van Rossum, *History of the Hour: Clocks and Modern Temporal Orders*, trans. by T. Dunlap (Chicago: Chicago University Press, 1996). Cf. Jacques le Goff, *Time, Work and Culture in the Middle Ages*, trans. by A. Goldhammer (Chicago: Chicago University Press, 1980).

authorities were in the forefront of clock developments and Travis cites
the example of clerics in the University of Oxford, who, by the end of the
fourteenth century, measured their daily academic exercises 'in equal
units of time [instead of] twelve liturgical hours which expanded to fill up
the time from sunrise to set no matter the day's length'.[3]

Thanks to Dohrn-van Rossum's work, one can see how early and how
widespread was the influence of clock-based timekeeping through the use
of sundials, bells, and mechanical timepieces. It can also be argued that
clock-based methods of recording and measuring time, particularly when
executed by signals such as bells, rather than by a circular dial, also
presented a *tabula rasa,* an objective context for transactions and their
record. The understanding of time which clocks produce is, on the whole,
linear and progressive, certainly in comparison with seasonal timekeeping, which interprets more than it measures. The meanings perceived
in each season depend on their relation to other seasons in the cyclic
movement; therefore the system is necessarily anti-progressive, continual-
ly reinforcing the perception that life is tied to a wheel. The Trinity
College, Cambridge MS 12 illustration accentuates this circular limitation
by making the naked baby and the naked corpse one and the same image
(Fig. 3, p. 31). Within the cycle there were moments of real celebration
as, for example, in the optimism of spring and the reward of harvest. But
seasonal evaluation of time tended to reflect the post-Adam view of a
fallen world, where achievement was judged, not as a success, but as sus-
pect self-aggrandizement which would, eventually, turn to dust. It is,
perhaps, ironic that today's disillusionment with the concept of progress
has led to a re-evaluation of cyclic time, seeing it as more stable because
recurring, so providing 'a sense of continuity, unity, and identification
with the history of mankind as a whole'.[4] In the Middle Ages, it was often
perceived to be a treadmill under Fortune's dubious control, with escape
only possible through Christian faith, bourgeois moderation, and, perhaps, the help of the more objective clock. This antifestive perspective
permeates the work of many writers and, as early as 1178, the progress of
Chrétien's Yvain was accompanied by a change from seasonal to clock-
based timekeeping. Yet the shifts were not all one way and in *Le Tournoi
de l'Antéchrist,* for example, it is a more precise hourly timing which

---

[3] Travis, p. 7.

[4] Hans Meyerhoff, *Time in Literature* (Berkeley: California University Press, 1960), p.
104.

records the moment of Antichrist's decline.[5] In practice, a pick-and-mix approach was logical and, while the clock's influence was more extensive than has sometimes been thought, the use of calendrical measurements did not die out, as the chapters above show. One of the most popular early printed works was a calendar: *Le Grant Kalendrier et Compost des Bergiers*, first printed in 1480 with subsequent reprints and translations throughout the sixteenth, seventeenth, and even the eighteenth centuries.[6]

Seasonal measurements obviously retained their value in the cultivated fields beyond the suburbs. In this rural society linear time tended to be only vaguely calculated: 'A father would indicate that his son was "about ten or twelve years old," [or] someone would be accused of a crime committed "from four to six weeks" before.'[7] Similar imprecision is found in the charge against Jean Le Doulx. Even though this was brought in the city of Lyon as late as 1466, Le Doulx was said to have been arrested *'dimanche derrenierement'* (Sunday recently past).[8] And among the bourgeoisie some aspects of the cyclic view appear to have held some sense. The wariness towards youths, expressed in Metz in 1551, was institutionalized in the gild system in Coventry at the same period. A man below the age of twenty-five was designated a 'young man', and not admitted to any offices. At about twenty-five he was redefined as a 'New brother', stable enough to be given responsibility. From there on the cyclic pattern was irrelevant and a man's career developed along progressive tracks, since achievement was only rewarded in later life, and those Coventry dignitaries made Sheriff or Mayor in their forties and fifties were obviously not languishing under Fortune's wheel.[9]

Towns themselves were relatively safe places, functioning according to statutes and laws, and behind protective walls, which formed 'not only a

---

[5] 'Li soleuz ot ja tant erré,/ Que par le grant chemin ferré/ Est venuz de medi a nonne.' ('The sun had already wandered so far along its road that it had travelled from midday to "none"' or 3 p.m.). Huon de Mery, *Le Tournoi de l'Antéchrist*, ll. 2901–03, ed. Orgueur, p. 220–21.

[6] See *Le Grant Kalendrier et Compost des Bergiers* (Paris, 1480), facsimile (Geneva: Slatkine, 1978), and *Le Grand Calendrier et Compost des Bergers* (Troyes, 1728).

[7] R. Muchembled, trans. Cochrane, *Popular Culture and Elite Culture in France*, p. 47.

[8] '"dimanche derrenierement". Cela peut s'entendre aussi bien du 29 juin que du 6 juillet.' L. Caillet, 'Projet d'Empoisonnement de Louis XI', p. 1, n. 2.

[9] Charles Phythian-Adams, *The Desolation of a City: Coventry and the Urban Crisis of the Later Middle Ages* (Cambridge: Cambridge University Press, 1979), p. 126.

physical, but also a psychological, frontier.'[10] Jacques Bruneau said that the summer games, which he did *not* write about, took place 'in the fields' 'outside the town'. City authorities had no jurisdiction over the open land beyond the suburbs. It was literally lawless, therefore, the one place where the enacting of challenges to law would not, in fact, be real rebellion against the town. Such a lawless area is presented as a perverted summer paradise in the setting for the 1507 *Sotise à huit personnaiges*, while in Huon de Mery's *Tournoi* Antichrist leads his hundreds of bachelor Vices out from the town of Despair into the fields. And it is a curious fact that, when the young Richard II confronted the Kentish rebels occupying the City of London on 15 June 1381, in those dangerous moments after their leader had been killed Richard is said to have won their trust with the words: 'I will be your chief and captain... Only follow me into the fields.'[11] He appears to have diffused the danger of further violence in the city by steering an actual rebellion back into the form of a game in the fields outside, and by replacing their mock-king leader with the real king for whom they still had loyalty. Turning politics into drama, here, worked in favour of authority.

Yet the possibility that violence, stemming from midsummer freedoms, might involve the town itself was always a danger, as happened the day after St John's Day in Metz, in 1405. Phythian-Adams has observed that in England, where carnival was not greatly observed, other seasons, such as midsummer, could well have been the outlet for excesses and John Stow's observation, in 1600, that the civic midsummer watches were established to bring about a sense of community and brotherhood leads to the possibility that, in England, this was another creative bourgeois idea for the rechannelling of such discordant energies:

> In the moneths of Iune and Iuly, on the vigiles of festiuall dayes, and on the same festiuall dayes in the Euenings... there were vsually made Bonefiers in the streetes, euery man bestowing wood or labour towards them: the wealthier sort also before their doores neare to the said Bonefiers, would set out Tables on the Vigiles, furnished with sweete breade, and good drinke, and on the Festiuall dayes with meates and drinks plentifully, whereunto they would inuite their neighbours and passengers also to sit, and bee merrie with them in great familiaritie, praysing God for his benefites bestowed on them. These were called Bonefiers... of good amitie amongest neighbours that, being before at controuersie, were there by the

---

[10] Ibid., p. 174.

[11] Charles Oman, *The Great Revolt of 1381* (Oxford: Clarendon Press, 1906), p. 76.

labour of others, reconciled, and made of bitter enemies, louing friendes.[12]

The midsummer practices, here, are designed to eliminate divisiveness in the hot months and they follow the sixteenth-century trend for English festivity to be divested of its rebellious potential. Political comment only appeared successfully in the festive histories and tragedies written for London's first professional theatre.[13] Seasonal activities on the Continent, however, were not so tidy, nor did Shrovetide ventilate all the year's licensed disturbances. From the twelfth century on summertime and carnival had distinct traditions and at midsummer the form of aggression considered integral to the season was verbal, resulting in political engagement rather than in a more physical attempt to overthrow the status quo. It is possible that William, Bishop of Mende, was well insulated from either, for he was sympathetic towards festive activity in general, drawing on the example of the Hebrews as well as of the Romans, and even quoting the pagan, Ovid, in support of the popular viewpoint:

> Salve festa dies, meliorque revertere semper,
> A populo rerum digna potente coli.
>
> (Welcome, festive day! and more welcome, ever returning!
> Worthy to be honoured by a prosperous people.)[14]

Until the end of the sixteenth century, and despite growing urbanization, life for most people still ran according to seasonal rhythms. Evidence from France and Britain shows just how reluctant city populations were to relinquish their festive liberties, still planning or saving certain activities for the season appropriate to them. In Laon, in 1587, this was to illustrate a political point, while London had a non-political and a more structured festive season. The concept of disorder was so integral to winter that lords of misrule were elected on 31 October because that was the night when disruptive elements were believed to be at large. These forces were then celebrated during the appropriate dark months of the year, and their reign ended at the festival of light on 2 February.[15] The importance of precise timekeeping did not mean the end of time's sea-

---

[12] John Stow, *A Survey of London Reprinted from the Text of 1603*, ed. by C. L. Kingsford (Oxford: Clarendon Press, 1908; repr. 1971), vol. 1, p. 101.

[13] See Billington, *Mock Kings*, pp. 128–38 and 218–39 and J. Dollimore, *Radical Tragedy* (Brighton: Harvester Press, 1984).

[14] *Rationale Divinorum Officiorum*, ed. d'Avino, p. 734.

[15] John Stow, *A Survey of London* p. 97. Billington, *Mock Kings*, p. 3.

sonal commemorations.

And, in answer to Jean-Claude Aubailly's question regarding the possibility of a period of festivities connected with the St John,[16] it is clear that there was one: a festive expression of divisiveness rather than of community. Yet Aubailly noted that May was a month sympathetic to women and his evidence suggests a cyclic development from 1 May to the end of June and beyond. At the beginning of summer when young men first begin to boil—turning into besotted suitors—women were in control. There are instances of girls, chosen for May garlands by would-be beaus, who returned the favour by speaking openly about the man's failings. The queen of the May was a more important role than was that of her festive spouse and, on St Agatha's day in May, wives had the right to give orders to their husbands (Aubailly, pp. 49–50). As the season progressed, its subject became the wilfulness of men, their power-hunger, the fragile nature of their youthful emotions, and the instability of more public success. The shift at midsummer was to include public as well as private concerns, with games focusing on individuals who were perceived to have abused their position and, where relevant, these exposés might continue until, or be resumed at, the *decollatio*.

Aubailly also queried whether there might have been dramas associated with a midsummer cycle. As well as improvised incidents, such as in Lyon in 1466 and Laon in 1587, it can be argued that the scripted plays consciously associated with this season were those Corpus Christi, Mystery, and Passion plays which contain a midsummer mockery of Christ in the summer game of torturers, and the eventual overturning of material power by spiritual forces. These plays appear to have been made integral to the midsummer cycle as part of the Church's ongoing attempt to re-Christianize the secular.[17]

Midsummer customs were seminal and it is not possible any more to say that of 'all the popular lay festivals Carnival presents the archetypical form against which others can be measured'.[18] The first festive novel was written in 1178 by Chrétien de Troyes and he took his inspiration from behaviour at, and around, the St John. It was this which provided the

---

[16] 'Théâtre Médiéval et Fêtes Calendaires ou l'Histoire d'une Subversion', p. 57.

[17] See Peter Happé's reading of 'cycle' in the context of religious drama in 'Cycle Plays: The State of the Art', in *European Medieval Drama*, ed. by S. Higgins, vol. 2 (Turnhout: Brepols, 1998), 63–84 (p. 64).

[18] E. Muir, *Ritual in Early Modern Europe* (Cambridge: Cambridge University Press, 1997), p. 86.

archetypical form for his plot structure and symbolic imagery. Chrétien's works are truly festive because his characters experience the season, ('*vivre le temps*', P. Walter, p. 10). In the first half of *Yvain,* all the main characters, but especially Yvain, live the arrogance, combativeness, and changeability of the St John's Day period while, the following year, Yvain's more humble experiences begin close to the *decollatio.* In *Erec and Enide,* Erec's courtly behaviour changes after Pentecost in an unexplained and perplexing way unless seen against festive principles. As Barber put it: if characters 'do not seek holiday it happens to them',[19] and this perception explains Erec's unreasonable volte-face. It is as though, on the wheel of life, Erec must change after Pentecost: the new season dictates his behaviour.

Yet, one may ask, why was it the post-Pentecost period which provided the archetypal festive experience, with carnival never mentioned by Chrétien, although it was in existence at the time? Two possible explanations come to mind. One is that midsummer games played out issues of power, frequently involving figures of secular authority, and the romances were for an aristocratic readership. This could explain why they were chosen by Chrétien, but not why they were so dominant that they were the obvious ones to choose. An explanation for this may lie in the comparatively liberal nature of the twelfth century. It was a time when many communities felt they could throw off the shackles of the feudal system and some succeeded for a while. The people of Troyes, for example, enjoyed more freedoms under its counts, Henri le Liberal and Thibaut III, than they were to know for many subsequent centuries.[20] And Louvain's celebrations of 1267 show how midsummer symbolism was used to express their change towards autonomy. When church and state power became more insistent from the end of the thirteenth century (so provoking satires such as that by Giélée) it would be understandable if carnival customs were found marginally more tolerable than was a challenge to, or satire on, actual men in power. The way that Adam de la Halle buries his verbal attack on the *échevins* of Arras in a more general, quarrelsome saturnalia, would seem to support this. Carnival is, at least, inclusive; it celebrates folly as a universal condition through generalized, symbolic names such as '*sot lunatique*', instead of singling out specific

---

[19] Barber, *Shakespeare's Festive Comedy*, p. 6.

[20] M. Boutiot, *Des Institutions communales dans la Champagne Méridionale aux XIIᵉ et XIIIᵉ siècles* (Troyes, 1865).

reprobates such as, 'sire Ermenfrois Crespins'. In Italy, the travelling *guillare,* who attacked great men by name, were executed if caught, while the generalized satire of *commedia dell'arte* flourished.[21] Erasmus, in his *Moriae Encomium,* included serious criticism of churchmen as part of an all-fool parade, and the work was said to have made Pope Leo X laugh.[22] Nine years later, however, the same Pope was rather less amused by Martin Luther's personalized, St John's eve attack. As Ben Jonson put it in the early seventeenth century: 'the age is grown so tender of her fame... I name no persons, but deride follies... vices generally'.[23] St John's day name-calling is, at its mildest, provocative; at its strongest the principle is revolutionary in both the ancient and the modern sense and, after their rebellion of 26 June 1405, the disenfranchised *métiers* of Metz attempted to establish a new, classless *commune.*[24]

The disorder of carnival can be uncontrollable or, by the sixteenth century, deliberately rebellious,[25] but its philosophy is more oblique, and the principle of total inversion is ultimately forgiving. This is not only safer, it can be more fruitful for comic drama, as Edwin Muir has noted.[26] To 'celebrate and deride' everyone produces a wide thematic range, a large canvas on which to explore human follies at all social levels and covering any subject.[27] The concept invites the audience to be self-critical, moving from an assumption that the inverted world is make-believe which can be laughed at while we remain safe in the real world, to an understanding that the *mundus inversus* is the real world stripped of pretence, as, for example, in the last line of Ben Jonson's *Bartholomew Fair*: 'We'll have the rest of the play at home' (V. 6. 111).

---

[21] T. Mitchell, *Dario Fo: People's Court Jester* (London: Methuen, 1984), pp. 11–12.

[22] *Praise of Folly and Letter to Martin Dorp,* ed. by A. H. T. Levi (Harmondsworth: Penguin, 1971), p. 8.

[23] *Ben Jonson's* Timber, ed. by F. E. Schelling (Boston, 1892), p. 72.

[24] F.-Y. le Moigne, *Histoire de Metz,* p. 156.

[25] S. Kinser, 'Why is Carnival so Wild', in *Carnival and the Carnivalesque,* ed. by K. Eisenbichler and W. Hüsken, Ludus, vol. 4 (Amsterdam: Rodopi, 1999), pp. 53–88. All Kinser's examples of specific carnivals come from the later Middle Ages and it is interesting to note that an earlier and challenging example Kinser includes is from Boccaccio's *Decameron.* Boccaccio set his tales during the hottest days of July; therefore, in this example (pp. 49–50), we see Boccaccio taking a carnival custom and making it more specifically personal and satirical, in his high summer context.

[26] Muir, *Ritual in Early Modern Europe,* p. 86

[27] M. Bakhtin, *Rabelais,* pp. 11–12.

The more pointed challenge to pride and power at midsummer was exclusive: it had an us and them mentality: or, as they say in the North of England, 'all the world's odd save thee and me, and even thee's a little odd'. The solsticial nature of the jokes also contains an implicit moral, which was avoided by writers from Chrétien to Adam de la Halle, since their multiple targets created a kind of universality which could be called midsummer saturnalia. Yet the follies exposed are limited to varieties of pride resulting in shame, both of which are derided. The whole point of the comedy is that it is one in which the reader laughs at, rather than with, the protagonists. And, in further contrast to the inclusiveness of carnival, these characters' actions are laughable largely because they arise from their wish to stand out as different from, and greater than, the rest of their society.

The wealth of evidence from 1500 on does then confirm that carnival replaced midsummer as the prime season of licence. Yet the *Sotise à huit personnaiges* (1507) contained elements from both, and it comes as more than a researcher can hope for to find another text which explicitly illustrates the transition from the dominance of St John's day to that of the winter season. The work, François Girault's *Chronicques admirables du Puissant Roy Gargantua*, is the one Rabelais was to use, and was based on the 1532 shorter text with the longer title, *Les grandes et inestimables Chronicques du grant et enorme geant Gargantua: Contenant sa genealogie; la grandeur & force de son corps. Aussi les merueilleux faictz darmes quil fist pour le* Roy Artus.[28] Praise of a giant is obviously an apotheosis of a young man, great and strong and tall: this time not an opponent to Arthur, but his rescuer. And the manner in which Girault continued the romance burlesque two years later suggests that he assumed the liberties of the winter season to turn those of summer into farce.

In chapter VI, Gargantua's parents are advised by Merlin to take the seven-year-old Gargantua to Arthur's court. They reply that, because of the monopoly on bread, they cannot afford to do this (see Appendix E). Merlin apprises Arthur who, immediately, hangs the offending courtiers, punishes the bakers and, for good measure, reforms the police. The giants eat their fill and prepare to leave, so causing great sorrow among the grateful people, and their hot tears create a fountain in which you could

---

[28] The text used is *The Tale of Gargantua and King Arthur by François Girault, c. 1534*, ed. by H. Brown (Cambridge, MA: Harvard University Press, 1932).

cook eggs on all the feast days from Christmas eve to the day after Epiphany. From this fountain, nine days before the St John, came a cock and a hen which laid eggs as large as bushels. On the eve of St John the people hurled these into the fountain and there emerged two chickens larger than hackney horses. Arthur cherished them because they were useful to him when he went to war. He could ride them into battle; their huge golden feathers provided his crest, which blinded the enemy when the rays of the sun reflected off them. The chickens were so huge that when they raised their wings they could overturn a fully armed man on horseback.

In the original romances Arthur is an inactive king, and it is a Gawain, or an Yvain, or a Fergus, whose adventures we follow. In Girault's parody, Arthur is in fact upstaged by a chicken. The bird, famous as a symbol of cowardice, is turned into a supra-natural warrior. Girault takes the burlesque found in *Fergus* one stage further by turning the familiar St John's day traditions of man's prowess and pride upside-down. And, since the section opens with a reference to both seasons, it would appear that he was signalling just such an intention to merge traditions.

Yet midsummer incidents still occurred, as the events at Laon show, and their ethos continued to feed into many works now thought of as carnivalesque. For example, the mockery between Hal and Falstaff in Shakespeare's *Henry IV, Part 1* (II. 5. 380–445) includes a scene of 'improvised' sketches, where each man abuses the other, and also the king. Such politically subversive, personalized, and challenging material originated not with carnival, but from midsummer liberties.

These freedoms, taken to their ultimate conclusion as in Louvain, Metz, and Laon, were a way of displaying the successful rejection of a hegemony. And the tradition still appears to have been in the popular repertoire during the French Revolution of 1789, for the treatment of some incidents which arose around midsummer in the years 1790–93 reveals their seasonal dramatization. The most notable incident occurred on 20 June 1790 when a group of *sans culottes* from the outskirts of Paris forced their way into the Tuileries, where Louis was under house arrest. They forced him to put on a red bonnet and cry, 'Vive la Nation'.[29] A cartoon of the time (Fig. 7) shows the inversion of actual power, resulting in the public humiliation of the one-time Sun King: an event not unlike the Prévôt's public humiliation in Laon in 1587. In 1792, after Louis's

[29] Georges Soria, *Grande Histoire de la Révolution Française* (Paris: Bordas, 1988), vol. 2, *Les Paroxysmes*, pp. 686–87.

*Figure 7: 20 June 17**92**, engraving. Louis XVI forced to put on a red*   ι 7؟υ?
bonnet and cry, 'Vive la Nation'.

attempted flight to Flanders on 20 June, he was brought back into Paris
on 25 June. His enforced return could have been the scene of a disastrous
and uncontrolled political *charivari:*

> The street was lined with immense crowds of tight-mouthed people, grim
> and reproachful. On the walls placards warned: Whoever applauds the king
> will be flogged; whoever insults him will be hanged.[30]

---

[30] S. K. Padover, *The Life and Death of Louis XVI* (New York and London: Appleton-

During the Revolution there were conscious attempts to leave feudal traditions behind. They only helped perpetuate the mindset which had maintained France's ancient social problems, and the Calendar itself was changed in 1794. Nevertheless, the year before this, there was a publication in Troyes, on 24 June, of the freedoms claimed by all the French. '*Souveraineté du peuple*' included the right for them to name their representatives, to be involved in the making of laws, and to choose administrators and judges. The document has much in common with the acts and declarations of self-government made previously on 24 June in Louvain and Metz.[31]

In more recent centuries, some use has been made of the theme of power at midsummer in plays such as Strindberg's *Miss Julie,* and, possibly, in Ibsen's *An Enemy of the People,* and Synge's *Playboy of the Western World.* The medieval element is also there in the satanic theme of Mussorgsky's 'St John's Night on the Bald Mountain'. However, such examples are no longer part of a commonly-held tradition, whereas in the Middle Ages, St John's day customs provided a unifying thread through disparate works, enabling the reader today to perceive them as a genre, instead of dividing all medieval literature into sections with nothing in common.

For in medieval and early modern society, where the lives of ordinary people held little value to their political masters, it is not surprising if people refused to relinquish traditions which not only gave their lives colour but, more importantly, empowerment. And, in view of this, it is surprising to find just how socially inclusive this divisive festive tradition could be. In the twelfth and thirteenth centuries in particular, the concept of one culture for the people and another for the upper classes appears to have been absent. St John's day traditions were acceptable to Chrétien's courtly readership even though the feudal system could be challenged in them and, in Louvain, in 1267, the Duke of Brabant accepted their incorporation as an expression of that city's political freedoms. Not every poet or playwright used them, but those who did provide twentieth-century readers with a chart of changing perceptions of man's place in relation to the cosmos, the Church, and the political system. Fortune's control of the seasonal progression of man's life from spring to winter was part of the

Century, 1939), p. 230.

[31] *Acte constitutionnel présenté au Peuple français, par la Convention Nationale, le 24 juin 1793: Déclaration des droits de l'homme et du citoyen*, Bibliothèque Municipale de Troyes, cat. no. 5658.

feudal perception of man's place in the fallen world, to be accepted as inevitable. But the stoicism was questioned by writers such as Giélée and de la Mote in their use of the midsummer turning point: it was also questioned from a religious point of view by Jean Michel.

Finally, we need not be surprised any more at the extensive use some writers made of Fortune and her principles, even her unprincipled principles, nor raise doubts over Boethius's fidelity to Christianity, because of his use of her in debate. Even though she was anathema to some churchmen, none of the examples examined here could be a threat to Christianity, nor to its central belief that this life is a preparation for the next. The placing of the Baptist's Nativity on 24 June created a buffer behind which Christian society never really disengaged from the perception that Fortune provided the most effective way of expressing the mutability of the material world.

Fortune Metaphors:
Wheel and Hill — Verbal and Visual

The wheel and the hill were not, of course, the only metaphors drawn to express Fortune's power: Boethius used diverse analogies in his *Consolation of Philosophy*. He wrote that Fortune is like the wind which carries your boat where it, not you, wishes,[1] for she turns her wheel like the tides in the Euripus estuary (II. i. 64–65), and like the good and bad years which come in farming (II. i. 56–57). With her wheel she takes pleasure in 'turning high to low and low to high' (II. ii. 29–30); while, in the last line of his opening complaint Boethius uses another metaphor which suggests the mountain: 'he who fell had not a secure foothold' ('Qui cecidit stabili non erat ille gradu' (I. i. 22). This describes a man undertaking his own ascent, not one subject to the rotation of a wheel, which usually involves an easy ride up until the man is pitched earthwards again as the revolve continues. The wheel provides the image for the cycle of inherited power of nation over nation, or of the succession of kings in one nation, as initially suggested by Tertullian and then by Alanis de Insulis, at about the time that Chrétien was writing: 'While Croesus is at the top of the wheel, Codrus is at the bottom. Julius is on his way up, Magnus on his way down, and Sulla is at the bottom'.[2]

---

[1] *Boethius: The Consolation of Philosophy*, II. i. 55–56, ed. by H. F. Stewart and E. K. Rand, LCL (London: Heinemann, 1918), p. 177.

[2] Alan of Lille, *Anticlaudianus, or the Good and Perfect Man*, Book VIII, Migne, vol. 210; trans. by J. J. Sheridan, *Anticlaudianus: or, the Good and Perfect Man* (Toronto: Pontifical Institute of Mediaeval Studies, 1973), p. 191.

The fact that men and women[3] can be passive and helpless on this circular journey accounts for the use of the wheel, by some illustrators and writers, as a symbol of Fortune's government over the seasonal progress through life which no individual can influence or change—called Fate in classical literature.[4] In the illumination on Folio 1^r of the Carmina Burana (Fig. 2, p. 30), the young man at the top of the wheel does not look like a real king. He sits inelegantly, his hose show beneath his crumpled tunic, and his sceptre is phallic—either a *fleur de lys* or *orchis morio*. His appearance is that of an ordinary young man raised to kingship at the midpoint of his life. As Michault Taillevent said, 'Fortune... par sa roe... fait... ung roy qu'ung populaire' ('Fortune, with her wheel, makes a working man a king').[5] The figures on Fortune's wheel in the Trinity College Cambridge MS 12 (Fig. 3, p. 31) also represent everyman in the four stages of life, and the naked figure under the wheel could be either the new-born baby, or the corpse to which he will return. The man on the wheel has no choice but to travel on it, yet, here, he is shown as a fool. The crown, on the head of the topmost figure, is shaped into fool's ears at the corners and he carries an eared replica of his own head, therefore a bauble, not a sceptre, while the man on his way up carries a dagger, and a wooden dagger was another fool's emblem. Some of the *Sotties* play on this inherent folly. For example, in *La Folie des Gorriers*, c. 1465, youthful courtiers behave ridiculously in pursuit of worldly avancement, dressing up, as they realize, in 'fool's clothes'. Yet Folie states the inevitability of the rise and fall in worldly fortune which they seek, the poor become great and the great decline (ll. 327–28). She trains the Gorriers in flattery, and *oultrecuidance,* and the end is an encomium on pride by a fool (ll. 611–12). Despite this advocacy of wheeltop success to men in their youth, what the audience sees is the Gorriers becoming fools, not gaining power.[6]

The most complete literary expression of the wheel-like movement

---

[3] Only men are shown in illuminations of Fortune's wheel, but Jean Michel includes a female example.

[4] As in *The Æneid,* Book VIII, l. 334. and in *The Astronomica* of Manilius, Book 4, l. 14. Cf. H. R. Patch, *The Tradition of the Goddess Fortuna in Roman Literature* (Northampton, MA: Smith College, 1922), pp. 141–42.

[5] 'Le Regime de Fortune', ll. 33–55, in *Un poète bourguignon du XVe siècle: Michel Taillevent,* ed. Deschaux, p. 233. See the Wheel of Life by William de Brailes in Burrow, *The Ages of Man,* p. 149, facing.

[6] E. Picot, ed., *Recueil général des sotties,* 1, pp. 137–75.

from birth to death, with its focus on folly at the topmost, midsummer, point, is found in the 'Passe Temps' of Michel Taillevent (see Chapter 1), while a more accepting version of the decline, along with the rise, appears in the anonymous sixteenth-century poem, 'Regne de Fortune': 'N'est il loysible ai diel donner clarté/ Et puis après de rendre obscurité/ Par noires nuyts? Pareillement l'année/ En quatre temps n'est-elle divisé?/ C'est le printemps, esté, autompne, yver;/ Chascun son cours fait sans rien estriver' ('Is it not lawful [for man] to give light to the sky and then give himself up to obscurity in dark nights?/ Similarly, isn't the year divided into four seasons/ spring, summer, autumn, winter/ Each runs its course without strife').[7]

On the other hand, the mountain which man sets out to scale, makes it the symbol for aspiration to a greater fame during the cycle of life than would fall naturally to him. As H. R. Patch noted: 'the concept of a mountain as a figure of inaccessibility and adversity is common enough. One speaks of "scaling" one's difficulties or "surmounting an obstacle"..., the mountain obviously can also symbolize degrees of exaltation and humiliation in worldly dignity'.[8] Yet, from the point of view of the man climbing, success appears to be the natural progression, and the fall into the valley turns Fortune into a force which disrupts his seasonal sequence. At the opening to *The Consolation of Philosophy,* in the same section where Boethius wrote that he 'slipped', he also says that his 'head is white before its time' (I. i. 9–11).[9] In Jean Michel's *Passion* (chapter 9) Lazarus and Mary, at the top of the wheel, are comparatively innocent because they revel in what has been given them without their seeking it, whereas the temptation of Christ on the mountain is a temptation to a more damnable ambition.

Needless to say, there was no law restricting use of wheel and mountain to separate meanings, and many variations can be found. Thus, in the illumination of the wheel in BL MS Royal 19 A IV fol. 13^v, competition to be the figure at the top involves active climbing and a struggle between contestants (Fig. 8). Alain Chartier attributed a disruptive effect to seasonal progression by Fortune, even while she elevated them: 'emong

---

[7]   *Recueil de Poésies françoises des XVe et XVIe siècles,* vol. 10 (Paris, 1875), p. 82.

[8]   *The Goddess Fortuna in Medieval Literature* (Cambridge, MA: Smith College, 1927), p. 132.

[9]   'Venit enim properata malis inopina senectus/ Et dolor aetatem iussit inesse suam./ Intempestivi funduntur vertice cani...', *Boethius: The Theological Tractates,* ll. 9–11, trans. by H. F. Stewart et al., LCL (London and Cambridge, MA: Heinemann, 1973).

Figure 8: Wheel of Fortune from the Saône et Loire: 1400–1425.

vs courtiers that be servants to fortune... we wexen old more by force of charges than by the nombre of years'.[10] And Alanis de Insulis's description of the kings on the wheel, quoted above, concludes with Fortune interrupting her own progress to reverse the expected movement: 'Marius is coming up but, with a turn of the wheel, Sulla is on his way back and

[10] *The Curial,* trans. by Caxton, ed. by P. P. Heyer and F. J. Furnivall, EETS ES 54 (London, 1888), p. 16.

Figure 9: Fortune with wheel and valley. Hortus Deliciarum, *fol. 215ʳ*.

Marius is being forced down'.[11] De Insulis says Fortune 'knows not how to be faithful; she remains true to this one tenet—that she always proves false' (Sheridan, p. 191): words which echo those of Boethius's Philosophy in II. ii. 29 of *The Consolation*.

The wheel and hill were often combined; again by Alanus de Insulis in the *Anticlaudianus,* where one part of Fortune's palace is said to sit 'atop the mountain rock, the other crouches on the rock's base.... The former part prides itself on its lofty roof: the latter stands uncovered in a gaping cleft' (Sheridan, p. 189). The contrast conveys her dual nature geographically and encapsulates her two extremes before the picture is complicated with specific examples of instability which build into the image of an ever-changing wheel: 'Thus the wheel sweeps everything up in turn and spiralling Fortune changes our fates' (Sheridan, p. 191). A thirteenth-century poem on the disgrace of Pierre de la Broce also combines the wheel with the hill. At one moment, Fortuna declares that Pierre's own evil ways caused his fall from the top of the wheel, and she was only God's instrument, but then she indulges in a personal triumph: 'Por quoi sui Fortune nammée,/ Quar je faz bien le fort tumber/ Et trebuchier en la valée' ('Why I am called Fortune is because I am good at making men fall catastrophically as I tip them into the valley').[12] The way the two symbols could be combined is captured in the twelfth-century illustration in the *Hortus Deliciarum* (Fig. 9) and they are wittily merged into one word, through the versatility of Scots spelling in a description of the Antwerp Ommegangen in 1562. The observer commented that a globe pageant represented 'þe vanitie of þe world, as it had bene þe quhill of Fortoun, sum tymes vp and sum tymes doun.'[13] 'Quhill', I would argue, can be pronounced as either wheel or hill.

And, although the mountain is reclaimed for Christianity in Jean Michel's *Passion,* in the *Hortus Deliciarum,* on the reverse side to the illumination of Fortune's wheel, an equation is made between the mountain and all earthly vice (Fig. 10). Christians must avoid the mountain altogether to reach heaven. The ladder, mentioned by Jacquemart Giélée in his *Renart le Nouvel,* lines 13–18, and implied at the end of Book IV of

---

[11] *Anticlaudianus,* trans. Sheridan, p. 191.

[12] F. Ed. Schneegans, 'Trois poèmes de la fin du XIIIᵉ siècle sur Pierre de la Broce', *Romania,* 58 (1932), 546–49.

[13] J. Cartwright, 'Forms and their Uses: The Antwerp Ommegangen 1550–1700', in *Festive Drama,* ed. by M. Twycross (Cambridge: D. S. Brewer, 1996), pp. 119–31 (p. 124).

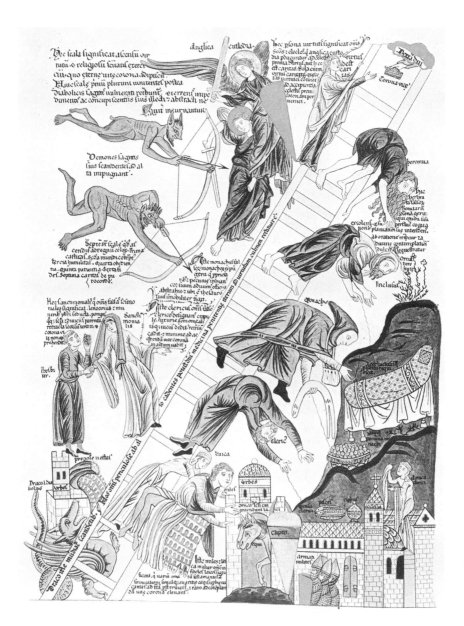

Figure 10: Earth and ladder to Heaven. Hortus Deliciarum, *fol. 215ᵛ.*

Boethius's *Consolation of Philosophy*, provides an analogy with a non-material ascent to salvation, though most men and women climbing it succumb to the 'snakes' on route, returning them to the path up the worldly mountain of damnation. The similarity between *monde* and *mont* —punned to the full by Giélée—appears to have been hard to resist.

Fêtes de Saint-Jean within the Church— Verdun and Metz

1)   Verdun, Collection Clouet, MS 183, fols 54^v–55^v: 'Fête de St Jean', transcribed by Charles Buvignier, *c.* 1890: (original manuscripts no longer extant).

23 Juin 1447   Capitulum dedit illis qui facerunt festum Sancti Joannis ad Supportandum expendas tres francos

19 juin 1455   les nouveaulx officiers élus à la Sainct Jean seront tenus de paier un franc pour faire la feste de Saint Jean

28 juin 1487   Aulx Acolytes de grace speciale pour aider à supporter les depens qu'ils ont fait et sustenu à la feste Saint Jehan derrien [sic] furent donnés deux francs

23 juin 1470   Pour l'absence de Mr de Verdun qui est en france détenu a esté ordonné de non avoir menestriers à ceste feste de Saint Jehan, et que ceulx qui ne l'ont pas faite l'an venant tous ensemble la feront

[23 June 1474—plague prevents it]

11 juin 1485   par Messieurs a esté conclu et ordonné qu'on fera ceste année la feste de la Saint-Jehan par M.M. qui la doivent faire, et y sont commis le prevost N. Matli et D. Troussuins avec Chaivart et Auchelin qui scavent les coustumes, et pour maistres d'ostel Honorati et Bultel

23 juin 1496   Conclusion est quod illi domini qui tenentur facere festum Sancti Johanni illud facient ut moris est

23 juin 1498   Conclu que M.M.J. Vaillant et C. Mileti fassent la feste de
                St. jean honorablement sans faire esclaundre (les deux
                messieurs étaient entrés en Stage en 1497)

14 juin 1501   Conclu qu'on fera la feste St Jehan, et ait ordonné aulx
                estagiers qu'ils facent en façon quil n'y a esclandre

10 Juillet 1501 Pourceque messieurs B. Dault et Nicol Guerard (entrés en
                Stage en 1502) ont refusé de payer les depens de la feste
                St Jean comme leurs compagnons et que complainte en a
                esté faite à Messieurs ce jourdhuy a esté conclu et ordonné
                quils satisfassent et paient selon l'arrest du compte

[18 June 1513—not to be performed, the money to go instead to repairing
                the chapel]

23 juin 1514   Messieurs ont conclu continuer la feste des estagiers de
                cette presente Saint jehan jusqu'à l'année venant

[6 June 1519—not to be performed because of the calamities of plague and
                war]

12 juin 1532   Pourceque de présent il est bon temps et a on [sic] bon
                marchié de vivre et aussi quil est paix et n'y a dangier en
                la cité conclu quon fera la feste à la feste Saint- jehan en
                ensuivant la bonne coustume ancienne

19 juin 1532   Ceux qui doivent faire la feste sainct Jehan s'estant excusé
                sur le peu de temps quils ont pour faire les préparations,
                on leur a permis de differer jusqu'à la nativité de la Sainte
                Vierge, feste de l'église

2)   Metz 1589. Archives Départementales de la Moselle G 499/8, fols
1^v–2^r. (Despite Church reforms a similar custom had continued. M^r
Pancellier was given leave to take part and his training for the priesthood
would be prorogued to allow for it.)

'... ascavoir que dedans la Veillee de La St Jehan Baptiste Prochainement
venant [1590] Il veriffiera et fera apparoitre de Son jngenuité Suivant La
Coustume de Ceance....'

Cheval -iers

(See S. Billington, 'The *Cheval fol* of Lyon and other Asses', in *Fools and Folly*, ed. by C. Davidson (Kalamazoo: Western Michigan University, Medieval Institute Publications, 1996), pp. 9–33.)

The horse was symbolic of man's own character to the point of anthropomorphism. For example, the twelfth-century *Bestiary* declares the animal unique because it 'feels the emotion of sorrow' and weeps for man, 'hence in Centaurs the nature of men and horses can be mixed'. Horses 'exult in battlefields;... Inflamed by the war-yell, they are spurred to charge. They are miserable when conquered and delighted when they have won'.[1] This perceived spiritednesss was most often used as a sign of pride, and Prudentius appears to have been the first to make the moral comparison. Superbia's horse, he wrote, was 'no less vainglorious... His mouth impatient of the curbing bit./ He foams with rage and turns from side to side,/ Galled at restraint and pressure of the reins.'[2] The illustrated psychomachia in the *Hortus Deliciarum* portrays Pride's horse as an extension of her own Vice and, when killed, the horse, too, dies a horrible death, while both are shown falling *aval* (Fig. 11). The twelfth-century *Vices and Virtues* warns: 'be not like the horse or the mule, which have no understanding',[3] and homiletic works empha-

---

[1] *The Book of Beasts*, trans. by T. H. White (Stroud: Sutton, 1992), pp. 84–85.

[2] *The Poems of Prudentius*, trans. by Sister M. Clement Eagen, vol. 2, p. 87. See Ovid, *Amores*, I. ii. 15 for classical use of the analogy.

[3] *Vices and Virtues*, ll. 3183–84, ed. and trans. by F. Holthausen, EETS, ES 105 (London: Trübner, 1905), p. 96.

Figure 11: The Fall of Pride and her horse, Hortus Deliciarum, *fol. 199ᵛ.*

size that Christ avoided this animal for his entry into Jerusalem. For example:

> [Our Lord] might ride, if he desired, on rich steeds, and palfreys, mules, and Arabs, but he would not, nor even upon the big ass, but upon the little foal that was still suckling—nor had ever borne any burden, nor had ever been defiled by any other ass. In so great humility did God Almighty place himself for us, and moreover set us example, that when we have wealth in abundance in this life be ye not therefore proud, nor wild (elated), nor stark (haughty), nor wayward, nor highminded.[4]

At the entry of Christ into Jerusalem in Michel's *Passion*, Simon says: 'There is no appetite for worldly honour when [Jesus] ascends into Jerusalem on an ass' (ll. 15299–300; see Chapter 9).

According to the moral analogy, *chevaliers* were identified with their horses in a less than complimentary way; centaur-like, man and horse embodied each other's failing. Hardibrans's horse in the summer combat in *Galeran* is called Orgueil while, in *Le Tournoi de l'Antéchrist*, Orgueil's warhorse is like Superbia's in Prudentius's *Psychomachia*, for it embodies the weakness of his vice. Had it not the habit of stumbling, it would have been a valuable racer: 'Li destriers orgeil si sovent/ Choupoit, quee ce n'estoit pas fins;/ se ce ne fust, il fust si fins,/ Qu'il vausist bien M. mars d'argent'.[5] In *Renart le Nouvel*, Orgueil's horse is described as pride and its fruits: 'hanist, grate, fiert et mort' ('Shame, graft or theft, arrogance, and death', ll. 571). In the *Passion de Semur*, at Lucifer's moment of revolt, the personification of Pride enters on horseback. He is a *chevalier* who treats heaven like a worldly court, where Lucifer would be the most appropriate king.[6]

The actual height to which the rider was raised on horseback above his fellow men also contributed to the image of arrogance. In romances and moralities, references to knights dismounting, voluntarily, often indicated humility, while if thrown in combat, they fell to shame since the weight of their armour made them helpless targets.[7] Also, in many of the moral

---

[4] *Old English Homilies and Homiletic Treatises,* ed. and trans. by R. Morris, EETS os 234 (London, 1868), Pt I, p. 4.

[5] *Huon de Méry: le Tournoi de l'Antéchrist,* ll. 642–45, ed. and trans. Orgeur, p. 75.

[6] *La Passion de Semur,* ll. 287, 294–98, ed. by P. T. Durbin and L. Muir, Leeds Medieval Studies, 3 (Leeds: Leeds University Press, 1981), p. 7.

[7] M.-L. Chênerie, *Le chevalier errant dans les romans arthuriens en vers des XIIe et XIIIe siècles,* p. 379.

Figure 12: The two horses of Lechery, Hortus Deliciarum, *fol. 202ʳ.*

analogies, one finds an underlying assumption that the peak of physical fitness is part of the waywardness, so suggesting the midsummer period of life. Méléagent is described as a more handsome figure than Lancelot, when they face each other for combat, while the religious English play, *The Conversion of St Paul*, opens with Saul, on horseback, described as *an aunterous knyght*, who boasts of his prowess in destroying Christians. By contrast, in the ascetic analogy in *Perlesvaus*, the spiritually dedicated Gawain rides a thin horse. Physical good looks and energy on proud horses might be an innocent part of a seasonal midsummer analogy, as at the end of Michault Taillevent's 'Passe Temps' where he wrote that in the chill of his winter, the old man 'ne lui convenient plus destrier/ Mais chevaulcher sur ung bas an' ('cannot ride any longer on a war horse, only on a lowly ass').[8] On the other hand, and more seriously, *The Conversion*

---

[8]   'Le Passe Temps de Michault Taillevent', ed. Deschaux, p. 150.

Figure 13: The fall of Lechery and her horse, Hortus Deliciarum, *fol. 202ʳ.*

of St Paul uses the proud horse as a symbol of the temporary nature of success in corrupt worldly ambition.

The wilful energy attributed to the horse also resulted in its being a symbol for lechery, closely associated with pride, and the love element of May can be attacked as Luxuria in the heat of youth. In illustrations where the horse depicts this there are, of course, two animals. Their placing at the foot of the mountain in Fig. 10 (p. 219), where two young people fall towards them, appears to symbolize this most common youthful tendency. (Cf. *Fools and Folly,* ed. C. Davidson, fig. 4.) In the *Hortus Deliciarum* flowers and the two horses form Luxuria's avant-garde against the Virtues, but she comes to as catastrophic a fall as that of Pride, though without the descent *aval* from a mountain top (Figs 12 and 13). The fact that Lancelot (Chapter 3) wears out not one, but two, horses in his pursuit of Guinevere could be humorous comment on this subject.

High Summer in Lyon, 1540–1604

Claude de Rubys, *Histoire véritable de la ville de Lyon* (Lyon, 1604)

P. 370: comments on popular traditions included in de Rubys's account of religious and secular plays put on by Jean Neiron during the summer months after Pentecost, from about 1540 to 1544.

Le peuple auoit là son esprit tendu les jours des Festes; Là où de present, priué de ceste maniere d'esbatement [p. 371] ils passent les Festes aux berlands, & aux tavernes, ou apres auoir bien beu, ils se mettent apres à dechiffrer le Roy, l'Estat, & le magistrat, qui sont semences de sedition.

P. 499: the start of more substantial description:

'De plusieurs resiouïssances publicques que se sont tous les ans en la ville de Lyon.'

(De Rubys begins with Pentecost and continues chronologically through the summer.)

[p. 500] Les Preuots des Marchands, & Eschuins (pour vne resiouïssance publicque de la bo[n]ne nouuuelle qu'apporta le Precurseur de Iesus Christ venant au monde, de sa prochaine venue...) font dresser la veille de la S. Iean au milieu du Pont de Saosne, vn beau grand feu de ioye, auec forces artifices de feu, puis sur le soir vont en corps, vestuz de leurs robbes vilettes, leurs [p. 501] Mandeurs deuant eux, querir le Lieutenant du Roy en son logis, & tous ensemble vont puis mettre le feu au buchier preparé sur le pont, suiuis de grand nombre de peuple. Le peuple de la ville souloit aussi pour se don[n]er du plaisir, faire quelque fois ce que les interpretes de droict appelle[n]t, la Charauary... Ces ioyeux esbateme[n]ts ont puis n'aguieres estez abolis, & le peuple au lieu de cela renvoyé aux tavernes, ou apres auoir bien beu, ils com[m]encent à cacqueter les pieds branslants soubs la table, comme pies en cage, dechiffrer le Roy, les Princes, le Gouuerneur, l'Estat & la Iustice, & minuter des Cartels scandaleux & diffamatoires, qu'ils vont puis afficha[n]ts par les carrefours, ou sema[n]ts par les rues. L'on faict souuent durant l'esté des esbattements sur la riuiere de Saosne, comme sont les ioustes que font d'ordinaires les Dimanches & iours de festes, deuant le logis du Lieutena[n]t du Roy, les bateliers des portes de S. George & de S. Vincent, armez de lances & de pauoys, allants de telle roideur & de telle vistesse sur leurs bateaux, & s'entrerencontrants auec leurs la[n]ces tendues les vngs co[n]tre les autres, q[ui] le plus roide faict tresbuscher le plus foible tout chaussé & vestu dans la riuiere, & quelque fois ils y tu[m]b tous deux, non sans gra[n]d risee de ceux qui les voyent & marche[n]t leurs trouppes auec le tabourin battant & l'enseigne desployee. Autres fois ils attachent vne corde trauersant la riuiere de bord en bord, au milieu de laquelle ils attachent vne Oye suspendue par les pieds: puis à course de bateau ils se vont attacher au col de l'Oye: auquel ils demeurent le plus souuent pundus, leurs bateaux s'en allant à val l'eau. C'estoit chose qui se souloit faire auec grand triumphe & resiouïssance, trompettes, clerons, cornets à bouquins, feux artificiels, & laschement de coleurines & petards: mais de present l'on se ressent de la pauureté de la ville, & perte du commerce. Les Eschevins souloye[n]t tous les ans par forme de resiouïssance, & pour s'entretenir tousiours en bon[n]e intelligence auec leurs concitoyens, au lieu de la dragee & confitures qu'enuoyent tous les ans aux Estreines ceux de Paris, faire deux festins solemnels, l'vn se faisoit en l'hostel de ville le iour de la feste de S. Thomas, au sortir de l'oraison, ou estoyent conuiez auec leur Orateur, quelque fois le Lieutenant du Roy: mais d'ordinaire les principaux Officiers & Magistrats de la Iustice, des Fina[n]ces, & quelque nombre des plus notables & apparents Bourgeoys de la ville.

Gargantua, 1534

Les chroniques admirables du puissant Roy Gargantua, from *The Tale of Gargantua and King Arthur by François Girault*, *c.* 1534, ed. by Huntington Brown (Cambridge, MA: Harvard University Press, 1932), chapter VI, pp. 9–12.

Grantgosier n'estoit point d'oppinion de partir de ce lieu là sans la présence dudict Merlin, car il luy dist: 'Gentil seigneur, tu scez que Gallemelle et moy sommes de grande stature, par quoy ne pourrions trouver de pain ne vivres facillement pour elle et pour moy: que veulx tu que nous facions, si tu ne nous y ordonne la manière d'en avoir, veu que tous les boulengiers de ce pays ict ne veullent faire du pain que par compas, à cause qu'ilz ont monopolle tous ensemble affin de le tenir tousjours chier, et d'aultre part ceulx qui y deusent mettre ordre sont ceulx qui en ont à vendre; parquoy ilz souffrent tout et ont nonchalloir de la misère et paovreté de la commune, mais, qui pis est, prennent argent des amasseurs de bledz qui tous les ans sont faictz et duictz de les serrer et amasser, de gentilz hommes et aultres personnaiges riches qui en ont. Et quant ilz ont ainsi tout desgarny le pays, ils tiennent leurs bledz en grenier et les mettent à tel pris qu'ilz veullent, dont le monde a beaucoup à souffrir.' Lors respond Merlin: 'Vous dictes la verité. Je m'en voys vers le roy de ce pays à celle fin de le advertir d'y faire pourveoir et mettre bon ordre.' Ce qu'il fist incontinent, car, la remonstrance de Merlin ouye, le Roy envoya ses commissaires par le pays, lesquelz firent pendre tous les courtiers de bledz aux goustières de leurs maisons et leur biens declairér confisquez; les boullangiers qui avoient monopolle ensemble furent pugnis du fouet et par la bourse; et fut toute la pollice reformée, dont tout le pays vallut beaucoup mieulx (si l'on faisoit ainsi par tout maintenant, ce seroit bien faict). Adoncques Grandgosier et Gallemelle chargèrent leur jument de grans pains, mais tout premièrement ilz en mangèrent plus de quatre mille pains. Alors Merlin leur mist leur jument appoinct et se voullut départir d'eulx comme dict est, et print congié, dont ilz demenèrent si grant dueil que en les eust bien entenduz de dix lieues, car ilz plouroient si tresfort que deux moulins eussent peu mouldre de l'eau qui leur sortoit des yeulx, et de leurs larmes se engendra une belle fontaine où l'on faict cuyre les oeufs la vigille de Noël, le jour de Noël et toutes les féries jusques au lendemain des Roys; et d'icelle fontaine sort, neuf jours devant la sainct Jean, ung coq et une poulle qui tous les jours ponnent gros oeufs comme boisseaulx, que ceulx du pays prennent et les gectent en lidicte fontaine la vigille de la sainct Jehan, desquel oeufz s'engendrent tout soubdain deux poullatrices, lesquelles sont plus grandes que hacquenées. Puis le Roy les prent et les faict nourrir bien chièrement, pour ce qu'ilz luy servent quant il veut aller en guerre, car ces poullatrices sont faciles à apprivoiser. Ilz se laissent monter sur le corps, sur lequel y a comme une chaire faicte, et ne fault synon que se bien tenir à de grandes plumes qu'ilz leurs procédent de la creste, la quelle est plus reluysante que fin or. Et puys quant ce vient qu'ilz s'en vont en guerre et que le soleil frappe dussus leur dicte creste, elle rend telle clarté que tous les adversaires sont aveuglés. Et lesdictes poullatrices sont de telle nature et proprieté que, quant elles haulsent leurs ongles elles renversent homme à cheval tous arméz, qui est une beste inestimable. Ledit Roy Artus en eut une, laquelle luy cousta bien ung milion d'or. Mais ceste poullatrice estoit si trèsvertueuse que elle portoit le Roy Artus de son royaulme d'Angleterre jusques à Paris en ung jour, car elle volloit en l'air comme ung canard de rivière; et si avoit les plumes des aesles si trèsfortes et si dures que, quant elle estoit en mutation et que ses plumes tomboyent, on en faisoit des pièces de artillerie, desquelles le Roy Artus se servoit en guerre, et estoit la meilleure artillerie qui fust pour ce temps là en tout le monde, car elle portoit bien vingt et sept lieues françoyses de droicte visée, et d'ung seul coup eust bien fouldroyé la tour de Babillone, et du vent du boullet eust bien traversé toute la ville de Paris et les faulx bourgs sainct Marcel sans la raye.

Select Bibliography

Manuscripts

Angers, Archives départmentales de Maine-et-Loire, MS 16. G. 9, fol. 127^v—*Comptes bursariales.*

Angers, Bibl. Mun. MS 994 [870]—Jacques Bruneau, *Philandinopolis, ou plus clairement les fidelles Amities, Contenons vue partie de ce qui estè & de ce qui peut estre, & de ce qui se peult dire & rapporter de la ville d'Angers, & pais d'Anjou.*

Verdun, Collection Clouet, MS 183, fols 54^v–55^v—Charles Buvignier, 'Fête de St Jean'.

Books—Primary Sources

(a) Ideological Context

Alanus de Insulis (Alain de Lille), *Anticlaudianus,* Book VIII, ed. by J. P. Migne, *Patrologiae Cursus Completus*, Latin Series, 210 (Paris, 1855), cols 559–66.

——, *Anticlaudianus: or, the Good and Perfect Man,* trans. by J. J. Sheridan (Toronto: Pontifical Institute of Mediaeval Studies, 1973).

Anon., *Acte constitutionnel présenté au Peuple français, par la Convention Nationale, le 24 juin 1793: Déclaration des droits de l'homme et du citoyen* (Troyes, 1793).

234

Anon., *Calendrier nouvellement reffait et autreme[n]t compose* [...] *au quel sont adioustez plusieurs choses nouuelles* (Paris, 1494): BL Ephemerides LR. 41. d. 2.

Augustine, *St Augustine: Sermons for Christmas and Epiphany,* trans. by T. C. Lawler (Westminster, MD: Newman Press, 1952).

Belethus, Johannis (John Beleth), *Rationale Diuinorum Officiorum Ionne Beletho Theologo Parisiense authore* (Antwerp, 1562).

Boethius, Ancius, *Boethius: The Consolation of Philosophy,* ed. by H. F. Stewart and E. K. Rand, LCL (London: Heinemann, 1918).

Chroniques Nationales Françaises:

    Enguerand de Monstrelet, *Chroniques d'Enguerand de Monstrelet,* ed. by J. A. Buchon, *Chroniques Nationales Françaises,* 26–40 (Paris, 1826–27).

    Froissart, Jean, *Chroniques,* ed. by J. A. Buchon, *Chroniques Nationales Françaises,* 11–25 (Paris, 1824–26).

    Jacques le Clerq, *Mémoires,* in Enguerand de Monstrelet, *Chroniques d'Enguerand de Monstrelet,* ed. by J. A. Buchon, *Chroniques Nationales Françaises,* 37–40 (Paris, 1827).

Coutumes des Pays, Duché de Luxembourg et Comté de Chiney, ed. by M. N. J. Leclerq, 4 vols (Brussels, 1867).

Enguerand de Monstrelet, see *Chroniques Nationales Françaises.*

Erasmus, Desiderius, *Praise of Folly and Letter to Martin Dorp,* ed. by A. H. T. Levi (Harmondsworth: Penguin, 1971).

Froissart, Jean, see *Chroniques Nationales Françaises.*

Guilelmus Durandus (Guillaume Durand, Bishop of Mende), *Rationale divinorum officiorum,* ed. by V. d'Avino (Naples, 1859).

Huguenin, J. F., 'The Diary of Philippe de Vigneulles', in *Les Chroniques de la ville de Metz,* collected by Huguenin, ed. by S. Lamort (Metz, 1838), pp. 125–804.

Jacques le Clerq, see *Chroniques Nationales Françaises.*

Jean de Roye, *Journal de Jean de Roye ou Chronique Scandaleuse,* ed. by B. de Mandrot, La Société de l'histoire de France (Paris, 1894).

Kirchmeyer, Thomas, *Popular and Popish Superstitions and Customs* [...] *in Germany and other Papist Lands,* trans. by Barnabe Googe (London 1570), in P. Stubbes, *Anatomie of Abuses,* ed. by F. J. Furnivall (London 1877–82).

La Hière, 'Annales de Metz', ed. by G. Zeller, 'Fragments inédits de chroniques messines (1553–1557)', *Annuaire de la Société d'Histoire et d'Archéologie Lorraine,* 33 (1924), 221–63.

Luther, Martin, *Luther's Works,* vol. 44, *The Christian in Society,* Pt 1, ed. by J. Atkinson, gen. ed. H. T. Lehmann (Philadelphia: Atkinson Fortress Press, 1966).

Miræus, Aubertus, *Opera Diplomatica et Historica*[...], 2nd edn, vol. 2 (Brussels, 1723).

Molanus, Jean, *Les Quatorze livres sur l'histoire de la ville de Louvain du* [...] *Jean Molanus,* ed. by P. F. X. de Ram, (Brussels, 1861).

Oudin, Guillaume, 'Extrait d'un manuscrit de Messire Guillaume Oudin,' *Revue de l'Anjou et du Maine* (1857), vol. 1, pp. 129–44; vol. 2, pp. 1–16; (1858), vol. 2, pp. 5–88.

Philippe de Comines, *Mémoires de Messire Philippe de Comines,* ed. by M. l'Abbé Lenglet du Fresnoy (Paris, 1747).

Philippe de Navarre, *Les Quatre ages de l'homme,* ed. by Marcel de Fréville, SATF (Paris: Didot, 1888).

Philippe de Vigneulles, 'The Diary of Philippe de Vigneulles', see J. F. Huguenin.

Rubys, Claude de, *Histoire veritable de la ville de Lyon* (Lyon, 1604).

Stow, John, *A Survey of London reprinted from the Text of 1603,* ed. by C. L. Kingsford (Oxford: Clarendon Press, 1908; repr. 1971).

Tertullian, *Ad Nationes*, II. 18. *Corpus Christianorum*, Series Latina, vol. 1, *Tertulliani Opera,* Pt 1 (Turnhout: Brepols, 1954).

The Theodosian Code and Novels and the Sirmondian Constitutions, trans. by C. Pharr (Princeton: Princeton University Press, 1952).

(b) Chansons de Geste, Romances, Poetry, and Narrative Satires

Alexandre de Paris, *Le Roman d'Alexandre,* ed. by L. Harf-Lancner, Le Livre de Poche (Paris: Librairie Générale Française, 1994).

Anon., *The Didot Perceval: According to the Manuscripts of Modena and Paris,* ed. by William Roach (Philadelphia: University of Pennsylvania Press, 1941).

——, *The Romance of Perceval in Prose,* trans. and ed. by D. Skeels (Seattle: University of Washington Press, 1961).

Anon, *La Chanson de Roland*, ed. and trans. by I. Short, Le Livre de Poche (Paris: Librairie Générale Française, 1990).

——, *La Chanson de Roland*, ed. and trans. by P. Jonin (Paris: Gallimard, 1979).

Anon. *Li chevaliers as deux espees,* ed. by W. Foerster, 2nd edn (Halle: Nieymeyer, 1877).

Anon, *Gliglois: A French Arthurian Romance of the Thirteenth Century*, ed. by C. H. Livingston (Cambridge, MA: Harvard University Press, 1932).

Anon., *Guiron le Courtois*, ed. by R. Lathuillère (Geneva: Droz, 1966).

Anon., *Hervis de Mes; chanson de geste anonyme (début du XIIIème siècle)*, ed. by J.-C. Herbin (Geneva: Droz, 1992).

Anon., *Les Livres du roy Modus et de la royne Ratio*, ed. by G. Tilander, SATF (Paris: SATF, 1932).

Anon., *Merlin: Roman en Prose du XIIIᵉ siècle*, ed. by G. Paris and J. Ulrich, SATF (Paris: Didot, 1886).

Anon., *Perlesvaus, Le Haut Livre du Graal: Perlesvaus*, ed. by W. A. Nitze and T. A. Jenkins (New York: Phaeton, 1972).

——, *The High Book of the Grail, a Translation of the Thirteenth Century Romance of* Perlesvaus, ed. and trans. by N. Bryant (Cambridge: D. S. Brewer, 1978).

Anon, *The Vulgate Version of the Arthurian Romances*, ed. by O. Sommer (Washington: Carnegie Institution, 1909).

Chrétien de Troyes, *Erec et Enide*, ed. by M. Rousse (Paris: Flammarion, 1994).

——, *Lancelot ou le chevalier de la charrette*, ed. by J.-C. Aubailly, (Paris: Flammarion, 1991).

——, *Perceval ou le Conte du Graal*, ed. by J. Dufournet (Paris: Flammarion, 1997).

——, *Yvain: ou le chevalier au lion*, ed. by M. Rousse (Paris: Flammarion, 1990).

——, *Yvain: le chevalier au lion: The Critical Text of Wendelin Foerster*, ed. by T. B. W. Reid, French Classics, 7th edn (Manchester: Manchester University Press, 1984).

——, *Arthurian Romances*, trans. by D. D. R Owen, Everyman's Library (London: Dent, 1993).

François Girault, *The Tale of Gargantua and King Arthur by François Girault, c. 1534*, ed. by H. Brown (Cambridge, MA: Harvard University Press, 1932).

Gervais de Bus, *Le Roman de Fauvel par Gervais du Bus, MS E*, l. 1102, ed. by A. Langfors, SATF (Paris: Picard, 1914–19).

Guillaume de Loris, and Jean de Meung, *The Romance of the Rose*, trans. by H. W. Robbins (New York: Dutton, 1962).

——, *Guillaume de Loris et Jean de Meun: Le Roman de la Rose*, ed. by D. Poirion (Paris: Garnier-Flammarion, 1974).

Guillaume le Clerc, *Guillaume le Clerc: The Romance of Fergus*, ed. by William Frescoln (Philadelphia: William H. Allen, 1983).

——, *Fergus of Galloway: Knight of King Arthur*, ed. and trans. by D. D. R. Owen, Everyman's Library (London: Dent, 1991).

Huon de Mery, *Huon de Méry: le Tournoi de l'Antéchrist*, ed. and trans. by Stéphanie Orgeur (Orleans: Paradigme, 1994).

Jacquemart Giélée, *Renart le Nouvel par Jacquemart Giélée,* ed. by H. Roussel, SATF (Paris: Picard, 1961).

Jean Renaut, *Jean Renart: Galeran de Bretagne*, ed. by L. Foulet, CFMA (Paris: Champion, 1975).

——, *Galeran de Bretagne, traduit en français moderne*, ed. by Jean Dufournet (Paris: Champion, 1996).

Jehan de la Mote, *La Voie d'Enfer et de Paradis: An Unpublished Poem of the Fourteenth Century,* ed. by M. A. Pety, Studies in Romance Languages and Literatures, 20 (Washington: Catholic University of America Press, 1940).

Jehan de Preis, *Œuvres de Jehan des Preis,* vol. 1, ed. by A. Borgnet and S. Bormans (Brussels, 1864).

Michault Taillevent, *Un poète bourguignon du XVe siècle: Michault Taillevent,* Publications Romanes et Françaises, 132 (Geneva: Droz, 1975).

Prudentius, *The Poems of Prudentius*, trans. by Sr M. Clement Eagen, 2 vols (Washington: Catholic University of America Press, 1965).

Raoul de Houdenc, *Meraugis de Portlesguez*, ed. by H. Michelant (Paris: Tross, 1869).

Recueil de chants historiques français depuis le XIIe jusqu'au XVIIIe siècle, ed. by L. de Lincy, First and Second Series (Paris, 1841–42).

Rutebeuf, *Œuvres complètes de Rutebeuf,* ed. by E. Faral and J. Bastin, 2 vols (Paris: Picard, 1969).

(c) Plays

Adam de la Halle, *Adam de la Halle: Œuvres complètes,* ed. by P.-Y. Badel (Paris: Librairie Générale Française, 1995).

——, *Medieval French Plays*, trans. and ed. by R. Axton and J. Stevens (Oxford: Blackwell, 1971).

——, *Le* Jeu de la Feuillée: *texte et traduction*, ed. and trans. by J. Rony (Paris: Bordas, 1969).

Anon., *Mystère d'Adam: texte du manuscrit de Tours,* ed. and trans. by H. Chamard (Paris: Colin, 1925).

Anon., *Le Mystère de la Passion d'Arras,* ed. by J. M. Richard (Arras, 1891).

Anon., *Le Mistere du Viel Testament,* ed. by Baron de Rothschild, SATF (Paris: Didot, 1878).

Anon., *La Passion de Palatinus: mystère du XIVe siècle*, ed. by G. Frank, CFMA (Paris: Champion, 1922).

Arnoul Gréban, *Le Mystère de la Passion,* ed. by Omer Jodogne, (Brussels: Académie Royale de Belgique, 1965).

Jean Michel, *Le Mystère de la Passion (Angers 1486),* ed. by Omer Jodogne (Gembloux: Duculot, 1959).

Recueil général des sotties, ed. by E. Picot, SATF, 3 vols (Paris: Didot, 1902–12).

Secondary Sources

Accarie, Maurice, *Le Théâtre sacré de la fin du Moyen Age: étude sur le sens moral de la Passion de Jean Michel* (Geneva: Droz, 1979).

Alain de Lille, Gautier de Châtillon, Jakemart Giélée et leur temps: Actes du Colloque de Lille, octobre 1978, ed. by H. Roussel and F. Suard (Lille: Presses Universitaires de Lille, 1980).

Audin, A., 'Les Rites Solsticiaux et la Légende de Saint Pothin', *Revue de l'Histoire de Religions,* 96 (1927), 147–74.

Aubailly, Jean-Claude, 'Théâtre Médiéval et Fêtes Calendaires ou l'Histoire d'une Subversion', in *Between Folk and Liturgy,* ed. by Alan J. Fletcher and Wim Hüsken, Ludus, 3 (Amsterdam: Rodopi, 1997), pp. 31–64.

——, *Le théâtre médiéval profane et comique* (Paris: Larousse, 1975).

Axton, Richard, *European Drama of the Early Middle Ages* (London: Hutchinson, 1974).

Bakhtin, Mikhail, *Rabelais and his World,* trans. by H. Iswolsky (Chicago: MIT, 1968).

Barber, C. L., *Shakespeare's Festive Comedy* (Princeton: Princeton University Press, 1959).

Bercé, Yves-Marie, *Fête et révolte* (Paris: Hachette, 1976).

——, *Histoire des croquants: étude des soulevements populaires au XVIIe siècle dans le sud-ouest de la France* (Geneva: Droz, 1974).

Berger, Roger, *Littérature et société arrageoises au XIIIe siècle* (Arras: Commission Départmentale... Pas-de-Calais, 1981).

——, 'Le *Jeu de la Feuillée*. Quelques notes', *Arras au Moyen-Age: histoire et littérature,* ed. by M.-M. Catellani and J.-P. Martin (Arras: Artois Presses Universitaires, 1994), pp. 221–22.

Billington, Sandra, *Mock Kings in Medieval Society and Renaissance Drama* (Oxford: Clarendon Press, 1991).

——, 'King and Queen Games in English Mystery and French Passion Plays', in *Custom, Culture and Community in the Later Middle Ages,* ed. by Thomas Pettitt and Leif Søndergaard (Odense: Odense University Press, 1994), pp. 85–104.

——, 'Social Disorder, Festive Celebration, and Jean Michel's *le Mistere de la Passion JesusCrist*', *Comparative Drama,* 29 (1995), 216–47.

——, 'The *Cheval Fol* of Lyon and other Asses', in *Fools and Folly,* ed. by C. Davidson (Kalamazoo: Western Michigan University, Medieval Institute Publications, 1996), pp. 9–33.

Bloomfield, Morton W., *The Seven Deadly Sins* (East Lansing: Michigan State College Press, 1952).

Blumenfeld-Kosinski, Renate, 'Arthurian Heroes and Convention', in *Meraugis de Portlesguez* and *Durmart le Galois', The Legacy of Chrétien de Troyes,* ed. by N. J. Lacy et al., 2 vols (Amsterdam: Rodopi, 1988), II, pp. 79–92.

Boutiot, M., *Des Institutions communales dans la Champagne Méridionale aux XIIe et XIIIe siècles* (Troyes, 1865).

Braet, H., 'Désenchantement et ironie dramatique chez Adam de la Halle', in *Between Folk and Liturgy,* ed. by Alan J. Fletcher and Wim Hüsken, Ludus, 3 (Amsterdam: Rodopi, 1997), pp. 89–96.

Burrow, John A., *The Ages of Man: A Study in Medieval Writing and Thought* (Oxford: Clarendon Press, 1986).

Caillet, Louis, *Projet d'empoisonnement de Louis XI en 1466: arrestation à Lyon de Jean Le Doux, dit Fortune* (Besançon: Jacques, *c.* 1909).

Carman, J. Neale, 'The Symbolism of the *Perlesvaus*', *PMLA,* 61 (1946), 42–83.

Carnival and the Carnivalesque, ed. by Konrad Eisenbichler and Wim Hüsken, Ludus, 4 (Amsterdam: Rodopi, 1999).

Casey, Maurice, *Is John's Gospel True?* (London: Routledge, 1995).

Champeaux, Jacqueline, *Fortuna* (Rome: École française de Rome, 1982).

Chênerie, Marie-Luce, *Le Chevalier errant dans les romans arthuriens en vers des XIIe et XIIIe siècles* (Geneva: Droz, 1986).

Cohen, Gustave, *Le théâtre en France au Moyen Age* (Paris: Rieder, 1931).

Collection de Mémoires relatifs à l'histoire de Belgique: XVIe siècle, Histoire des Troubles Religieux de Valenciennes 1560–1567, ed. by Charles Paillard (Brussels, 1874), vol. 1.

Collection de Mémoires relatifs à l'histoire de Belgique: Mémoire de Pasquier de la Barre et de Nicolas Soldoyer 1565–1570, ed. by A. Pinchart (Brussels, 1859).

The Conflict between Paganism and Christianity in the Fourth Century, ed. by A. Momigliano (Oxford: Clarendon Press, 1963).

Courcelle, Pierre, *La Consolation de philosophie dans la tradition littéraire: antécédents et postérité de Boèce* (Paris: Études Augustiniennes, 1967).

Cuvelier, Joseph, *Les institutions de la ville de Louvain au Moyen Age*, Mémoires de l'Académie Royale de Belgique, 2nd series, 11 (Brussels: Palais des Académies, 1935).

——, *Documents inédits concernant les institutions de la ville de Louvain au Moyen Age* (Brussels: Palais des Académies, 1935).

Davis, Natalie Zemon, *Society and Culture in Early Modern France* (London: Duckworth, 1975).

Darrah, John, *Paganism in Arthurian Romance* (Woodbridge: Boydell, 1994).

Dohrn-van Rossum, Gerhard, *History of the Hour*, trans. by Thomas Dunlap (Chicago: Chicago University Press, 1996).

Dufournet, Jean, *Adam de la Halle: à la recherche de lui-même, ou le jeu dramatique de la feuillée* (Paris: Société d'Édition d'Enseignement Supérieur, 1974).

Evans, J. M., *'Paradise Lost' and the Genesis Tradition* (Oxford: Clarendon Press, 1968).

Flinn, John, *Le Roman de Renart dans la littérature française et dans les littératures étrangères au moyen âge*, University of Toronto, Romances Series, 4 (Paris: Presses Universitaires de France, 1963).

Frakes, Jerold C., *The Fate of Fortune in the Early Middle Ages* (Leiden: Brill, 1988).

Gaidoz, Henri, *Le Dieu gaulois du soleil, et le symbolisme de la roue*, Études de mythologie gauloise, Extrait de la *Revue Archéologique* (Paris, 1886).

Gennep, A. van, *Le Folklore du Dauphiné,* vol. 2 (Paris: Librairie Orientale et Américaine, 1933).

Girard, F. M., Baron de Hannoncelles, *Metz ancien,* 2 vols (Metz, 1856).

Grimbert, Joan T., *'Yvain' dans le Miroir,* Purdue University Monographs in Romance Languages (Philadelphia: John Benjamins, 1988).

Guigue, M.-C., *Recherches sur les Merveilles* (Lyon, 1887).

Guilland, R., 'Étude sur l'Hippodrome de Byzance', *Byzantinoslavica,* 27 (1966), 288–307.

Haidu, Peter, *Lion Queue-coupée* (Geneva: Droz, 1972).

Histoire générale de Metz, ed. by Jean François (Metz, 1769–90).

Hunt, Tony, *Chrétien de Troyes: Yvain (le Chevalier au Lion),* Critical Guides to French Texts (London: Grant and Cutler, 1986).

Kelly, Thomas E., *Le Haut Livre du Graal: Perlesvaus, A Structural Study* (Geneva: Droz, 1974).

Kernan, Alvin B., *The Cankered Muse* (New Haven: Yale University Press, 1959).

Kolve, V. A., *The Play called Corpus Christi* (Stanford: Stanford University Press, 1966).

Le Goff, Jacques, *Time, Work and Culture in the Middle Ages,* trans. by A. Goldhammer (Chicago: Chicago University Press, 1980).

Lepage, H., *Les communes de la Meurthe,* vol. 2 (Nancy, 1853).

Le Roy Ladurie, Emmanuel, *Le Carnaval de Romans* (Paris: Gallimard, 1979), trans. by Mary Feeney (Harmondsworth: Penguin, 1981).

Lives of the Popes in the Middle Ages, ed. by H. K. Mann, 19 vols (London: Kegan Paul, Trench, Trübner, 1925–32).

Lyons, Faith, *Les Éléments descriptifs dans le roman d'aventure au XIIIᵉ siècle,* Publications Romanes et Françaises, 84 (Geneva: Droz, 1965).

McGinn, Bernard, 'Portraying Antichrist in the Middle Ages', in *The Use and Abuse of Eschatology in the Middle Ages,* ed. by Werner Verbeke et al. (Leuven: Leuven University Press, 1988), pp. 1–48.

Ménard, Philippe, *Le Rire et le sourire dans le roman courtois en France au Moyen Age (1150–1250)* (Geneva: Droz, 1969).

Meyerhoff, Hans, *Time in Literature* (Berkeley: University of California Press, 1960).

Le Moigne, François-Yves, *Histoire de Metz* (Toulouse: Privat, 1986).

Muchembled, Robert, *Popular Culture and Elite Culture*, trans. by L. Cochrane (Baton Rouge: Lousiana State University Press, 1985).

Muir, Edward, *Ritual in Early Modern Europe* (Cambridge: Cambridge University Press, 1997).

Nicholas, David, *The Growth of the Medieval City* (London: Longman, 1997).

——, *The Later Medieval City* (London: Longman, 1997).

Oman, Charles, *The Great Revolt of 1381* (Oxford: Clarendon Press, 1906).

Padover, Saul K., *The Life and Death of Louis XVI* (London: Appleton-Century, 1939).

Patch, Howard Rollin, *Fortuna in Old French Literature* (Northampton, MA: Smith College, 1923).

——, *The Goddess Fortuna in Medieval Literature* (Northampton, MA: Smith College, 1927).

Peignot, Georges, *Histoire morale, civile, politique et littéraire du Charivari depuis son origine, vers le XIVe siècle* (Paris, 1833).

Petit de Julleville, L., *Les comédiens en France au Moyen Age* (Paris: Cerf, 1885).

——, *Histoire du théâtre en France: les mystères,* 2 vols (Paris: Hachette, 1880).

Pickering, F. P., *Literature and Art in the Middle Ages* (London: Macmillan, 1970).

Piot, G. J. C., *Histoire de Louvain depuis son origine jusqu'aujourdhui,* Pt 1 (Louvain, 1839).

Ribard, J., 'Théâtre et Symbolisme au XIIIe siècle', in *The Theatre in the Middle Ages,* ed. by H. Braet et al., Mediaevalia Lovaniensia, Series I/ Studia 13 (Leuven: Leuven University Press, 1985), pp. 103–18.

The Romances of Chrétien de Troyes, ed. by Douglas Kelly (Lexington, KY: French Forum Publication, 1985).

Rubin, Miri, *Corpus Christi: The Eucharist in Late Medieval Culture* (Cambridge: Cambridge University Press, 1991).

Schlumberger, Gustave, *L'Épopée byzantine à la fin du dixième siècle,* 3 vols (Paris: Hachette, 1896–1905).

Schmolke-Hasselmann, Beate, *The Evolution of Arthurian Romance: The Verse Tradition from Chrétien to Froissart,* trans. by M. and R. Middleton (Cambridge: Cambridge University Press, 1998).

Schneider, Jean, *La Ville de Metz aux XIIIe et XIVe siècles* (Nancy: Georges Thomas, 1950).

Sears, Elizabeth, *The Ages of Man: Medieval Interpretations of the Life Cycle* (Princeton: Princeton University Press, 1986).

Soria, Georges, *Grande Histoire de la Révolution Française* (Paris: Bordas, 1988).

Sponsler, C., 'Festive Profit and Ideological Production', in *Festive Drama*, ed. by M. Twycross (Cambridge: D. S. Brewer, 1996), pp. 66–79.

Stallybrass, Peter, and Allon White, *The Politics and Poetics of Transgression* (London: Methuen, 1986).

Travis, Peter W., 'Chaucer's Chronographiae, the Confounded Reader, and Fourteenth-Century Measurements of Time', *Disputatio,* 2 (1997), 1–34.

Uitti, Karl D., and Michelle A. Freeman, *Chrétien de Troyes Revisited* (New York: Twayne, 1995).

Ungureanu, Marie, *La bourgeoisie naissante: société et littérature bourgeoises d'Arras aux XIIe et XIIIe siècles* (Arras: SEDES, 1955).

Walter, Philippe, *La mémoire du temps: fêtes et calendriers de Chrétien de Troyes à la Mort Artu* (Paris: Champion/Geneva: Slatkine, 1989).

Woolf, Rosemary, *The English Mystery Plays* (London: Routledge and Kegan Paul, 1972).

Index